Intercultural Communication

A Critical Perspective

SAN DIEGO

Dedicated to Leah Vande Berg

scholar, teacher, and mentor
who tirelessly enacted a
critical perspective of the world

———————

Bassim Hamadeh, CEO and Publisher
Todd R. Armstrong, Publisher
Tony Paese, Project Editor
Jess Estrella, Senior Graphic Designer
Sean Adams, Production Editor
Danielle Gradisher, Licensing Associate
Natalie Piccotti, Director of Marketing
Kassie Graves, Vice President of Editorial
Jamie Giganti, Director of Academic Publishing

Cover image copyright © 2017 iStockphoto LP/Aleksei_Derin.

Printed in the United States of America.

ISBN: 978-1-5165-2052-7 (pbk) / 978-1-5165-4526-1 (al) / 978-1-5165-2053-4 (br)

3970 Sorrento Valley Blvd., Ste. 500, San Diego, CA 92121

Intercultural Communication

A Critical Perspective

Rona Tamiko Halualani

San José State University

Brief Contents

Detailed Contents

Chapter 3
Re-Thinking Communication   49

Chapter 6
Identity Layers and Intercultural Communication   119

Chapter 7
Historical Memory and Intercultural Communication   139

About the Author

Rona Tamiko Halualani is a professor of intercultural communication in the Department of Communication Studies at San José State University. She also served as the special assistant to the president, director of inclusive excellence and institutional planning for San José State University from 2007 through 2009. Dr. Halualani is the author of *In the Name of Hawaiians: Native Identities and Cultural Politics* and is the co-editor (with Dr. Thomas K. Nakayama) of the *Handbook of Critical Intercultural Communication*. She has published numerous articles in the *Journal of International and Intercultural Communication, International and Intercultural Communication Annual*, and *International Journal of Intercultural Relations*. Dr. Halualani is also the former editor in chief of the *Journal of International and Intercultural Communication*. She teaches courses on intercultural communication, critical intercultural communication, globalized intercultural communication, and culture and gender identity.

Preface

What Inspired This Book

I remember the first time I experienced a critical (or power-based) view of the world. It was as an undergraduate student in a rhetoric and communication course (in my major) at the University of California at Davis. The amazing professor (Dr. Julie Brown) was discussing one of my favorite movies, *Pretty Woman* (with Julia Roberts and Richard Gere), and how beneath the "fairy tale" plotline that I loved, there was a deeper hegemonic ideology at work that framed women as "sexual objects" as well as a dominant patriarchal, heteronormative, and capitalistic framing of romance. I was floored. I had never thought about this movie or the world in this way. I was intrigued and yet unsure. A critical view of the world seemed heavy and a bit harsh. Even though I had numerous disconfirming experiences with gender and racial marginalization, I just did not have a developed critical sensibility. I wasn't sure what it meant for me to see the world in this way. It almost seemed easier to not have this view and see the world so differently.

Then, my fate as a critical scholar became sealed in the spring of 1993. I was a beginning graduate student in the Department of Communication Studies at California State University, Sacramento. I was taking Critical Theory in the Media with the inspiring Dr. Leah Vande Berg. We examined all sorts of media texts, such as the news, sports commentary, and popular television shows at the time such as *The X-Files*, *NYPD Blue*, *Roseanne*, *Will and Grace*, *Star Trek*, and *Murphy Brown*. Dr. Vande Berg showed us how power forces framed and constituted our world. I was mesmerized with every insight shared from that class—from how camera angles objectify women, how plotlines elevate male characters and maleness over women, and how characters of color and gay, lesbian, queer, and transgender persons are subordinated in a variety of ways (content-wise, visually, discursively).

I was indeed changed. This view of the world was not just something I was going to do for this class. My sight on everything became different at that moment. I knew that I had to go about life differently. It would affect everyone around me: my family, my significant other, my friends, and my community—all of who witnessed me becoming "overanalytical" and "intense."

I was hungry to learn more about this seemingly hidden way of understanding the invisible and visible (albeit normalized) structures and ideologies of power. Fast forward three years to my time at Arizona State University under the mentorship of Dr. Tom Nakayama as a PhD student. At that time, I suddenly entered the world of critical intercultural communication, or how culture and identity were framed by unseen forces of power. My mind was blown. As a multiracial woman who strongly identified with my Native identity and my Japaneseness, I realized then that I wanted to work with others to share this critical intercultural communication perspective—a perspective that was missing from my everyday life. I wanted to be in the classroom and in the community with this critical intercultural communication perspective.

This perspective helped to clarify ideas and insights with regard to my own intercultural relationships and my own cultural experiences. It also showed me some painful and negative dimensions of society. I was heartened to push for clarity, complexity, and the need to transform the problematic aspects of our social hierarchies.

My own journey as an undergraduate student led me to this book—to envisioning and writing this book for you.

As a diasporic Native Hawaiian, fourth-generation (Yonsei) Japanese American, and part White/European American woman who was born and raised in San Mateo, California in a two-parent home, a critical intercultural communication perspective has given me the tools and language through which to see my world in a clearer way. By "clear," I mean "sight" that is unobstructed by my own fears or denials of larger societal forces, power interests, and racial, socioeconomic, gender, global, and sexual orientation hierarchies of difference. "Clear sight" also refers to a new type of lens that confronts my own power interests, privilege, and historical placement that disempowers others around me. Such a lens optimally positions us to work for social change and intercultural justice. This bestows on us the space and opportunity to connect and help others around us (and especially those whose interests are marginalized) in a real and authentic way.

About This Book

While I have reflected on, crafted, and composed this book over the last 14 years, I have been accumulating ideas and concepts for this book since that fateful day in 1993 when re-engaging the *Pretty Woman* film and the "absence" of Asian American characters on the screen. However, writing a book for students about power is difficult at best. There is a specific jargon that critical scholarship employs (with its obtuse words and abstract and unexplained concepts) that make it "unfriendly" and "inaccessible" for today's students and everyday individuals. I wanted to write this book in a way that understanding high-level concepts was relatively easy (although there is still some jargon attached to concepts in this book). Such translation between complex concepts of power in relation to intercultural communication takes time, careful thought, effort, and energy—14 years of time, careful thought, effort, and energy. I have created this book to welcome you into critical intercultural communication studies and to do so in a compelling and understandable format.

Intercultural Communication: A Critical Perspective stands as one of the few intercultural textbooks for undergraduate intercultural communication students that primarily examines contemporary dimensions of intercultural communication with regard to the trope of power. This book frames intercultural communication through a power-based perspective that highlights how macro structures and forces (governmental, historical, economic, media, institutional forces) interrelate with micro-communication acts, encounters, and relationships between and within cultural groups. Such a macro-micro power focus reveals the complex, dynamic, and multi-layered nature of contemporary intercultural communication.

Intercultural Communication: A Critical Perspective is the only dedicated textbook to date that articulates and translates a focused critical intercultural perspective to intercultural communication for college students.

Approach of the Book

The approach of this book is grounded in a framework based on key dimensions of power in relation to intercultural communication. In so doing, a macro-micro focus is applied throughout the book to theorize the ways in which (macro) larger structures of power intermingle and reconfigure (micro) private/individual encounters and relations between different cultures, both domestically and internationally (especially as these terms become muddled due to globalization). In terms of the book coverage, I employ theory, research findings, and guided examples on critical intercultural communication studies. I especially focus on explaining and translating often abstract and difficult-to-understand theoretical concepts of culture and power into accessible and interesting notions.

Keep in mind that the majority of intercultural communication textbooks focus on an interpersonal approach to intercultural communication, emphasizing individual and group-centered attitudes and communication skills. While useful and important in its own right, such an approach glosses over the larger macro-micro process of intercultural communication, or the ways in which larger structures of power (governmental, institutional, legal, economic, and mediated forces) intermingle with micro-acts and encounters among/within cultural individuals and groups. This book proffers an equally valuable perspective of macro-micro processes that frame intercultural communication through the framework of "in/visible dimensions" and power—meaning that this textbook will introduce you to both the hidden (beneath the surface) and visible (what we see but take for granted, given its naturalized appearance) aspects of power that constitute intercultural communication encounters and relations.

Features of the Book

The book includes several important features as delineated next:

- User-friendly and accessible language regarding the critical intercultural communication perspective. For example, a user-friendly and accessible tone regarding in/visible dimensions of power in intercultural communication is threaded throughout the book. This feature of accessible language and explanations for often theoretically dense, critical concepts, makes this text unique among all of the other intercultural communication textbooks. It is my hope that in the book, important high-order power-based/critical theories can be shared with undergraduate students in an exciting and understandable manner.

- Focused connections between the unit of focus and intercultural communication. Each chapter includes a section that directly states the relationship between the unit of focus and its impact on intercultural communication, so as to foreground the link in the reader's mind. I find this feature to be important because it is difficult to conceptualize the intricate connections between power structures and forces and private intercultural encounters.

- A narrative opening for each chapter. Each chapter begins with a narrative about how that chapter focus is lived on an everyday basis by individuals across different cultures. You will engage personal and individual narratives more as way to understand the material (and especially high-level material) and in a more compelling and accessible fashion. These narratives will relate directly to the chapter topic and focus. Through such narratives, I hope that you will be able to gain a better sense of how concepts are lived and experienced in different ways.

- Uniquely offered chapter content. Another distinctive feature of this book is that it features a power-based, critical perspective on topical clusters that have been long neglected in other intercultural communication textbooks (and courses) such as structures of power, communication as a power-based act, ideologies, representational politics and speaking for others, social/structural and personal layers of identity, historical memory and historical amnesia, racialization and the racial state, and intercultural relationships and intercultural desire.

Moreover, great attention is paid to each of these topic clusters in terms of singular attention in an entire, dedicated chapter as opposed to just a brief section among other concepts within a chapter.

- Guiding examples. Each chapter features several key guiding examples through which to understand and absorb the concepts of focus. These examples are directly incorporated into the chapter material and content coverage. Such examples are historically important ones and/or contemporary ones that illustrate the emphasized concepts.

- Interactive and curated Web examples. I have incorporated interactive Web examples in the active learning and instructor resource areas through which students can interact with digital content that demonstrates the chapter concepts in a concrete way. Today's students are used to reading from multi-platforms (text, social media, internet, Web links, and examples). In the electronic version of this textbook, this will enable a streamlined way for students to interact with chapter content and web-based content (and not in a disjointed or distracting manner).

- Active learning material. I have incorporated substantial activity guides for instructors as a way to get students actively involved in understanding and employing the concepts of power and intercultural communication discussed. These activity guides will be electronic versions with digital content, which will speak to both the instructor and technologically savvy students. Additional resource material (with digital content) will be highlighted for students in this area as well. Additional resources can be readings, articles, newspaper articles, and/or websites.

- End-of-chapter material. Each chapter will conclude with a summary, key terms, discussion questions, and possible activities.

My Invitation to You, the Instructor

Consider this book as an invitation to engage a unique and yet meaningful power-based perspective—critical intercultural communication studies—of our intercultural world and relations. With this invitation, you are officially ushered into a community of scholars and social actors to help re-think and transform our social ideas, power arrangements, systemic/institutional forces, and historical habits that marginalize various groups and positionalities. The work needs to be done by all of us across all social identities and differences. No one is exempt from such hard work. Together, we can reimagine and re-work our society to be more just, meaningful, and empowering for us—as cultural members, allies, advocates, and social partners in the world.

I am so excited to be in this community and in this particular moment of learning with you.

—Rona Tamiko Halualani

Acknowledgments

This book—*Intercultural Communication: A Critical Perspective*—has been a passion project of mine over the last 14 years. It was only made possible through the efforts, insights, support, and love shared by many people in my life.

First, I am grateful for the encouragement and guidance of Todd Armstrong who first urged me to write this unique book back in 2004. He has always believed in this project, and me, and continued to offer unwavering support (across two different presses) even when others claimed that there was no real need or market for a book on critical intercultural communication. I am thrilled that the project that started out with Todd will culminate under his editorship, guidance, and care. I am forever indebted to him.

I also need to express thanks to Tony Paese, my project editor, for his attention, support, and excellent facilitation of this book project. Leah Sheets, Jamie Giganti, and the entire Cognella Academic Publishing team supported me at every stage of the manuscript.

My work in this book is the direct product of wonderful insights from excellent intercultural and critical scholars. These wonderful scholars who reviewed drafts of this manuscript, include the following:

- John Chiang (SUNY Oneonta)
- Jolanta Drzewiecka (Università della Svizzera italiana)
- Lisa Flores (University of Colorado Boulder)
- Elisabeth Gareis (Baruch College)
- Krishna Kandath (Central New Mexico Community College)
- Etsuko Fujimoto Kinefuchi (The University of North Carolina at Greensboro)
- S. Lily Mendoza (Oakland University)
- Dreama Moon (California State University, San Marcos)
- Jennifer Huynh Thi Anh Morrison (San José State University)
- Kent Ono (The University of Utah)
- John T. Warren (late, Southern Illinois University, Carbondale)
- Gust Yep (San Francisco State University)

These scholars provided important suggestions and made this book stronger. I especially acknowledge my friend, John T. Warren, who died too soon and encouraged my work. He was and is a constant source of inspiration for me.

I feel extremely fortunate to have been a part of a PhD program at Arizona State University with the brightest scholars in the discipline. These individuals—Anu Chitgopekar Khanna, Jola Drzewiecka, S. Lily Mendoza, Etsuko Kinefuchi, Regina Spellers Sims, Dreama Moon, Michelle Holling, and Tim Kuhn—are not just my peers, but my close friends whose work is awe-inspiring. They have helped me in their critical insight, praxis for a better world, and generosity of spirit.

Stacy Holman Jones, Brenna Curtis, and Penny Pearson were with me at the beginning at California State University, Sacramento when I realized that I wanted to be a critical scholar. I thank them for their wisdom, gifts, and time. We shared a special time in our lives and were part of a graduate program that was second to none.

There are so many colleagues in the discipline who have helped me along the way—too many to thank here. I highlight the mentorship of Leah Vande Berg and Nick Trujillo—both of whom left the world too soon but invited me into the discipline and tirelessly encouraged my voice as a scholar and teacher. In addition, Jolene Koester and Ron Lustig have always been there for me (and are to this day) and generously gave me their time, advice, and mentorship. I would also not be the scholar I am today without the active support of Kent Ono, Lisa Flores, Alberto Gonzalez, Belle Edson, Judith Martin, and David Theo Goldberg. I am forever indebted to the advice and wisdom of Tom Nakayama, my doctoral adviser, who was and is ahead of his time, contributing so much to intercultural communication and providing me with the space to do the work that I love and teach.

The colleagues in my home—the Department of Communication Studies at San José State University—have always given me examples of excellent scholarly work and authentic teaching. I especially highlight Deanna Fassett, who is not only my close friend and department chair, but serves as an example of strength, wisdom, and praxis in her work as a critical communication scholar.

My family—my parents, Ronald Alohikea and Jennie Halualani, and my brothers Roger and Michael Halualani—shaped my life experience, and from those experiences, helped me write this book. I am who I am today because of my wonderful life partner and spouse—Kung Chiao. Kung has listened to every idea and theory that I wanted to put in this book. He displayed patience with every idea and also contributed to the formation of those ideas. Kung has become a critical intercultural communication scholar even though he may not realize it yet! Our twins—Kea and Keli'i—are the lights of our lives and truly inspire me to be better, truer, and more critical as their world and lives depend on it.

And finally, I am so grateful to the many wonderful students who I have been privileged to have in my courses over the last 24 years. These students gave me the courage to complete this work and showed me their experiences of struggle, triumph, and transformation. This work would not be possible without all of my students.

In gratitude,

Rona Tamiko Halualani

Chapter 1

Introducing Critical Intercultural Communication

Learning Objectives

> To introduce this textbook

> To understand a critical approach to intercultural communication

> To examine the larger, unseen contexts and structures of power in our lives

Introduction: A Day in the Intercultural Life of Jenny

Jenny, a Filipina American college student, is about to start her day in New York City. She gets up in her tiny apartment and prepares to go to class at a nearby state university. Jenny slings her backpack strap over her shoulder and smooths out the wrinkles on her Indian sari-styled blouse that she picked up at a swap meet last weekend. This sari blouse in a deep shade of burgundy with ornate beading on the hem and is not just a mere piece of clothing; indeed, it represents the spread of culture (in this case, Indian culture) across borders, nations, and continents. In Jenny's world, cultural items and styles become trendy, commodified, and ready to be consumed for a price. Though she didn't know much at all about Asian Indian culture, Jenny loved wearing this sari blouse.

Fully dressed, Jenny leaves her apartment building. One block later to the east, she waves to the same elderly Chinese man who she sees everyday on her way to campus. At this moment, Jenny officially enters the new "Chinatown," or the ethnic enclave established and settled by a growing Chinese American community. As she passes the Hong Kong Flower Lounge Restaurant (best known for its dim sum) and the Eastern Tea store, Jenny remembered hearing that this Chinatown area had only been around for the last 20 years, a relatively short period of time. Before that, as early as the 1940s, only Whites had lived in this area, which, at that time, was a new, developing residential community of affluent White professionals. Gradually, in the 1960s, the surrounding New York City neighborhoods became heavily populated by Black residents from Harlem and new Asian and Latino immigrants from the Bronx. Long-time White residents had moved out of the

1

Jenny begins her day in bustling and diverse New York City and experiences many intercultural aspects.

and began to play her new songs while checking her Instagram. In addition to fashion, cultural influences definitely spread through music—whether it was Samoan rap, Jamaican reggae, French pop, Black gangsta rap, or the British punk sound. Jenny did not know much about these different cultural groups, but she wanted to. She actually had never thought about it before—it was just her music on her phone. Her thoughts were interrupted by a familiar voice.

"Hey," said a tall man. It was Kevin, Jenny's boyfriend of about a year. He attended the same university as she did and was Puerto Rican. Jenny beamed as he greeted her and they clenched hands on their way to campus. Jenny had not told her family about Kevin. She wasn't sure how they would react to her dating someone from a cultural group that they did not know much about. Her father had always said negative things about other cultural groups, including Puerto Ricans who lived nearby. According to her parents, they were too "different" and "no good" for Jenny. Her mother would always say that where they were from, you wouldn't mix with other "kinds"—it was too risky. Your own family would disown you because your line was no longer "pure" and/or you would experience harsh treatment by society for being in an intercultural relationship or marriage. Jenny would always meet Kevin on her own and not with any family members present. She didn't want to risk a scene and the glaring disapproval from her parents. It was better that they not know. Besides, it is 2018! People date outside of their group all the time! Sometimes Jenny thought that she only seemed interested in dating people of other backgrounds because it went against her father's beliefs.

Together, hand in hand, Kevin and Jenny walked toward campus. They arrived at the student lounge where a group of their friends—all psychology majors—hung out and waited for their classes to start. Most of these friends were either Latino/a or White/European American—Jenny had never seen

area (in a movement pattern known as "White flight"), and Blacks and Latinos moved into the area. It was known then as the "good area" that was once desirable and pristine and had since become a dangerous, crime-infested ghetto. Jenny thought for a moment about all the different ethnic groups that had lived in the area she was walking through. The racial and ethnic differentiation of urban spaces and neighborhoods was not some impersonal topic that Jenny learned in school; it was all around her and strangely enough, she had only now stopped to think about it. Sometimes what is close is overlooked.

Five blocks later, Jenny's iPhone tumbled onto the sidewalk. "Ahh!" she yelled. She knew her phone case was slippery. Earlier that morning, Jenny had downloaded several new songs for her morning walk—some from the Hong Kong pop scene and others from the newest craze among her friends, KPOP (Korean Pop) music. As she picked up her iPhone, she reached for her BEATS headphones them this way. They only talked about school and life together, never about their own cultural and family backgrounds. Why should they? It seemed everyone wanted to get "racial" these days—some of her professors were obsessed with talking about race and difference in the classroom; her university had all those "diversity" events and mandated GE courses. Her friends in the psychology department didn't need to get into issues about race or diversity; they were beyond all that "PC" ("political correctness") stuff. They talked about other, more important things and what they had in common: school.

After her last class, Jenny walked back to her apartment with Kevin—he left her at the Mason interchange so she could head home alone (without her parents knowing of their meeting as they often made surprise visits to her apartment). As she walked into the house, Jenny greeted her grandmother, who was visiting that week from California. She greeted her grandmother in what little Tagalog she knew. All of her life, Jenny had not learned much of the language or customs about her Filipino background. Both her parents were born and raised near Manila and came to the States in their 30s. It was not an easy road; Jenny had heard her parents talk about how rough it was to get US citizenship and that there was a lot of discrimination when they first moved to New York and had a family. They had vowed to not let their children experience that hardship. Jenny was the oldest child of four and was always told by her parents that she was "American" and to never forget that. Her parents never spoke or taught Tagalog or their Ilocano dialect to any of the children. They never practiced any Filipino customs; they didn't even talk about it. To Jenny, this was just the way it was. It made it awkward when she first met other Filipinos her age in high school and college—all of whom assumed that she was "Filipino" like they are. Jenny didn't want to talk about her background with other Filipinos; she felt judged by them. She didn't talk about her background at all—in or outside of the home. It was just the way it was.

Locating Intercultural Communication in Our Lives

In so many ways, intercultural communication pervades our lives. We typically think of intercultural communication as being those face-to-face interactions between and among culturally different persons and/or the exchanges that occur when traveling to a different region that features unfamiliar cultures and languages. But, the notion of intercultural communication also touches our lives in multiple and shifting contexts and by larger, unseen structures of power in ways that we may not even notice.

In the featured narrative over the last several pages, Jenny's life is saturated with issues of culture, intercultural communication, and power, both directly and indirectly. The clothes that Jenny wears derive from larger global capitalistic contexts in which ethnic fashion trends enable individuals to dress exotically, even without a solid understanding of the culture that is being portrayed. The cultural items themselves may not even be made in the country of presumed origin or by the cultural group being portrayed. It is a representation of culture that Jenny and others around the world consume, circulate, and participate in. Larger structures of power, such as global capitalism and economic modes of production, touch Jenny's life in a way that she does not even fully know.

Likewise, as Jenny makes her way to school, she walks through a racially/ethnically diverse neighborhood setting that has gone through several historical changes in the racial/ethnic and socioeconomic composition of residents. By passing through a neighborhood that was settled first by Whites, then Blacks and Asian and Latino immigrants, Jenny does not fully realize how the areas in which she and others live are deeply impacted by historical and economic moments. Some groups move into areas that are deemed more "affordable," while others leave because the community has become too racially mixed and associated with crime and low-income housing (Ellen & O'Regan, 2011; Hwang & Simpson, 2014; Kim, 2000; Lees, 2016).[1] Historically, groups had also moved into specific neighborhoods because of the difficulty in gaining equal access to stable housing and jobs, and extreme housing discrimination was brought on by economic and institutional structures as well as the larger societal attitudes toward Blacks, Asians, Latino/as, and other cultural and immigrant groups. Thus, historical and economic contexts have placed individuals, families, and groups in specific neighborhoods and regional areas, thereby delineating which groups will live near each other and kept separate. Again, larger, unseen structures help to shape our intercultural communication zones, participants, and the kind of intercultural relations in which we engage. Jenny comes into contact with only a few groups—Asians, Blacks, and Latino/as—because of the historical and economic positioning of these groups in specific neighborhood spaces.

Even the music that Jenny listens to on her iPhone relates to issues of culture and intercultural communication. Her tunes, ranging from Hong Kong pop, KPOP, Indian Bhangra fusion, Samoan rap, Jamaican reggae, French pop, Black gangsta rap, and British punk, all derive from a melding and blending of different global cultures and musical forms. Various cultural music genres expose Jenny, and the rest of us, to images, symbols, and lyrics of cultures we may not know much about. Thus, music can serve as the gateway into learning more about a cultural group or at least being curious about it. It also may shape how we perceive the cultural group from which the musical genre derives. Meaning, we consume the music of other cultures without thinking about how perceptions of these cultures are shaped by such music (and often popular trends of music) (Guilbault, 2006). Jenny is interested in listening to different blends of music but may not fully consider the myriad of cultural issues involved in such popularized music. For example, cultural groups may be depicted in specific ways through different musical forms: rap and hip hop as creating strong, masculine images of cultural groups. In this way, then, musical forms, such as hip-hop from Black/African American communities, reggae from Afro-Caribbean groups, and punk from the British/European scene, can

---

1   You will see these in-text citations (Author Last Name, Year of Source) throughout this book. In-text citations are provided to identify key scholarly works or sources that shape and inform the ideas presented in that part of the chapter. These citations are formatted in APA (American Psychological Association) which is used throughout the social sciences. All citations are featured in the References section at the back of this book.

enable other cultural groups, such as Asians, Pacific Islanders, Middle Easterners, and Europeans, to express their cultural identities in different ways from their traditional cultural forms.

Jenny's personal life also highlights the role of intercultural romantic relationships in everyday life. She dates someone of a different background, Kevin of Puerto Rican descent, and carries on a secret relationship for fear of disapproval by her parents. Jenny is mindful of her father's perceptions of and feeling toward different groups, as is evident in his personal comments spoken in the privacy of their home. She feels that these beliefs are too "traditional" and not reflective of the modern times. Jenny's parents explain to their daughter that those mixed or intercultural couples would experience discrimination in larger society. Thus, the societal view that racially/ethnically pure blood lines and unions are "necessary" and "right," frames how Jenny's parents negatively view intercultural relationships as well as influence Jenny's rebellious attitude toward her parents' views. These views emerge in specific historical and political contexts in which contact or union with specific groups on the basis of race, ethnicity, religion, gender, or sexuality is deemed impermissible or prohibited with other groups (Washington, 2012). For example, interracial marriage in the U.S. was legally allowed in the *Loving vs. Virginia* case since only 1967 (Hoewe, 2016; Wildman, 2002). Jenny and her parents are therefore greatly impacted by the power of larger, below-the-surface societal views of who is appropriate to marry whom and behave in response to these larger views.

When Jenny interacts with her friends at school, she socializes with a diverse group of friends who are all psychology majors at the same university. Jenny explains that she and her friends do not talk about their cultural backgrounds or about diversity. Instead, they like to talk about things they have in common and not get so "racial," like her professors and the university seemed to always want to do. Jenny and her friends want to move beyond the "pc" ("political correctness") stuff. The intercultural contact that Jenny has with her friends, therefore, seems directly separate from any discussion of "political correctness," "race," "difference," or "diversity" (Halualani, Fassett, Morrison, & Dodge, 2006; Halualani, 2010). Instead, these societal discourses and viewpoints on political correctness, race, difference, and diversity, as created by national governments, courts of law, politics, and public institutions, are very much impacting how individuals like Jenny go about socializing with friends and on what level. Meaning, because of US society's focus on colorblindness, or the notion that we should not highlight cultural difference but rather treat everyone as equals and without cultural reference (Omi & Winant, 2014), it has become difficult and uncomfortable for individuals to confront, head on, issues of difference and diversity with one another. As a result, larger societal viewpoints about race, difference, and diversity again close off the realm of dialogue and exchange about individuals' cultural backgrounds and the similarities and differences traversed through cultures. Jenny and her friends do not want to engage these issues for fear of divisiveness and hostile relations and prejudice. But, they are not actually moving "beyond" or outside of these issues of difference and diversity; through their acts of avoidance and dismissal, they are responding in direct relation to these issues and actually giving power to the very logic that they oppose: the notion that race, difference, and diversity are negative, divisive, and all-powerful. To not talk about these issues does not mean that prejudice, discrimination, or hostile relations will automatically or even gradually end (Omi & Winant, 2014). How we choose to interact with culturally different persons is often influenced by societal attitudes and viewpoints about culture, race, difference, and diversity (Halualani, 2008).

Finally, Jenny's own relationship to culture is influenced by her parents' experiences. She shares that she does not speak Tagalog or know very much about her Filipino background. Instead, Jenny's parents emphasize her "Americanness" and do not share much of the culture with her. Their behavior is influenced by the way in which they were treated by US society upon their immigration. As acclaimed sociologists Portes & Rumbaut (2001) uncovered in their exhaustive study of immigrant families, because of their negative experiences of societal discrimination and acceptance, Jenny's parents decide to raise their children without a focus on "culture" and more of an emphasis on their "Americanness" so that their children will be more accepted by society (Rumbaut & Borgen, 2011). Again, experiences of societal oppression and discrimination can inform how a culture is passed on or the extent to which it is, which reflects not just on the culture itself, but also by the societal and historical treatment of the culture. How we are positioned in relation to our own cultural backgrounds and identities comes in large part from our own family members' experiences of acceptance, inclusion, exclusion, and marginalization. This also plays into how Jenny is able to relate to other Filipinos of her age group and triggers a politics of authenticity within her cultural community, or a debate over what it means to be a "true" or "real" Filipino. Our experiences in society and in relation to specific historical, political, and economic structures, shape how we see our own culture and how we choose to pass it on to the next generation. As you can see in this example, a day in the life of Jenny is greatly embedded by intercultural communication and by larger, unseen structures of power, which make up the **critical intercultural communication** approach that is the focus of this book.[2]

In this chapter, you will be introduced to a unique approach to understanding intercultural communication: that is, a **critical approach**. This approach explores and views intercultural communication encounters through a specific focus on power and how cultural groups are positioned in different ways through larger, unseen sociopolitical structures, histories, and conditions. These unseen or invisible structures of power that play out in intercultural communication are the taken-for-granted shapers of intercultural relations such as the media, government, economy, history, global markets, and popular culture. A critical approach to intercultural communication will heighten your awareness and analytical skills, as well as raise new and interesting questions to explore. Moreover, a critical approach to intercultural communication enables you to make important observations about the world around you and equips you with insights so that you can

---

2   You will see bolded terms throughout this book. These bolded terms represent "Keywords" that are defined in the Glossary for your reference and knowledge.

take meaningful action and change in improving our world toward more positive and equitable intercultural relations. We *all* can make a difference in this world, and this book will guide you on this path.

In order to fully understand a critical approach, we will first take a "tour" of how intercultural communication embeds our lives and experiences. In this "touring," you will notice how contexts and structures of power touch our lives and shape our intercultural communication encounters with one another.

What Is Critical Intercultural Communication?

A critical approach to intercultural communication provides a perspectival view of the world in terms of the structures and contexts of power that surround us and impact our lives and experiences. This approach examines the invisible dimensions of intercultural communication, or the taken-for-granted shapers of intercultural relations such as the media, governmental institutions, economic structures, historical memories, global markets and brands, and popular culture (television, film social media, fashion, cultural trends). The key highlighted element through a critical approach to intercultural communication is power, or the constraining force by which larger dominant structures, and sometimes, groups and individuals, are able to gain in position and achieve their aims and interests over or against the will of others. It is important to note that whether we notice or not, invisible dimensions of power constitute and frame our intercultural communication encounters, relationships, and everyday experiences.

As stated earlier, intercultural communication is much more than in-person, face-to-face contact between two or more persons or micro interactional episodes. Instead, a critical approach to intercultural communication expands this focus to encompass all multi-layered dimensions of power that reside in specific contexts and operate beneath the surface of intercultural communication in hidden and subtle ways.

Contexts of Power in Our Lives

There are several overlapping contexts of power in our lives that shape intercultural communication encounters and relations in unique ways. These are as follows:

- The economic context
- The governmental context
- The legal context
- The educational context
- The family context
- The media context
- The tourism context

These settings are constituted by larger, unseen power forces that help to demarcate how we understand and approach culturally different persons and communities. All contexts of power share three noteworthy characteristics:

1. A context of power is based on an obvious and/or subtle (visible and or hidden) hierarchy of dominant and subordinate parties.

2. A context of power revolves around an ongoing struggle for power between dominant and subordinate parties/interests.

3. Each context is both independent and interdependent of each other.

1. Hierarchy of power. This first characteristic highlights how a context of power is based on an obvious and/or subtle (visible and or hidden) hierarchy of dominant and subordinate parties. A dominant party can be defined as one that possesses the legal, economic, and governmental authority to enforce rules, laws, policies, taxes and fees onto others—a trait that most individuals do not themselves possess. In addition, this dominant party (or parties) wields great influence in widely projecting and circulating specific ideas and views about what the "truth" is—how the nation and its government should be viewed and how others are to be seen. A dominant party benefits the most economically and socially, given that its position and power capacities allow it to maintain, reproduce, and strengthen its own supremacy and authority over others. A subordinate party is defined in opposition to that of a dominant one, meaning that a subordinate party does not possess the larger authority to make and enforce laws (and imprison individuals), impose fees, or control media content, nor does it have the great financial and political resources of a dominant party at its feet to exert influence over society. A subordinate party (an individual, a group or community), instead, is often the one who is at the other end of (and who experiences the brunt of) the dominant party's full reach of power and authority and who must creatively use its own resources to fight domination and marginalization in society.

As an example, in many cities throughout the U.S. (and possibly in other countries as well), housing developers and city "revitalization" programs (which are funded by state and local grant monies), have targeted rundown, crime-infested, dilapidated, and economically struggling city spaces for the building of "new" residential communities that can take advantage of more affordable land and housing prices. Such a process is also known as gentrification, in which housing developers and urban planners make over and re-occupy a city composed of poor and struggling minority groups, such as East Palo Alto in California or Harlem in New York. In such a context, the housing developers (who are mostly White/European American-run corporations that make billions of dollars in revenue), as well as the city/urban planners and redevelopment agencies, represent the dominant parties, while those at the other end, the longtime racialized minority residents (most often Black/African American, Latino, and Southeast Asian communities), who are pushed out of the housing market and eventually out of the new, gentrified cities, represent the subordinate party. The hierarchy of power between these two interests, in this context, positions them in starkly unequal positions, with city developers and planners making all the decisions about redevelopment and with longtime minority (non-White) residents excluded from the planning process and the economic benefits of gentrification (for they cannot afford to buy the new homes in their own area). Moreover, there are tense and often hostile interactions and economic competition among the historically established minority (non-White) residents and those new residents (who are mostly professional class White/ European American and Asian Americans) who buy into homes for more reasonable prices and can experience the benefit of remaking a new city (that is, by taking over seats on city councils and enlisting the help of local police officers to watch over and protect their new neighborhoods over the under-resourced areas). Changes in neighborhoods, therefore, inscribe a specific hierarchy of socioeconomic class and racial/ethnic interests as intercultural interactions among these parties are, at the outset, already skewed, imbalanced, and unequal.

In 2017, the giant electronic commerce company, Amazon, moved into East Palo Alto, California, which signaled the height of this city's gentrification. A hierarchy of power has developed among the nearby corporate newcomers, Amazon, Facebook, and Ikea, and longtime African American, Latino/a, and Pacific Islander residents, and incoming White and Asian American residents and renters.

Contexts of power with their embedded hierarchy of power interests make seemingly equalized and balanced intercultural interactions more complicated and questionable in terms of mutual understanding and agreement. Instead, the contexts of power that touch intercultural communication encounters and relationships require us to unpack the hierarchies involved that can frame and push an intercultural interaction in a specific direction (and toward affirming one party over the other).

2. A struggle for power. A context of power revolves around an ongoing struggle for power between dominant and subordinate parties/interests. In this hierarchy, dominant and subordinate parties compete with one another to gain societal power. Dominant parties (large structures, such as governmental administrations, court system, corporations, and educational institutions, among others) work hard to establish and maintain the power they have over smaller communities and cultural groups in terms of race, ethnicity, gender, sexual orientation, nationality, region, and socioeconomic class, among others. The moves by dominant parties are not always guaranteed in exacting power over others with less power resources; instead, subordinate parties/interests also participate in this feud for power by creatively and strategically using their resources at bay, such as community organizing and mobilization, intergroup alliances with other marginalized communities, the right to protest, media coverage of the "little person" versus "the overpowering force"—government, corporation—in order to resist such dominant parties and liberate themselves. Thus, this struggle of power is characterized by an unpredictable fight for, on one hand, in terms of dominant parties, domination and control, and, on the other, in terms of socially marginalized groups, freedom, resistance, and transgression. No one side is guaranteed of always winning the fight, which is ongoing with new challenges and obstacles. Of course, dominant interests have more wide-reaching resources and capacities of power to make and enforce laws, policies, and taxes, but this does not mean that individuals and groups naturally succumb to such forces. Through alternative forms, such as music, art, writing, independent media, the power of protest and mobilization, as well as crafty usages of dominant law and policy, individuals and groups can indeed resist and defy dominant forces, but with great risk and costs to them, including societal rejection, imprisonment, and even death.

Using the aforementioned context of power—redeveloping neighborhoods—the struggle occurs among the housing development corporations, city planners, and the longtime minority residents who are economically pushed out of their homes to make way for more affluent homeowners. As city planners and developers remake certain aspects of a neglected community for upper middle-class homeowners, focus on revenue, push for redistricting changes, and solicit retail franchises to establish businesses in the area, minority residents circulate petitions and create propositions that resist the gentrification process. In addition, minority residents also invite local media coverage to "hear the true story" of how the city (and the housing developers) are "chasing us" out of our homes. Here, housing developers work for profit and territorial control over a neighborhood with the interests of new, affluent residents in mind while current (non-White) residents fight for the preservation of their communities.

Contexts of power, therefore, stand as arenas where struggles of power play out and dominant parties/interests and subordinate parties/interests vie for power—more specifically, for the former, the power to rule over and control all others, and for the latter, the power of freedom and independence from dominant forces.

3. An independent and interdependent context. The third characteristic of contexts of power in our lives is that each context is both independent and interdependent of each other, meaning that contexts of power typically have their own unique attributes and envelop specific forms of struggles between dominant and subordinate parties/interests. At the same time, these contexts also work in cooperation with one another, providing support for similar and/or shared struggles of power. In the neighborhood context, for example, the city government creates and operates a city redevelopment agency to increase revenue for its fledgling city and attract new and more affluent homeowners (and taxpayers). As an independent unit, the city government context, therefore, possesses its own tailored interests in making profits and stabilizing its community base. Within the

Japantown in San José, California, represents one of the oldest Japanese American ethnic enclaves (ethnic neighborhoods) in the U.S. with its 126-year-old history. It highlights the economic context in that this residential area housed working class Japanese immigrant families, who developed businesses and service companies for their community, and separated such a group away from others.

city context, there also lies an ongoing struggle between city leaders and planners who have made commitments with housing corporations, incoming retail businesses, and city officials and workers who fear that all of these "redevelopment" changes will displace the majority of the residents in the community. Thus, this context is driven by its own interests of power and is characterized by specific struggles over power, such as those between city leaders and other leaders and city workers, as well as a struggle between minority residents and new residents.

But, contexts of power also become intertwined with one another and become interdependent in terms of a shared interest in making money, establishing generic communities that "sell," increasing tax revenue, and securing state monies to help support a stable and growing city. Thus, the contexts of local government and economic corporations work together to "redevelop" a racialized neighborhood into an attractive, marketable, and non-minority-focused living community (with the potential to appreciate in equity over time given increased gentrification efforts). Such an alliance makes the contexts of local government and economic corporations even more formidable and powerful than when each works alone. Contexts of power often operate in cooperation with one another so as to achieve shared interests and goals, especially in terms of gaining and maintaining power and control in a particular setting.

The next section features several main contexts of power that operate in our lives in terms of culture and intercultural communication.

The Economic Context

The context of the economy affects how we live day to day, influencing everything from how much money we make in our jobs to what products or items are deemed important to consume, to which region we will live in based on our socioeconomic class. The economic context is based on material capital (money) and a shifting global/national/regional marketplace of consumer services and goods in which the public (always marked as consumers), in some way, participates, some more than others. The main unit of material capital and how much of it one has, outlines intercultural communication relations by "classing" specific racial/ethnic groups into a hierarchy of socioeconomic classifications—lower class, working class, middle class, upper middle class, upper class. These classed distinctions determine the type of neighborhoods that individuals will live in, as cities represent complex "racial maps" of ethnic enclaves separated from one another. This impacts our intercultural communication encounters because the economic context influences some cultural groups living in one part of town and away from others. Ethnic enclaves are located in differentially classed areas such as the "slums," "the ghetto," "the suburbs," and the "metropolitan downtown," which also further label its residents in racially spatialized ways (Goldberg, 2002). The economic context, therefore, places cultural groups in specific areas and in contact with only one to two different groups (or in some cases, such as in the wealthier parts of town, where there is limited contact with culturally different groups). In the greater Bay Area in Northern California, for instance, inner city "ghettoes" and "dilapidated" areas house mostly Blacks/African Americans and Latino/as (and Southeast Asians and Pacific Islanders as well), while the suburbs and ritzier "residential communities" enclose mostly Whites, African Americans, and, in some cases, Asian Americans. Residents, therefore, tend to interact mostly with those other cultural groups that live within their racialized space, and beyond these, many do not have any interactions with other cultures. The economic context also plays a role in placing us in certain professions and jobs, schools and universities, and in friendships and romantic relationships with individuals within our own class designation. The economic context therefore frames who and which cultural groups will interact with each other and how often.

The Governmental Context

There are several overlapping levels of governmental power that impact us. Our national government engages in foreign relations and diplomatic missions with other nations. These specific foreign relationships that are forged, and the way in which the US government perceives these relations (as "friendly," "cordial," "tense," "hostile," "at a standstill") inevitably frames our perspective of the world's nations and their culture(s).

The mood that is set through foreign relations not only touches on nation-nation dealings on a formal level, but also how we view their national and ethnic counterparts who have emigrated to the United States. In the case of World War II, when the United States faced off against Japan, the government launched a massive detainment of all Japanese who lived in the country, even though the majority of them had been born as American citizens. In the midst of our proclaimed "war" on Iraq, individuals of Middle Eastern descent, many of whom came to our country more than 10 years ago, become easy targets of anger and resentment that stem from our government's view and approach to the Middle East. How our country treats and interacts with other nations historically also affects how these nations perceive America and by extension, Americans. We, as private individuals who do not operate at the governmental level, are therefore always considered aligned with our government and thus, their "relational baggage" becomes our own as citizens from other nations may grow to emulate and or scorn our government and culture. The enormous power of governmental structures to solidify nation-to-nation relations, organize alliances with specific nations, and declare war on others, greatly frames and configures our views and attitudes about other national cultures and our private one-on-one relationships with individuals who come from (by citizenship) or descend from (by ethnicity/ancestry) other countries.

As another example, state and local governmental bodies also work in tandem with the legal system to define the cultural meaning of marriage. From 2008 through 2012, many state governments and supreme courts reasserted their definition that marriage is a legalized union between a biological male and female. The state and legal denials of gay couples who wanted to get married, also formalized the construction of marriage in a specific way, marginalizing gay, lesbian, and transgender couples whose identities did not fit neatly into any one cultural box. Moreover, the state and court system legally defined a "family" to be a unit composed of a male and female and their children, thereby outlawing gay and lesbian adoptions. There is no question then that the governmental context (along with the legal context) shapes our cultural definitions of marriage and family, which greatly structure our cultural views of these notions and those individuals who do not fit neatly into the state's definitions. Thus, although same-sex marriages have been federal recognized in recent years, this context has pre-determined our contact with and shaped our understanding of same-sex couples before any interaction has taken place in the past and still can today.

The Legal Context

As the arm of the government, our legal system is based on the principles of equal treatment and opportunity and fairness and objectivity. The court proclaims itself to be a neutral and rational order that does not privilege or harm one cultural group over another. Such a self-declared role of neutrality, however, can be questioned when considering the court's rulings on issues of racial discrimination, for example. In the US legal system, antidiscrimination law defines a hate crime as an action inflicted on a victim by a perpetrator (U.S. Legal, 2012). The law's focus hones in on wrongful perpetrator behavior that is visible, direct, and intentional; anything else fails to present itself as "racist" or "discriminatory." Racial discrimination is therefore assumed to be merely the misguided and irrational behavior of a few, while "fault" is conceptualized as proof of intent to carry out a discriminatory action. Those who do not behave within this narrow and difficult-to-prove criteria for intentional racist behavior are not deemed racist. This legal logic, then, does not pay attention to hate crimes or violent and slanderous acts by individuals who, when viewing all the evidence, did not "plan" via intent to commit such an act but were driven by a deeply engrained brewing hostility toward a specific cultural group. In addition, antidiscrimination law fails to consider the surrounding social structures, such as governmental and educational institutions, that foster and reproduce conditions of discrimination in what is known as institutional racism. In this way, cases of structural racial discrimination done to individuals fly over the legal "radar" of visible, direct, intentional, and irrational behavior and are rarely critiqued or addressed. The legal context operates from the presumption that all individuals live in a society that is neutral, equal, and just, which belies the disproportionate experiences and realities of marginalized groups based on issues of culture, gender, age, nationality, race/ethnicity, sexual orientation, and socioeconomic class, among others. The fact that oftentimes we invest our faith in a legal system without question is troubling, given that this context creates legal precedents and prohibitions in intercultural matters (such as the state recognition of tribal identities, the constitutionality of same-sex marriage, racial/gender discrimination, affirmative action, or race-conscious programs) that are sanctioned by the government and enforced by law enforcement agencies and public entities.

The Educational Context

The educational sphere is a major setting that sets into place our knowledge about other cultures and culturally different persons, as well as how we approach diversity and intercultural interactions. Elementary, middle, and high school social studies curricular materials are not neutral, comprehensive resources that describe other nations, their specific histories, and the historical and contemporary role of the United States in relation to the rest of the world. Individuals employed by public/state school districts and who come from specific cultural vantage points (in terms of gender, age/generation, race/ethnicity, nationality, regional origin, languages spoken, sexual orientation, and socioeconomic class, among others) determine and compose such curricula which in turn, shape our views and perceptions of different nations, cultures, and even languages. What we learn during our childhood education about, for example, the Native Americans and their contentious history with early European settlers in North America, or the Second World War and the designated "allies" and "enemies" of the United States, therefore is not the sole definitive account of "what actually happened" and "how cultures truly are." Instead, the public educational system, with its bureaucratic structures, political interests, and dependency on governmental funding, selectively constructs a specific version of knowledge about other nations and cultures. Under the guise of state-approved curricular standards (which mandates the dissemination of uniform teaching materials to students), unvarying versions of knowledge are continually reproduced throughout schools and with successive generations. It is questionable as to why many parents and students do not question the supposed "facts" about history and culture that are repeated year after year. Other questions with regard to this context include "Why are only the languages of French and Spanish taught at most public schools, as opposed to other European, African, Asian, and Pacific Islander languages? Why do we only read literary accounts from the "classic" White American writers such as John Steinbeck and Ernest Hemingway? Who makes these curricular decisions? Why did we not learn more about the original inhabitants of the Americas and how their lives changed when Columbus arrived? (Richter, 1998; Taylor, 2011)

The Family Context

The sacred space of family is also a context of power in ways that are not completely obvious. Our parents, grandparents, and other family members greatly influence how we see the world and other cultures by enculturating us into their shared world views and attitudes about others. Rejecting our family's views is not an option, as our families possess great resources of power: their approval, love, financial support, and recognition of us as true family members. Certainly, none of us want to alienate ourselves from the caring and security and emotional/financial support that our family can provide us. But, this becomes difficult when it relates to how to choose to live our lives, the professions we strive for, and the relationships that we build with others. For example, parents and family members have already selected professions for their children before they even enter high school—doctors, engineers, lawyers, business entrepreneurs, teachers, and so on (Fouad & Byers-Winston, 2005; Mau, 2000). Their decisions about their daughter's or son's future determine the kind of schools she or he is to enroll in and the type of social networks she or he must engage in. Racial/ethnic groups seem to have preferred professions and careers for their children, which derive from cultural and community expectations and priorities (Fouad & Byers-Winston, 2005; Mau, 2000). Many Asian Americans, for example, have shared that their parents wanted them to be doctors, engineers, or lawyers as opposed to teachers, social workers, and artists. This creates tension and conflict within families as the children break away from their parents' expectations and pursue different venues. Difficult relations between parents and their grown children are linked to societal beliefs that benefit certain power interests. Racial, ethnic, and cultural communities invoke the societal belief that if children enter the fields of medicine, science, or business, lucrative and socially elevated positions will follow, resulting in financial prosperity and social mobility. These beliefs are not just isolated views of a group that serve only those directly involved; in the larger picture, these beliefs also "feed" the science and business arenas (which are aligned with the governmental context), with a tailored workforce, and help these sectors gain immense esteem (and social respect), privilege, and, of course, profits. Thus, societal structures, such as the economy and government, indirectly and directly touch on our family units and relations.

Throughout our childhood, there may also be ongoing conversations with our parents and elders about who is "appropriate" to befriend, date, and even marry. Seemingly innocent comments such as "You should hang out more with your own kind and not those _____" or, "Those _____ are not good for you" may slip by without notice. Comments such as these may reflect on how a family and or a cultural group view and perceive specific racial, ethnic, religious, socioeconomic, or sexual-identity groups. Learning about their parents' intercultural do's and don'ts of friendship and marriage creates enormous pressure for individuals, and oftentimes forces them to have to choose between their families (and even culture) or their friends, romantic partners, and/or spouses from different backgrounds (Chung & Ting-Toomey, 1999). There is much at stake in these relational decisions wrought by familial and cultural pressures. Even to this day, parents worry that intercultural and interracial marriages (with specific racial/ethnic group members) will threaten their cultural and religious beliefs and that such unions will not be accepted by society. Cultural communities fear the dilution of cherished cultural traditions and practices and the loss of language over time due to growing rates of intercultural relationships and marriages. Intercultural dating and marriage taboos then indirectly serve to maintain ideals of cultural, racial, or ethnic purity and discourage relationships across difference, which reproduces the already fragmented ethno-racial order of the United States.

We are exposed to certain representations of the world and cultural groups through various media outlets (print, electronic, internet).

The Media Context

The media context is undoubtedly a powerful shaper of intercultural communication and relations, given the overly media-saturated world in which we live. With access to radio, television, film, and the internet, individuals all over the world are exposed to representations of the world and its many different cultural groups. We may not see such mediated images, content, and portrayals as representations embedded with specific world views, cultural/national slants, and power interests of capitalism. Instead, more often than not, these images are accepted and invoked with little critical analysis, which could be largely due to the seductive nature of hyper-real, almost life-like, and visually stunning moving images captured on the screen. But when peering closer at mediated images and content, we must remember that these are created in a context driven by economic motives, governmental control (the FCC in the United States. or the BBC in England), and nationalistic interest in negatively depicting certain nations over others. Thus, given this backdrop of power, the local and national news coverage that we receive often provides imbalanced and distorted views of world events and national occurrences. How, for example, the US media depicts and discusses the war in the Middle East, or the relations between the United States and North Korea, China, Mexico, France, and other national powers with a vested interest in positively valorizing U.S. world views (of democracy, equality, and freedom) and justifying past and present governmental actions—how we understand the depictions of foreign nations and their cultures depends largely on the kind of knowledge constructions and representations that are circulated in various forms of media. For many individuals, with limited economic capital to traverse the world and little leisure time to gather alternative perspectives, the news, therefore, becomes the primary source of supposedly neutral and truthful "information" about other cultures. The power of the media also lies in our own willing suspension of critical judgment regarding news coverage because of the immediate trust that we place in the journalistic principles of objective fact and the responsibility to tell the truth. How do we really know what is going in the world's wars and hostile confrontations and what constitutes those conflicts? What ultimately lies beyond the image of nations who supposedly clamor for United States' intervention, aid, and liberation from tyranny? How does news coverage depict and portray immigrants as always "illegal" and swarming and desperate to realize the American dream? How are specific minorities portrayed in terms of being "criminals," "poor," and/or "model citizens"? What do media enterprises and national governments gain by producing certain kinds of representations? Taken together, these questions encourage us to see our media in a different light and in terms of how mediated images reveal different, vested views of cultures, nations, and world events.

The Tourism Context

With the development of advanced aircraft, train systems, and cruise ships, we are able to travel to different parts of the world and the farthest corners of the globe to encounter new and exciting cultural lands. Consider, for example, that you can catch one of the daily flight routes to Tahiti, Bali, Nepal, Greece, China, and Singapore, as well as thousands of other fascinating destinations. The context of tourism and the travel industry stands as a unique setting through which we can, for a price, experience other cultures and possibly interact with the "natives." The notion of "going native" and delving into the local and indigenous cultures of faraway lands reveals the tourist fascination with "getting close to culture." Thus, individuals join tour groups that take them through the jungles of the Amazon, on African safari, and even to tour rumored cannibalistic lands (MacCannell, 1999). For most of us, our jaunts to common destination sites, such as Mexico and Hawai'i, also stem from a tourist fascination with the indigenous peoples: to see where and how they once lived in the past (and not in contemporary form) and the ultimate demise or decline of the native via tours of once-thriving historical native villages (as if we are witnessing the "death of a culture").

The context of tourism is first and foremost based on economic profit and an elaborate system of commodification that is fused with cultural symbolism, meaning that certain cultural icons, symbols, and meanings are commodified: They are economically valued in terms of a consumer price and exchanged as marketable goods to the tourist. This fast-paced and lucrative travel and tourism industry positions tourists as consumers but in such a way that they experience pleasure and delight in partaking

Performances or displays of cultural traditions and symbols are presented and reconstructed in tourist sites and locales. Thus, we are exposed to specific versions of a culture and what it represents through tourist venues (which could be informed by the cultural group but may not necessarily be so).

in commodified cultural rituals and spectacles. It's vacation and leisure, after all; how could such an industry be harmful when it creates enjoyable travel experiences? The tourism industry ultimately commodifies and sells cultural experiences, images, and representations that are quickly consumed (and in many cases, for exorbitant prices). But tourism is not so straightforward; it is a complex arena in which travel companies, marketers, hotel and show management, and cultural groups themselves (in the destinations) participate in the construction of touristic representations and delights. For example, consider the ways in which native groups themselves work with hotel chains, transportation lines, and travel agency outfits to shape an "authentic" native experience (a meal, ritual ceremony, dance, and/or tour). All of these parties expend great energy in incorporating only the most authentic and native-like elements so as to bring travelers closer to the land and the surrounding culture. As another example, in Bali, a Hilton hotel showcases a Balinese dance by native peoples that actually was created by the Balinese for the sole purpose of entertaining tourists. Thus, a native dance was created within the Balinese community and used in tourist shows at the mainstream Hilton hotel in Bali. What is also interesting is that this "constructed-for-tourists dance" is also being practiced and displayed in private Balinese community festivals and celebrations (outside of the tourism industry). Here, then, an internal/native cultural ritual is specifically created for the external tourist industry and then re-incorporated back into the culture itself. The routes of cultural meanings and representations therefore zig-zag unpredictably through the private and public spheres and the inside and outside of a culture, thereby illustrating the complex and multi-layered dimensions of the tourism industry. Native groups may feel pressured to comply with the tourism industry's practices (and commercialized focus) so as to economically benefit (via state monies, travel industry kickbacks, jobs for native persons as tour guides) their own people, who are often the most economically and socio-politically marginalized groups in their region (as for example, in Australia, Fiji, Mexico, Hawai'i, Guam, Puerto Rico, and South Africa). The cost of participating in the tourism industry, however, may be too high as cultural groups "sell" off their native images and cultural knowledge while also becoming dependent on the influx of tourists and the success of the travel industry. This vicious cycle often dilutes and waters down cultural meanings and provides too much "access" to outsiders, so much so that the cultural community fails to preserve and cherish its own indigenous symbols, meanings, and way of life for itself. The tourism industry makes ample profits and, because of their economic profit base and structure, this context undeniably impacts how cultural groups understand and see their "cultures," what aspects of their cultural knowledge will be commodified, and how we, as tourists, perceive and experience cultures different from our own. All of this, in turn, frames our intercultural communication encounters with these cultures.

The aforementioned contexts of power shape and delimit our intercultural encounters and relationships as well as our own cultural memberships and practices. Reflecting on how certain contexts of power touch our lives is vital for our own critical awareness and future social action.

A Sense of Urgency: A Call for Your Critical Reflection and Action

Because we exist in a globalized, media-saturated, and profit-centered world, we stand at the crossroads of great uncertainties, complex questions, and difficult times. The uncertainty lies in the kind of life we can have for ourselves and loved ones in this complex power-laden world in which we, and cultural groups and nations, may have limited resources of power (money, influence, authority) at our disposal. In addition, there is great angst over issues of war and hostility as we consider the many historically-based and "new" conflicts between, among, and within nations and cultural groups. Will only the military-strong and rich nations prevail, while all others are doomed to cultural decimation? Are there actually some cultural differences that cannot be worked out and mediated no matter how much we try? And, what of the cultural groups and nations whose voices are silenced and not considered—what happens to them? How do oppressed cultural groups and nations resist, remake, and tip the contexts of power in their favor? What interpersonal acts and larger efforts can be made to bridge cultures and bring about conditions of equality and empowerment for all cultural groups? How might we incorporate a more just and transformative way of approaching cultures and intercultural communication in our lives?

All of these questions further emphasize the importance of critical intercultural communication as an area of study. Simply put, we need to examine, study, and care about intercultural communication in terms of issues of power because there is a great deal at stake if we do not. With a great sense of urgency, then, there is a need for us to enact a critical intercultural communication approach in our lives. This perspective enables us to look beyond and beneath the obvious aspects of power (or what is in front of us) as well as dig down into the hidden dimensions.

This entire book is written from a critical intercultural communication perspective and will help guide you through this lens of seeing and knowing. This perspective requires that we seriously consider and engage the following questions as we go about our daily routines and encounters:

- What dimensions, structures, and forces of power are embedded in my own intercultural encounters and relationships? To what extent are these dimensions, structures, and forces of power invisible and/or obvious?

- What kind of power dynamic deeply exists in these encounters and relationships, meaning, what is the hierarchy of power interests and how are different individuals and cultural groups positioned in relation to one another? To what extent does one individual or group have more power than the other?

- How am I positioned in the intercultural relationships and encounters in my life? In different contexts (family, work, school, and to the government, corporations, courts of law, and the media)? To what extent do I gain a power advantage over others in some contexts than in others? To what degree am I marginalized and put at a disadvantage in certain contexts over others?

- What can I do to change and mediate the power differences between individuals and cultural groups? How might I help others who are marginalized and oppressed in society? What are some small and large acts that I can engage in to bring about equality, reconciliation, positive/cordial relations, and build strong communities?

- How can I take advantage of my own position in specific contexts (economic, social, organizational) that may be used to help marginalized communities?

- How can I raise important questions about culture and power with those around me (my family, friends, classmates, co-workers, and community/cultural members)?

These questions encourage us to seriously consider the different power dimensions that occur in intercultural interactions and relations. Think of how much we all could help one another if we made it a practice to step out of our normal routines and conveniences to question and analyze issues of intercultural interaction in terms of power. We may gain great insight on others from different backgrounds and the experiences they are having in relation to structures of power. We may also learn about our own selves and the taken-for-granted aspects of our cultural identities and experiences. Herein, we can become more attuned thinkers, analysts, cultural members, and societal participants as humans attached to larger communities. These gains represent only some of the amazing gifts that can be proffered through the active practicing of the critical intercultural communication perspective in our lives and, more specifically, in terms of our intercultural communication encounters and relationships (Halualani, 2011a).

Purpose of This Book

This book was written for the sole purpose of having you envision your role in contributing and building a more just world and engaging in intercultural justice. Intercultural justice stands as the notion of taking action to help culturally different communities, groups, or persons (of your own or outside of your group), whose identities and lives are negatively impacted by structures of power. Another term used is social justice, which refers to the ways to positively transform society by working toward the re-distribution of advantages, disadvantages, benefits, and resources to those in need or left without these forms.

The ACT Framework for Intercultural Justice

A useful framework for intercultural justice is ACT, with each letter representing a specific component and step, delineated as follows:

A refers to the steps in raising one's **awareness**. This requires us to revisit certain contexts and structures in our lives that we have taken for granted. The goal here is to be open to reflecting on and re-examining one's deeply held beliefs, views, and knowledge of cultural concepts, even if such reflection is difficult and or even face threatening to one's self.

C speaks to the next step of considering, questioning, and **critiquing** invisible dimensions of power. This book's chapters provide examples and topical information to break down and uncover, in terms of complex concepts of power at play, and evaluate these concepts in terms of the impact on our lives.

T addresses the stage of **thoughtfully taking action,** individually and collectively. It is also important to conceptualize action in terms of two aspects: individual action and collective action.

- Individual action refers to those acts that you can plan and enact on your own in terms of pushing for a change in the status quo.

- Collective action represents work that can be achieved with others in a formal or informal organization, collective effort, or association in order to challenge a structure of power and advocate for and assist a cultural group in terms of their needs and struggles.

The ACT framework for intercultural justice reminds us to be mindful of the issues and complexities here, and how not everything can be "solved" with a single action. Instead, this framework proffers a continual and ongoing process of becoming open to and aware of structured inequalities and disproportionate power relations, engaging in deep consideration and critique of structured oppressions, and thoughtfully taking up such action that will have a positive impact on others in our intercultural world.

The ACT framework for intercultural justice is what cultural studies scholars refer to as "agency" or the socially shaped capability to act and make a difference against a structure of power or practice of domination. This framework represents a way to counteract and challenge forces of power that affect our intercultural lives.

Summary

Power is embedded in many visible and invisible aspects of our lives. A critical intercultural communication approach allows us to examine how power plays out in our intercultural communication encounters, contexts, and relationships. We are surrounded by contexts of power (economic, governmental, legal, media, family, tourism) that possess a hierarchy of dominant and subordinate interests. Through the ACT framework for intercultural justice, this book invites us to take action to help culturally different communities, groups, or persons (of your own or outside of your group) whose identities and lives are negatively impacted by structures of power.

Keywords

ACT framework for intercultural justice

Collective action

Contexts of power

Critical intercultural communication
   approach (or critical approach to
   intercultural communication)

Dominant party

Individual action

Intercultural justice

Power

Social justice

Subordinate party

Unseen or invisible structures of power

Questions and Activities

REFLECTION activity on your intercultural life:

Think about your own life and experiences. Ask yourself the following questions:

- What aspects of culture and intercultural communication play out in your own life?

- What about those aspects have you not thought of before?

- Why do you think these aspects were not noticed before?

- What larger structures and contexts are also embedded into your own experiences—family, neighborhood, school, and work life?

DISCUSSION activity on contexts of power:

What other contexts of power (not covered in this chapter) do you see as impacting intercultural communication? How so? Think of specific examples.

DISCUSSION activity on ACT framework for intercultural justice:

Discuss the following questions in class/online: What are some examples of individual action and collective action that you see in society in terms of intercultural justice? How do you see yourself using the ACT framework for intercultural justice?

Chapter 2

Culture, Power, and Intercultural Communication

Learning Objectives

➤ To understand the notion of culture through a power-based perspective

➤ To explore the key characteristics of power

➤ To re-think culture as a field of forces

Introduction: Vu's Search: What Is Vietnamese Culture?

Vu is a first-generation Vietnamese American high school senior in Chico, California. His parents were both born in Vietnam and emigrated to the US in the 1980s. As an only child with no surviving grandparents, Vu had always wanted to know more about his Vietnamese background. Though his parents taught him how to speak some of their native language, he rarely used it. There were no relatives living nearby, let alone in the States, and he had never been to Vietnam (as his parents wanted him to "look at the future and not the past"). Vu felt hungry for knowledge about his culture. However, finding out about the Vietnamese culture was no easy task. Vu explains, "I remember I started looking up different newspaper articles online—any reference to Vietnamese culture or people—and most of the stuff that came up was about

Vietnamese refugees. About the Vietnamese as a war-torn people who endured French colonialism and a Communist regime and had to flee for safety to this country. I don't know. Reading about that—it made Vietnam seem pretty messed up, like you would go there and see nothing good. It seemed completely destroyed by war."

Vu had moved from newspaper articles to actual history books—texts that his social studies teacher recommended for him—and others available in his local library. Again, for Vu, the focus on Vietnam always seemed to be about war, namely the Vietnam War with the U.S. There were details about how Vietnam was torn apart by way of a conflict between the north (the Communist regime) and the south (a pro-U.S. administration) and how the U.S. intervened by sending military troops to aid the southern part.

Vu shares what he found in these accounts: "When it was a historical account from an American, it was about saving and liberating the weak Vietnamese from the evils of Communism, but I found some stuff from the Vietnamese in the States and from movement groups in Vietnam and that stuff talked about how the Vietnamese were a strong people—that they fended off French and Japanese colonizers and then, through Communism, fought off the U.S. You get very different perspectives. Are the Vietnamese passive and in need of help, or more assertive and strong?"

Vu still had questions and it was made more complicated as he looked at books or research reports that discussed the beliefs and values of Vietnamese culture. "I looked up information from anthropology, sociology, anything I could find, and what I got was some knowledge about the Vietnamese beliefs in animal and ancestor worship and that there is a mix of folk beliefs with other religions within my culture (Buddhism, Taoism, Confucianism, Catholicism, Protestantism). It sounded really cool and pretty complicated. But when you compare that stuff to tourist accounts or guide books (which came up in my search), Vietnamese are just this friendly, carefree people who greet and interact with visitors all the time. They are happy and carefree, you know? There are pictures of Vietnamese in these tour guides smiling, laughing, which is so different from the pictures in the newspapers or history books—those Vietnamese were crying and looked lost. And then Vietnamese scholars and activists have different images—that of Vietnamese standing tall and proud with their fists up with patriotism and with this real sense of pride and strength in keeping Vietnam a strong, independent nation. So, which is it? Which image best fits my culture? What is my Vietnamese culture really?"

This example demonstrates that culture is defined in various ways and by multiple structures of power such as the government, legal system, economy, educational institutions, and media, as well as by cultural communities as a whole and individual members themselves. In light of this example, several questions arise: How can this be? Isn't culture a consistent and uniform set of meanings shared by all members across contexts? Why are there different versions of what a culture entails? Why does Vu encounter such varying definitions of Vietnamese culture? Aren't the meanings of culture consistent within and across cultural groups? These questions problematize the notion of culture, especially in terms of its predominant conceptualization as a set of meanings purely created by and shared among cultural groups as a whole.

A Power-Based Perspective: Re-thinking Culture and Intercultural Communication

The concepts of culture and intercultural communication are difficult to define and reveal a multi-layered nature that is often forgotten or ignored. We learned from chapter 1 that power is the constraining force by which larger dominant structures, groups, and individuals are able to gain in position and achieve their aims over/against the will of others. This chapter will focus on the power-based perspective of culture that will be used throughout this book and help ground our understanding of intercultural communication. Several examples of how a power-based perspective frames culture differently from our everyday outlook will be shared. After reading this chapter, you will be anchored in the notion of culture as a field of forces that encompass multiple layers, contexts, and elements of power.

A perspective that focuses on power reveals great insights about aspects of culture and intercultural communication relations (Gibson, 2007). But, what exactly is power? Is it something we all have, or just something some of us engage in? Is power an entity that we can see and touch? Is it a positive or negative force? The next section delineates a power-based perspective as it relates to understanding culture, communication, and intercultural communication in a different light.

Typically, individuals view power as "physical coercion" in which one individual dominates over another. In addition, for many, power seems to connote a type of social influence over others to act and think in a specific way. The underlying assumption of these popular conceptions is that power is defined from the standpoint of someone who is exerting or enacting power, or someone who is deemed *powerful*. But, lest we forget that

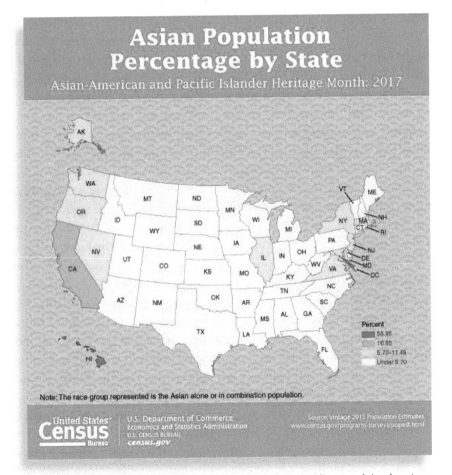

Asian Americans continue to grow in number in the U.S. and while some Asian American groups and generations experience upward socioeconomic mobility, others do not. Moreover, many Asian Americans, despite their socioeconomic class standing and generational status, still experience systemic and social discrimination.

power is multidimensional, it can push and be pushed. Power can destroy and create. These dimensions are grounded, though, in the specific context of power at hand and the position one occupies in relation to dominant power.

For example, Asian Pacific American communities occupy a unique position in relation to dominant power. Within the last 15 years, a multitude of East Asians—Chinese, Taiwanese, Koreans, Japanese—and Asian Indians, who have recently emigrated into the US and conduct transnational business around the globe, have emerged as the upper professional class among all racial/ethnic groups (e.g., Cross, 2017; Kim, 2000; Ong, 1999; and Zhou, 2004). Many members of these groups have purchased expensive homes in largely White/European American affluent neighborhoods and gained high-profile leadership positions in city and state government. These Asian Americans also enroll their children into prestigious schools and universities, many of whom go on to earn scholastic honors (e.g., academic awards and valedictorian status). With such increased affluence, society has labeled Asian Americans as the new "Whites": an ethnic group that has achieved economic and political success and, in turn, pushed out all other racial/ethnic groups from gains in power (as well as replacing majority groups at the top of the hierarchy). This example belies a more complex relationship between Asian Americans and their relationship to dominant power (Chou & Feagin, 2015). While they may have financially established themselves, Asian Americans, especially those that have emerged in the upper, professional, and middle classes, still experience systemic and social discrimination.

As a contrast, Southeast Asian communities (e.g., Vietnamese, Laotians, Hmong, and Cambodians) have established a presence in the U.S. with population numbers running at two million and residing in states such as California, Illinois, Minnesota, and New York, among others (United States Census Bureau, 2017). However, according to a 2000 report jointly released by the Asian Pacific American Legal Center, Asian Law Caucus, and National Asian Pacific American Legal Consortium, Southeast Asians stand as one of the poorest Asian groups in California, with Hmong, Cambodian, and Laotian communities being the poorest (Kula & Paik, 2016; Mio & Fu, 2017; Tang, 2000). Thus, Southeast Asians do not have the economic and political resources that other Asian Americans do, which means that they are relegated to dilapidated neighborhood areas, lower-tier jobs, economically deficient schools, and diminished means to voice their needs to governmental and social agencies. All of this translates into a heavily imbalanced relationship between this cultural group and the larger structures of power and dominant interests. However, it is important to note that while Southeast Asians face more significant challenges to financial and political empowerment, they *do have the power* to express their frustrations, voice their concerns, resist institutional and economic racism, and push for transformation, albeit in more confined channels. Thus, the particular relationship between a cultural group and dominant power, therefore, determines the kind of push-pull dynamic a cultural group will face in a power-laden world. Meaning, the degree to which a cultural community (or even a member) will face resistance from structures of power and dominant parties will determine how much leeway it can have for resistance and how creative it must be in overcoming structural and power obstacles. Given their limited hold on formal power resources such as economic and political influence, Southeast Asians have relied on the one resource in their favor: community mobilization. They have been able to bring together and mobilize Southeast Asians across regions to protest societal dominance over them. One example of this can be seen in the collective organization, SAKHI for South Asian Women, a community-based organization in the New York metropolitan area committed to ending the exploitation and violence against women of South Asian origin. Another stands in the form of the Southeast Asian Resource Action Center (SEARAC), which is a national organization that advances the interests of Cambodian, Laotian, and Vietnamese Americans through advocacy and leadership development.

Somewhere in between the struggling Southeast Asian groups and the upper-class East Asian Americans and Asian Indians, there lie several other Asian American groups who have lived in this country for over 20 years (and, for the children, all of their lives), and bought homes, settled into stable jobs, and managed to send their now-grown children to college. Chinese Americans, Japanese Americans, and Korean Americans have, for example, established a presence in the United States since their initial period of immigration (Cross, 2017; Hwang & Jaimes, 1999; Kula & Paik, 2016; Omi & Winant, 2014).

Given their settled status in the US, middle class Asian Americans stand in a tricky position in relation to dominant power. They feel vested in the American system of power given their hard work and sacrifice all these years and thus, work hard to strike a balance between gaining societal acceptance (and improving their social status) and resisting persistent discrimination issued against them for being "forever foreign" immigrants. Thus, these middle class Asian Americans are not likely to express outright hostility against and make trouble for structures of power; instead, they feel compelled to protect what they (and their families) have and blend into society as Americans as best as possible. Though middle class Asians Americans face similar discrimination like all other Asian American groups (but in different ways), they still feel more attached to and dependent on dominant power and thus will behave in ways that do not threaten that relationship (although, when needed, these communities will protest and demand recognition as hard-working ethnic Americans). Again, the position a cultural group occupies in relation to dominant power and structures of power helps to shape that group's relationship to dominant power and larger society, as well as the kind of push-pull dynamic (whether in the extreme, medium, or subdued sense) that will ensue.

These examples, therefore, demonstrate that the power dynamic between cultural groups (and members) and structures of power and dominant parties can vary from context to context and from group to group. In addition, the aforementioned examples illustrate the double-sided nature of power, or the constraining and enabling aspects of power. Power can be both a controlling force that seeks to restrict the movements and experiences of individuals and groups as well as an enabling force that individuals and groups can deploy in dramatic or subtle form against larger structures (Chen & Morley, 2006; During, 2004; Hall, 1996c; Popular Memory Group, 1982).

With this in mind, power can be defined as the following:

1. A constraining force by which individuals, groups, and structures are able to achieve their aims and interests over/against the will of others, and

2. An enabling and creative force that individuals and groups can use against larger structures.

Characteristics of Power

Power is characterized by several attributes or qualities that solidify its force (Thompson, 2013). There are several key characteristics of power that complicate the relationship between cultural groups, dominant parties, and structures of power:

Power Is Invisible and Hidden

As discussed in chapter 1, we cannot see all of the power structures in our lives. Think about the set of friendships that you have in your life. These friendships are special, precious, and very private. It even seems that we voluntary choose, out of all the possible options, who our friends will be based on common interests, personality, group associations, and similar backgrounds. However, friendships remain a hidden context shaped by historical, economic, and power forces. The settings through which we forge friendships are not neutral, blank slates. Rather, without our conscious attention, these settings are already layered over with power influences such as history, economics, and cultural/social inequalities (influences that are deeply engrained and difficult to see on the surface). For instance, the neighborhoods that we reside in, the workplaces that we are part of, and the social outlets to which we attend have a predetermined set of relations laid out for us due to history and economics. Through historical patterns of migration and conflict, certain cultural groups have been placed in closer contact and shared settings with one another. In specific cities, one or two cultural groups stand as the primary residents of particular areas—Whites/European Americans dominating one area and in another, Whites/European Americans, Asian Americans, and Latino/as. Economics further shape these settings because

Similar to the "yin and yang" dialectical and complementary system, the characteristics of power as constraining and power as enabling, together capture the interlocked complexity of social power in today's world.

economic cycles and hierarchies of people place us in neighborhoods, schools, workplaces, and social outlets with other individuals of *similar socioeconomic status* (and detach us from individuals outside of our class status). Thus, if historical and economic cycles and hierarchies position us with one or two other racial/ethnic groups, it is likely that most of our everyday contact and friendships will occur with members of these groups. Friendships, then, are social contracts that are based on some degree of limited choice and are invisibly framed by historical and economic conditions and the resulting cultural/social inequalities. This example suggests that power dimensions are unseen, invisible, and untraceable. Ponder other everyday experiences, choices, relationships, and interactions that fill your life and how these may be framed, to some degree and in invisible form, by macro-power influences. Just because we do not "see" such power domination or daily wars in our streets does not mean that they do not exist. Social control and power gains even more potency through its invisible nature. Power can move swiftly and easily when unsuspected and forgotten, especially when it touches our intercultural and interpersonal relationships and interactions.

Power Is Material

Power also manifests itself differently within and among groups, creating inequalities and a society of haves and have-nots. Power is material in that it results in concrete, tangible consequences for all those involved, especially in terms of economic implications, or the amount of money we have, the type of jobs that we are able to enter in, the kind of lifestyle we are able to lead, and how we, as different groups, are economically exploited (Hall, 1996; Storey, 2016; Van Dijk, 2015). Simply put, the degree of material power that you possess (or do not) determines, in part, how you are able to live, how others (and even yourself) view you, and society's valuation of you in terms of the economic context. Material power, while operating mostly through the economic mode of production, also impacts the social spheres of our lives: how we think and relate to one another through issues of money, status, and economic gain/loss at home, school, work, places of worship, and in times of leisure. In its materiality, power then carries real effects on individuals and groups; it can hit a person hard in his or her pocketbook and affect how society treats him or her. Material power can even determine that person's very survival in, for example, war-torn countries and top-heavy national economies that exploit the working and immigrant classes.

Cultural group members are undoubtedly affected by material power in that there are distinct economic differences among, between, and within specific racial, ethnic, religious, and regional groups. Ponder how, in the US, certain racial/ethnic group members, such as Mexicans/Mexican Americans, Southeast Asian Americans, and under-classed Whites/European Americans that make up the working class, take on "blue collar" tier manual labor (housekeeping, janitorial services, gardeners, construction) and factory jobs and are often treated with disdain, avoidance, and pity (Waisman, 2015). Because of material power, these groups often experience social marginalization and economic exploitation (as they are paid small wages for taxing labor in horrific working conditions). The experiences of these groups are markedly different from those of their racial/ethnic group counterparts (of all different backgrounds but most notably Whites/European Americans, Asian Americans, and Asian Indians) in the upper professional classes (doctors, lawyers, engineers, and business executives) who are in a position to practice more economic freedom and enter and participate in American society and institutions (although minority upper professional classes still experience discrimination and resentment from society because they are posed as "economic threats"). Thus, in comparison to the upper professional classes, the working class is looked down upon and they are deemed "lowly," as well as the professions associated with them, which become racially/ethnically marked jobs, and receive limited (if any) medical and family benefits and protection on the job. Likewise, this class is considered to be a disposable and easy-to-replace labor force and is granted a disproportionate amount of power to influence the political, economic, and social arenas of society with little money (and no increasing cycle of wages), and possess limited political representation as well as a restricted voice to express discontent with jobs (Bell, 2017; Waisman, 2015). These material differences set the stage for often tense, contentious, and even a lack of intercultural encounters and relationships between different economic classes (who scholars suggest may only interact in economic-based service transactions with individuals locked into their economic positions). Power and domination are not light matters; these forces, especially in the material sense, affect every fiber of our being and carry real implications for various cultural groups in different ways.

Power Is Constraining

When we are placed in a subordinate social, economic, or political position to a larger power—like when a manager reprimands an employee for critiquing the company's weak organizational culture or when a parent disciplines a daughter for being too "bold" and aggressive for a "girl"—we are made to feel repressed, punished, and inferior. The taxing and painful experience of being dominated reveals the constraining and dominating tendency of power. For example, Filipinos all over the world have been made to feel dominated for several decades, first with colonization by Spain and then colonization by the US (which still has a military presence in the Philippines, although hostile threats are minimal) (Mendoza, 2002; Mendoza & Strobel, 2015). Such domination has reverberated throughout the hearts, minds, and souls of Filipinos for centuries. Filipinos punish themselves for being naturally "weak" and "inferior" to colonial powers, questioning the value of their culture, language, and traditions (which become a form of internal colonialism in which the oppressed marginalize and rebuke their own selves).

Consider also the African and Asian slave trades throughout Europe, Asia, and across the Atlantic, which today still have far-reaching effects throughout the world (across all of the main continents) and how individuals were stripped of their rights and individual freedoms as humans, and their citizenship and power to control aspects of their lives (physically, socially, economically, and politically). The toll exacted on enslaved individuals by colonialist (and greedy) governments is unimaginable as they experienced, according to Mendoza and Strobel (2015), a form of epistemic violence that undermines and devalues their own cultural identities. Through such epistemic violence and extreme subjugation, individuals and cultural groups are constrained by governmental, legal, economic, institutional, and social forces, as their movement, desires, and perceptions are contained. The conceptualization of power as constraining, therefore speaks to the type of power—one through coercion, force, and violence—that has been historically established in the age of exploration, conquest, and domination and is synonymous with martial states and colonialist administrations. However, constraining types of power still linger and seep into the experiences and lives of many different cultural groups and countries. Thus, given its long-established and still-active presence, the constraining and dominant mode of power must be named and exposed as it relates to intercultural communication encounters and relations.

Power Is Enabling and Creative

In the same turn, though, while power can restrain, limit, and contain us, power can also be productive and creative. It is not just a force that subjects us to top-down configurations. Instead, individuals' capacity to change, or at least challenge, their dominated structures and conditions can be enabled through power. We, as individuals and cultural groups, possess a different type of power than larger power structures and forces. We have the ability to resist and act through social means, meaning, oppressed cultural groups can mobilize members and protest structures like the government, law enforcement, military, and corporate powers via rallies, picketing, strikes (which shut down businesses), marches, riots, and activist organizing. In regard to the earlier example of the Filipinos, Filipino communities in the Philippines and the US have used their power to develop a grass roots indigenous Filipino movement that renews the "original" languages, traditions, and practices that were cast aside by colonial powers. Filipino movement groups challenge the Westernized constructions of Filipino culture and re-narrate their indigenous historical origins. It is their hope to recreate the Philippines as an indigenous sovereign nation, much like the Native Hawaiians seek to do with Hawai'i. The Filipino case illustrates that even in the most repressive conditions of domination, power can be remade by marginalized individuals and groups in creative and complicated ways.

Dominant forms of power can even be re-deployed by individuals and groups to work in their interests. Indigenous Native American and Latin American groups, for example, use the prevailing courts system (a dominant structure of power), and international law and legal loopholes to stop corporate development, modernization, and encroachment of their sacred cultural lands (Bonvillain, 2016; Lobo, Talbot, & Carlston, 2016). In the U.S., during the 1960s, Chicano/as used group mobilization and activist organizing to resist dominant society's unfair and harsh treatment of Mexican migrant workers. These activists also used the power of the law in a resistive way to charge police with excessive force and brutality during peaceful protests. Hawaiian nationalists have used the state and federal supreme court venues to "sue" the United States for illegally seizing Hawaiian land in 1893 and demand that Hawai'i be returned completely to the Hawaiian people as a separate nation from the US (Silva, 2004; see Halualani, 2002, for a detailed analysis of Hawaiian cultural politics). Thus, there is wiggle room within

Native American tribes have engaged in collective protest to creatively resist larger forces of power that usurp their cultural rights to land, water, and sovereignty.

dominant contexts, structures, and conditions to maximize the enabling aspect of power; power—even dominant forms—can be used to recreate and remake conditions for marginalized cultural groups.

These last two attributes—power as constraining and power as enabling—seem, at first glance, to be contradictory. How can power be both extremes? Such a contradiction represents the dialectical tensions of power. We feel overwhelmed and determined by power at times (and constrained), but we also can use power productively, strategically, and creatively in any setting and circumstance and within the terms of our individual lives and experiences to fight against power domination (and thus be enabled). These two linked dimensions capture the complexity of social power in today's world as critical scholars have attributed to and highlighted as deriving from theorist Karl Marx:

Individuals "make history in conditions not of their own making." (Hall, 1980b). That is, we work within the parameters of the power dynamic that are embedded in our lives (De Certeau, 1984). Thus, hope is not lost in that cultural groups who live amid power forces and structures can maneuver around (though not escape) and maximize the power-laden conditions of their lives. Individuals and cultural groups have agency or the ability to act and possibly change their lives for the better. It is important to remember that our experiences as cultural group members are structured and embedded by dimensions of power that frame but do not dominate or lock in our actions.

A power-based perspective therefore enables a uniquely rich view of intercultural communication and the concrete power pressures, demands, and realities of individuals and cultural groups in their intercultural communication relationships and encounters.

What Is Culture?

What truly constitutes culture? Is it a complicated system of world views, beliefs, values, and attitudes that are passed down from one cultural generation to another? Is culture a shared mindset and outlook on life created and solidified through the cohesion of cultural group membership? Do we automatically inherit or learn culture, or the world views, beliefs, and practices of a group/community? Conceptualizing and defining culture seems to be an insurmountable task as it seems to encompass so many attributes, perceptions, behaviors, and traditions, leading to the question: Where does culture begin and where does it end?

For the scope of this book, let us think of culture as a set of meanings that result from a social process of meaning-making. More specifically, culture is a socially constructed system of meanings among group members who collectively shape world views, perceptions, beliefs, values, attitudes, cultural practices, and identities that bind them together and toward one particular way of life. Members of a group, therefore, participate in the creation and circulation of a set of meanings that constitute their culture. For example, individuals in a particular racial or ethnic community co-construct meaning by discussing, debating, and sharing with others what their group stands for and how they see the world, as well as the specific rituals and customs that represent their group's core values and demonstrate loyalty to and pride for one's group. A set of meanings is socially created by individuals *and* passed down and enculturated among later generations through the social process of communication. Culture is therefore both the product and process of individuals and groups coming together and making meaning around a way of life. And while it seems as if culture is a neatly packaged system that gets reproduced time after time (as if we automatically know and inherit culture), it is important to note that the social processes and relationships that occur around and within and give meaning to culture are often overlooked.

The social processes and relationships that give meaning to culture do not occur in a vacuum; they are situated in a particular historical, socioeconomic, and political moment. Indeed, while it stands as a group or socially constructed system of meaning, culture is also created within specific historical and political conditions and contexts, meaning culture is not just limited to those meanings created and shared by its group members; it is a set of meanings constituted in negotiation and contest with overseeing national and state governments, larger world and political trends (for example, in times of war), economic markets and modernization (technology, late capitalism, competition), legal systems, and international, interethnic, and interracial hostilities.

In other words, culture is not an essential (natural/internal) set of traits or characteristics or psychological tendencies possessed by and shared within a group of individuals merely by virtue of their geographically "belonging together." To assume this would be to believe that culture is an automatic given among its members and internalized as a whole without much variation or disagreement. Intercultural communication scholar Dreama Moon (1996) reminds us that culture is not "unproblematically shared" and is constituted by multiple parties and power interests. Think about the cultural memberships that are most salient to you. Ask yourself: Is there a consistent set of meanings, world views, beliefs, values, and attitudes shared by all cultural members? Are your cultural group's meanings uniform in content, function, and form? Do all of your cultural group's members possess the same views and engage in the same culturally appropriate behaviors? Do all of your cultural group's members reach consensus about what their culture entails? It is likely that you answered "no" to a few, if not all, of these questions. How can this be? How can we have disagreement within our own cultural groups and yet at the same time believe that our own cultural system is coherent and unified in meaning and equally shared among its members? The image of culture is mystical in this way; it seems to be all-encompassing, "natural," and widely shared within a community, which obscures what occurs beneath the surface of culture: the construction of an invisible hierarchy of meanings created by different power interests that articulate what a culture stands for (its main essence).

Thus, from a power-based perspective, **culture** is a system of meanings and representations created in an entangled field of forces through which differently positioned entities (i.e., dominant government, legal, economic, mediated, institutional, and educational structures), groups, and persons compete for the power to define, represent, and even own a culture and its resources (land, artifacts, and cultural practices).

As a guiding example to better understand this reconceptualization of culture, let's consider Native American Indian culture, which is represented through 562 federally recognized tribes in the US (Bonvillain, 2016; Lobo, Talbot, & Carlston, 2016; Waldman, 2014). The culture of Native American Indians spans more than just a singular group with a specific cultural way of being and form of expression. Social scientists, communication studies scholars, and anthropologists have studied Native American communities and concluded that Native American culture consists of a world view based on nature and spirituality as connected to land and animal life. According to these studies, for Native Americans, human existence is to be in balance with the surrounding nature and land. While these nature-based representations of Native Americans have dominated academic research, newspaper coverage, and media representations in television and film, the image of Native Americans as deeply connected to nature and land stands as just one of the many configurations of Native American culture, or the set of meanings that constitute this cultural group.

There is a more expansive and enmeshed field of forces through which the US government, local and state governments (with the spread of Indian gaming and casinos), native agencies created by the government (Bureau of Indian Affairs), anthropologists, archaeologists, historians, tribal governments, and Native American communities are all (and have been historically) vying to define the culture of "Native Americanness," native belonging, and entitlement (Bonvillain, 2016; Lobo, Talbot, & Carlston, 2016; Waldman, 2014). For example, there is a contentious history between early European explorers (and later American colonialists) and Native American Indians (self-proclaimed as the peoples who are indigenous to the territory known as the United States of America). In the 1500s, European explorers on the North American continent believed that "some men were inferior by nature to uphold the view that Indians were slaves by nature" (Parker, 1996, p. 2). Europeans, at the time, felt that Native American Indians were much like "children" and therefore needed protection from larger, superior Christian nations. There existed the imperialist view during this period that a Christian nation had a natural right to conquer Indians and seize their lands. Christian European nations therefore deemed themselves as superior to Native American tribes, thereby possessing the right to rule over all non-Christian inhabitants and territories. Throughout the 18th and 19th centuries, American colonialists employed this imperialist view and claimed exclusive title to Indian lands gained by early European explorers. In past treaties with Native American Indians and federal legislation that delimit Native American tribal reservations and Native American "rehabilitation" programs, the US government repeatedly characterized the Native American culture as a savage, barbaric, and undeveloped group inferior in intelligence, civility, and the ability to govern themselves (much like children) compared to European American colonialists.

According to the federal government, Native American culture stood as a "weaker," "inferior," and "uncivilized" group that could not survive in the modern world. As such, the US federal government solidified this representation of Native American culture by legally defining Native Americanness as being attributed to only those individuals who can prove blood parentage (with verifiable documents). Thus, Native American culture is further delimited as a people made in the "blood" or based on biological heritage (Pearson, 2017; Wilkins & Stark, 2017). Such a representation becomes important to the federal government as it struggles to claim rightful ownership of all Native American land, which is deemed the property of the true indigenous settlers of American land: Native Americans. In order to make claims to the large tracts of Native American land, the colonialist federal government would have to depict Native American culture as not "fit" to take care of such land (nor manage a large civilization) and as a race that is dying out and nearing extinction (as evident in the decreasing number of members who can prove actual blood parentage). Today, the blood quantum requirement imposed on Native Americans stands as a difficult-to-meet criterion that excludes many Native Americans from claiming any right to their heritage, tribal membership, and tribal land lots. Native American Indian reservations were also created to seemingly furnish this cultural group with some land, but the reservation system was actually set up to contain, racially and spatially mark, and "rehabilitate" and "modernize" Native Americans (Dippel, 2014; Waldman, 2014). Thus, the meaning of Native American culture was not solely created or represented by Native American Indians themselves. Native American culture is therefore defined in a specific way by past colonialist and present federal governmental administrations for a specific power aim: to gain land and power (and simultaneously displace a cultural group deemed to be inferior and soon to be extinct).

A Native American member showcases aspects of his cultural identity and world view, which have also been historically and currently framed by the larger US media and government.

In a similar vein, in 1824, the US federal government created an agency—the Bureau of Indian Affairs (hereafter BIA)—"charged with enhancing the quality of life, promoting economic opportunity, and carrying out the responsibility to protect and improve the trust assets of tribal governments, American Indians, and Alaska Natives" and assist Native Americans with benefits, services, loans, and education and employment opportunities (https://www.bia.gov/bia;). However, this agency that seems to serve and protect the interests of Native Americans, largely works in the interests of the federal government. For instance, the BIA requires that Native Americans who receive services and opportunities provide proof that she or he is listed as an Indian by blood on a base roll of a federally recognized Indian tribe. Through such a requirement, the BIA is clearly aligned with the federal government's aim in containing Native American culture spatially and socially.

Likewise, cultural anthropologists in the past have also participated in defining and representing Native American Indians as a culture, in terms of shaping their histories and identifying the "true" markers of Native Americanness (world views, belief system, cultural and communication styles) (Lobo, Talbot, & Carlston, 2016).

In turn, Native American Indian communities have redefined their culture in response to the governmental and academic constructions of them. As early as the 1800s, Native American Indian tribes took legal action through the US court system to challenge the US government's appropriation of their lands and the government's construction of them as undeveloped and unfit landowners. Several tribes even composed a constitution that redefined their communities as independent, sovereign nations who had been historically oppressed by dominant society.

Culture as a Field of Forces: Four Premises

Different power interests shape uneven, contradictory, and even contentious framings of cultures, which carries serious political and social implications for those cultural groups. Culture, in this way, should be viewed as a larger field of forces. This reconceptualization rests on four premises that merit discussion.

First premise: The core meanings that make up culture derive not just from the cultural group itself, but from a myriad of competing structures and parties that seek to define culture in a such a way that privilege their own interests. Meanings that constitute the "face" of a culture come from a variety of power sources and do not merely serve the needs of a cultural community. Instead, meanings and representations of culture that are created and circulated by specific structures and parties of power enable these entities to, above all else, meet their needs and advance their own agendas. Dominant structures of power prioritize the goals of maintaining and increasing their dominance in society and thus, participate in the act of defining, constituting, and representing cultures with these goals in mind (Said, 2012). For instance, governments can justify tighter control and restrictions over cultures that they deem (and in turn come to define) as a people "in need" or that pose as militaristic or economic threats to the nation. African Americans, Native Americans, Puerto Ricans, and Hawaiians have historically been labeled and defined by the federal government as "inferior people" who are in need of "rehabilitation," "development," and "guidance" by US governmental bodies (Ashcroft, Griffiths, & Tiffin, 2013). Such definitions have served as vehicles to justify slavery, segregation, illegal annexation, and the containment and dispersion of peoples in specific cultural ethnic enclaves, villages, homesteads, or reservations.

Second premise: The meanings of culture that are created by structures of power mostly benefit these dominant structures rather than the actual cultural groups that are being represented. Indeed, meanings carry political weight and are considered to be the driving "capital" for some structures of power to gain much more than the actual cultures being depicted (During, 2004; Hall, 1980b). Thus, cultures that are being represented and depicted by specific structures of power gain little, if any. The definitions created do not contribute to the substance and structure of a cultural group in such a way that the group benefits economically and politically. For instance, consider the corporations and retailers who create and promote specific economic profiles of culture groups and how much money they make from ethnic marketing strategies. Such revenue is not apportioned out to, or even enjoyed by, the cultural groups of focus. Oftentimes, the representations are created at the expense of the cultural group and end up stereotyping or simplifying the nature of that group's cultural system. For example, fast-food chains such as McDonald's have advertisements that feature (and thus presume) only Latino or African American patrons, while Whole Foods ads display only younger White customers. Basketball shoe and apparel companies have advertising campaigns that showcase African American hip-hop and rap artists and influencers and African American customers. Corporate brands have long created Spanish language advertising campaigns to "court" Latino consumers and thus, presume that all Latino/as speak Spanish and/or want to be reached through that language. These marketing representations work to benefit the corporate brands and do not fully consider the needs of the cultural groups themselves.

Third premise: The meanings created by influential structures of power tend to "stick," gain more credibility, and therefore, are considered to be the "real" face of a culture. Ironically, although structures of power are external sources of representation for cultural groups, there is no way to differentiate between externally created meanings (those created by forces other than the group itself) and internally created meanings (those created by the actual groups themselves) of culture. Instead, all the meanings seem to

McDonald's glocalizes its products for its surrounding specific national/ethnic group or country. For example, McDonald's sells Greek Mac pitas in Greece or sandwiches with Tikka or Indian spices in India. This move of glocalization allows a global brand to appeal to a specific ethnic/national audience which can also reproduce global and Westernized culture.

be "natural," "truthful," and "real," and as if they originated from the groups themselves. What occurs here is that the meanings created by structures of power may incorporate the culture's native language or imagery (or, in mediated forms, actors who descend from that group) and therefore become blurred and naturalized as authentic reflections of that culture. With access to money and resources that enable the circulating of specific images of culture, dominant structures and parties of power gain a foothold. In addition, dominant structures of power, such as the government and the media, often rely on the authoritative discourses of "scientific fact" (through which scientific studies are cited as evidence for how a culture "naturally is") and "cultural expertise" (through which cultural members "narrate" the internal truths of their culture, and social and cultural researchers who have studied the group at hand, point to the inner workings of that culture at hand).

A culture is continually perceived and valued based on the more sensationalized and widely reproduced meanings and the incorporation of seemingly authentic elements, such as symbols, imagery, and voices that come from within that cultural group. With culture as a field of forces, there is a dual process at work: Structures of power create definitions of culture to meet their own needs and goals, and, in turn, these definitions take on a life of their own and are widely reproduced by these structures and society as the actual reflections of that culture.

Complicating matters, what also happens is that cultural groups being represented often internalize these meanings and project these as their own "authentic" reflections of who they are. Meanings and images created by structures of power enter in and become fused with a larger collection of representations, portrayals, world views, and beliefs of a cultural group. There are no distinctions between these meanings in terms of their source of origin; instead, they all appear equally convincing, credible, and "real." Cultural group members, therefore, internalize meanings and representations that may not have derived from their own cultural systems and may, in fact, benefit others rather than themselves.

Native Hawaiian culture stands as a primary example of the naturalization and incorporation of externally created meanings. To this day, Hawaiians believe that one of their most important cultural values is the "Aloha spirit" (or what is also known as "Hawaiianness at heart"), which is based on the notion that the Hawaiian culture (meanings, world view, cultural practices, and even resources such as land and artifacts) is to be equally shared, not only among all Hawaiians, but also among non-Hawaiians (Halualani, 2002). Think about the reproduced notions that you hear about when you travel to Hawai'i: "Hawaiians are inherently generous" and "the Hawaiian culture is about giving and sharing." This widely held interpretation of the Aloha spirit represents a meaning shaped by external structures and parties of power, such as the colonialist government in Hawai'i (the British and the US) that mimics a "native" value within the Hawaiian culture and distorts such a value for economic and social gain.

Native Hawaiians are most often associated with the popularized touristic image of "lovely hula hands" or as a fully open and benevolent culture through the distorted notion of "Aloha." This has grated against the notion of Native Hawaiians as a strong, proud, and sovereign people whose native rights to land, culture, and belonging have been usurped.

Asian American television and film representations have been limited to stereotypical portrayals of villains, martial arts experts, or "sidekick" characters (ones assisting other main characters who are often White). Although he was a featured actor in the popular series *Lost*, Daniel Dae Kim played more sideline characters in *Hawaii Five-O* and appeared as part of larger ensemble casts.

The colonialist government from the 18th and 19th centuries, and foreign business representatives in the Hawaiian islands, extracted and re-interpreted the notion of "Aloha" from the Hawaiian philosophical concepts of aloha ʻaina (love and respect for the land) and *Aloha* (sharing, exchange in reciprocity), so as to guarantee and naturalize a one-way line of compassion and charity between foreigners and Hawaiians. Consider also that the Aloha spirit was created during a time when Hawaiian warfare was at its height (during King Kamehameha's rise to power and ongoing battles between Hawaiian chiefs), which suggests that the Aloha spirit was distorted and then used to depict and naturalize the inherently "friendly" and "peaceful" nature of Hawaiians at a time when it was in the best interest of the colonialist government to tame native unrest. This dominant representation of the Aloha spirit is slippery because Hawaiian culture does indeed invoke values based on caring, unity, collectivity, and giving (Halualani, 2002).

Hawaiian Studies scholar and historian Lilikala Kameʻelehiwa describes *Aloha* as it was meant in the Hawaiian culture: as a relation of reciprocity between status-similar Hawaiians who would exchange goods and resources with one another (Kameʻeleihiwa, 1992). This was to *Aloha* your neighbor. Thus, the cultural value of *Aloha* was appropriated by Western outsiders as an a means of power to naturalize Hawaiian giving (once a practice of exchange between social equals) for the benefit of colonial explorers, American business representatives and government interests, and even tourists. Thus, *Aloha*, as the distorted Aloha spirit, stems from a structure of power rather than a cultural essence of "Hawaiianness." As a result, the representation of Hawaiians as naturally benevolent and willing to share everything (culture, land, and native sovereignty) further opens and extends native belonging and residency to all non-Hawaiians.

Fourth premise: The power imbalance between structures of power and the cultural group being represented has a major impact on the cultural group itself and its ability to define itself on its own terms and for its own needs. Representations created and projected by structures of power carry serious consequences for the cultural groups being represented. Cultural groups have a challenging time trying to shake off these external representations of their cultures, especially those that incorporate historically based stereotypes and myths and do not provide a full portrait of their cultures. For instance,

Asian Americans have been depicted by mainstream film, television, and music culture as one-dimensional caricatures such as ancient or evil villains, Kung Fu masters and martial arts fighters, foreign immigrants, asexual nerds or geeks, and, in the case of Asian American women, docile and subservient (Hamamoto & Liu, 2014; Nguyen, 2014). These images of Asian Americans, through persistent reproduction over time, have come to represent Asian American cultures (and their members) and stand in the place of other meanings and representations.

Such depictions have plagued the Asian American community over the years as they constantly face these stereotypes in all aspects of life. For example, Asian Americans in classified government positions (such as scientist Wen Ho Lee) often fall under suspicion by the US government because of the long-held representation of Asian Americans as foreign immigrants whose national loyalty rests with their homeland. The stereotype of the Asian American model minority labels all Asian Americans as "aggressively driven overachievers who assimilate well" and as "super-intelligent students" (Lowe, 1996, p. 24), meaning that this group represented the model immigrant minority via its successful educational, economic, and social integration into US society. These dominant representations of Asian Americans cast a negative light on those Asian Americans who do not fit the profile of being assimilated, economically successful, and demonstrating academic excellence. Many Asian American immigrant families explain that they are often mocked or ridiculed for not having a command of the English language or adopting the American lifestyle as the model minority should. Asian American students who academically struggle in elementary and high schools are often left at a disadvantage because their teachers place higher educational expectations on them than other students because of the model minority representation.

As yet another negative consequence of the representations of Asian Americans created by dominant structures of power, Asian Americans have experienced physical acts of prejudice because of the reproduced meaning of Asian Americans as foreign economic threats. The 1980s marked a tumultuous economic time for the US, which was fledgling and relied on foreign investment from Japan and other nations. Auto plants in Detroit were bought out by Asian companies and moved out of the country, which displaced thousands of US autoplant workers. As such, in 1982, a Chinese American named Vincent Chin was mistaken as a "Japanese" person by two recently laid off White/European American auto workers and severely beaten and killed. This incident sent a message that all Asian Americans (despite the many different Asian ethnicities) were considered to be foreign threats who were not welcome in this country.

Due to the overwhelming reproduction of Asian/Asian American stereotypes, it has been difficult, then, for Asian American communities to redefine their images and cast more complex mainstream representations of their cultures. The question becomes: How can cultural groups ever step outside of the externally created meanings that depict their cultures? Thus, specific cultural groups struggle economically, politically, and socially with external representations of themselves and work hard to redefine themselves.

These four premises illustrate that cultural groups are not singular and self-contained entities; they are fields of forces, as well as constellations of competing representations and meanings from structures that are vying for control over cultures. As intercultural communication scholars Judith Martin & Thomas Nakayama (2000) explain, "culture ... is not just a variable, nor benignly socially constructed but a site of struggle where various communication meanings are constructed" (p. 8). Cultures are differentially positioned in relationship to one another within societal structures, material conditions, and power relations, and, as such, culture becomes a field of forces where competing interests vie for dominance and control. Thus, to say that culture is "a site of struggle" is to point to the process whereby competing interests (dominant structures and cultural communities) shape different representations of culture from different positionalities of power (Hall, 1980a, 1985).

Summary

A power-based perspective to culture and intercultural communication highlights how there are constraining and enabling forces in how we experience culture and interact with others. Power is also invisible and hidden and concrete and material in our lives. From this perspective, culture is a system of meanings and representations created in an entangled field of forces through which differently positioned entities (i.e., dominant governmental, legal, economic, mediated, institutional, and educational structures), groups, and persons compete for the power to define, represent, and even own a culture and its resources. Culture should also be viewed as a field of forces in which competing interests (dominant structures and cultural communities) shape different representations of culture from different positionalities of power.

Keywords

Culture

Culture as a field of forces

Culture as a site of struggle

Power

Power-based perspective

Questions and Activities

REFLECTION activity on power in your life:

- Reflect on how a power-based perspective brings out new insights on your life. What are the ways in which power is invisible and hidden in your life?
- What are the constraining (limiting, controlling) aspects of power in your life?
- What are the enabling (empowering, creative) aspects of power in your life?

REFLECTION activity on culture as a field of force in your life:

- Reflect on how your own culture is a field of forces between dominant structures or interests in your own cultural group.
- Is there a difference in terms of how your culture is defined or understood among these interests? How does that make you feel?
- Why do you think there is that field of forces? Whom does that benefit?

DISCUSSION activity on culture as a field of forces and the ACT framework for intercultural justice:

- Think back to the ACT framework for intercultural justice (as discussed in chapter 1).
- What are the ways in which cultural groups can resist and oppose the dominant representations of their own culture by governmental bodies, media outlets, and/or other structures of power?
- What are the ways in which you, as an individual, can resist as well?
- To what extent is confronting and resisting larger dominant framings of culture difficult?
- What could help chip away at this challenge?

Chapter 3

Re-Thinking Communication

Learning Objectives

> To re-think what communication is from a critical intercultural communication approach

> To situate what an intercultural relationship looks like through a power-based perspective

> To become familiar with how historical context and sociopolitical context frame our intercultural communication encounters

Introduction: A Portrait of Intercultural Communication Between Marissa and Kelly

In San Francisco, Marissa, a 22-year-old Mexican-American/Latina female from Oakland, California, and Kelly, a 25-year-old African American woman from Los Angeles, met over a year ago at an employee training day at a coffeehouse and eventually started conversing and socializing together. However, they come from very different backgrounds. Marissa was born and raised in a working class neighborhood in Oakland and works two jobs to help pay her way through school at the local community college. She lives with her parents and three younger brothers in a neighborhood of mostly other Latino and African American families.

Kelly, on the other hand, is from a moderate-size suburb of mostly Asians and Whites/European Americans in the San Fernando Valley in Los Angeles and is the only child. Her parents are both professionals: her father is a lawyer and her mother is a director of fundraising at a private university. Kelly is attending school at University of California, Berkeley and is working at the coffeehouse for some extra money and to have another social outlet. This portrait presents Marissa and Kelly's perceptions of their friendship.

First Meeting

An employee training session at the Bean marks the first meeting between Marissa and Kelly.

> MARISSA: It was during a training at the Bean when I first saw her. We were both new. And when I did see Kelly, I thought, "Thank God! There is another minority!" Pretty much all the other people there were the White Berkeley, hippie type. So, I remember thinking that I wasn't totally alone. I was kinda stepping back, was more cautious because she was so distant and to herself. Plus, my track record with other Blacks hasn't been too good.

> KELLY: Marissa was sitting in the back watching everybody and checking out the scene. I knew she was Latina or Mexican. She did seem pretty tough—no smiles, no words, nothing. She just looked around. She looked at me a little with a hard look, and I just looked away. Marissa seemed pretty tough and intense. That's how I saw her. That's how a lot of people see her at first.

Relating to One Another

Two weeks later, Marissa and Kelly worked the same shift and ended up closing the Bean together with the manager. On that shift, they begin to talk to one another.

> MARISSA: We immediately bonded over liking the same stuff. Like working out, going to the gym, dancing, all that stuff. We even shopped at the same places. Liked the same music. That was really cool and I felt at home with her. I watched her at first. Like I kinda expected her to not have many friends like me or where I come from and who I am. That history I am sure is between our communities. But, I just had to kinda jump in after awhile 'cause we are working together and in that same space you know.

> KELLY: Marissa was not totally friendly at first. I understood that reluctance at first. I am like that too. But we somehow got on the topic of music and hobbies. That was cool. She did ask me questions like, "You like rap/hip hop stuff or certain stores that minorities go to?" I don't know if she just thought that was what I like or that she thought that of me because I am Black. She kinda spoke to me like I was from the "hood" or something—just the tone and the swagger. I didn't like that at first. I expect it no matter what though. We had more in common and being at work together as some of the only people of color, that was something good. I was open to that part.

Points of Tension

Marissa and Kelly built their friendship over the next year and experienced connections over similar interests and experiences, as well as points of tension.

MARISSA: Kelly always assumes the worst about me and my friends. I get it. I really do, but she doesn't want to come out with my friends and me and I don't get that. I ask and she just seems resigned to the fact that we hate Black people or that it is all about her race. I have reservations about other people and even Black people treating me a certain way. I try to not let that totally come into our friendship. I want to connect with her over how we experience a lot from people who aren't brown or black, who aren't minorities in this area.

KELLY: Marissa would say that I tend to alienate myself from her outside of work. If it is one on one, I am more comfortable with her. I know that she is getting to know me piece by piece. But I don't know her friends or her family and maybe I don't fully know her. That is a real possibility. Because, yeah we are both from diverse racial groups, but I feel like right now it is about my community being treated differently and separately from everybody else.

This chapter re-conceptualizes communication from a critical intercultural communication approach based in power. We anchor this chapter around a portrait of a friendship that crosses socioeconomic and cultural lines.

The portrait of Marissa and Kelly's intercultural friendship reveals many important layers about communication and intercultural communication. This chapter focuses on this portrait in order to help you re-envision communication as more than just an interactional (in the moment) process of relating between individuals in an immediate context. Just as we did with the notion of culture in chapter 2, the process of communication itself can be seen anew through a power-based perspective. Rather than focus solely on the typical sketch of the communication process learned in other classes through a traditional interpersonal model, this section features key definitions of these concepts in relation to power. Here the concepts of communication and intercultural communication will be re-conceptualized from a power-based perspective. Through a new power-based lens, the larger structural, historical, and power-laden influences that configure communication and intercultural communication will be revealed.

Re-Conceptualizing Communication From a Critical Perspective

From a power-based perspective, communication is framed as being more than a neutral channel of expression. Such a view may defy our common sense. After all, when we are communicating with others, we tend to focus on the obvious factors in the conversational exchange at hand (i.e., what was said, with whom, where, when, and how). What escapes

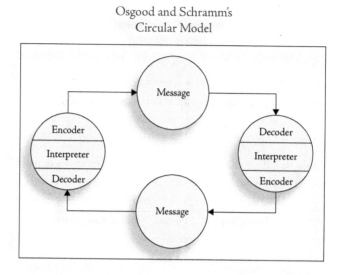

Osgood and Schramm's
Circular Model

Communication has been understood and theorized through the
traditional sender-receiver model of communication or a circular
model of communication.

our attention are all the under-the-surface layers of meaning—the surrounding historical
and political contexts and personal experiences that have been framed by historical and
sociopolitical conditions—that play into and shape what we think of as straightforward
communication interactions. After all, according to popular view, the communication
process seems to be direct, linear, and on the surface (meaning, what transpires during
the communication process defines the entire communication process). Over time, the
notion of communication has come to represent a direct, immediate, and easy-to-read
channel of expression and meaning between two or more individuals. This representation of communication, however, obscures the many different and complex factors that
constitute communication as process, act, precursor, and outcome.

You may have learned about the different models of communication that are discussed
in other communication studies courses. For instance, think back to the famous sender-receiver model that explains how a sender communicates a message to a receiver who
understands the sent message (in the same way as intended by the sender) and responds
accordingly. As other scholars in communication studies argue, such a model fails to
capture the multifaceted and circular nature of the communication process in which all
interlocutors (individuals who participate in a conversation, interaction, or dialogue) are
sending and processing messages at the same time and that these messages are mediated
by subjective factors. As a result, circular models of communication have been created.
Though the modeling of communication has changed, remnants of the older communication model still linger, as the communication process is positioned as being a neutral
space that is untouched by historical and political contexts, meaning that the communication process has, in the past, been framed as an immediate, direct one-to-one exchange,
untouched by any surrounding contextual forces of power and solely dependent on the

interlocutors' communication behaviors in the moment. What this implies, then, is that if a communication encounter is awkward, difficult, or even hostile, that the source of the problem mostly lies in some deficiency in the communicators themselves. Thus, the other layers of meanings that derive from an interlocutor's past experiences, cultural background, and the historical and political factors that surround the communication encounter and the interlocutor's cultural identities and behaviors, are forgotten with regard to the communication process.

The sender-receiver model's conceptualization of communication carries implications for intercultural communication encounters. In following this model, the presumption is that one only needs to learn and master the correct communication skills practiced by cultures A, B, and C in order for positive intercultural communication and mutual understanding with those cultures to occur. This model oversimplifies the complex and multifaceted nature of communication with both process and outcome and does not seriously consider the issue of power.

In conceptualizing culture as a larger field of forces (as we did in chapter 2), this chapter therefore frames communication as more than a neutral channel for expression or in-the-moment message-related behaviors. Instead, communication from a power-based perspective is based on multiple layers that merit discussion and reflection.

What Is Communication From a Power-Based Perspective?

Communication encounters are not neutral, clean slates; these exchanges are already situated in specific historical and sociopolitical moments and contexts.

Indeed, communication encounters are not neutral exchanges and thus are already historically and politically contextualized prior to the communication exchange, and continue to be so during and after communication takes places between and among individuals of different cultural backgrounds. As a starting point, let us consider Stuart Hall's (1980a) perspective on communication and apply it to the process of communication. In his important essay "Encoding/Decoding," Hall (1980a) argues for a different way of conceptualizing communication, particularly for mass communication and media studies. Hall explains that the process of communication is not a neutral and de-historicized linear circuit among sender, message, and receiver, but rather as a complex structure of relations created and framed by macro-entities such as history and structures of power. In other words, the components of communication (e.g., through sender, receiver, communication medium, message, meaning) do not automatically exist or naturally emerge; these elements are shaped by structures of power. Moreover, the interlocutors (known more traditionally as "sender" and "receiver") do not act in predictable ways (with predetermined behaviors) nor are their meanings and exchanged messages clear-cut. Even the relation between interlocutors is always uncertain and shifting in meaning before, during, or after the interaction has occurred. The elements of interlocutors' messages and meanings do not always correspond with one another, nor do they exist in and of themselves. Instead, power, history, and context are "behind-the-scenes" factors that create and seamlessly "stitch" together speakers, messages, and meanings.

According to Stuart Hall, communication refers to the specific arrangement of messages, meanings, and social relations between individuals, as shaped by the surrounding historical and political contexts and power forces (Hall, 1980a; Slack, 1996). In other words, the components of communication (e.g., sender, receiver, message, meaning) are themselves "social productions" that are configured and framed by larger power forces but made to appear "natural," "immediate," and "on the surface." Thus, we focus on the immediate aspects of communication exchanges without realizing how these are situated in larger, unseen contexts and historically and politically shaped meanings.

If we apply the traditional sender-receiver model of communication to the friendship between Marissa and Kelly, the first presumption is that Marissa and Kelly are equal to one another in terms of socioeconomic class; cultural, racial, and ethnic background, and social acceptance. How could we not presume this? We mostly see connections and similarities with the individuals in our social networks. Differences are either avoided or can't be discerned on first glance; they are deeply embedded into our backgrounds, identities, and the surrounding historical-political context. This stands as the ideological power of communication through which it is naturalized as a neutral, equalized, and on-the-surface process.

In addition, through the traditional model of communication, our focus would be solely on the immediate communication exchanges that take place between Marissa and Kelly, as with the following:

MARISSA (places her backpack on the table): How long you working today?

KELLY (sighs): Like four more hours.

MARISSA (nodding): I have about two more and then I am supposed to go to my friend's party.

KELLY: Which friend? Out here?

MARISSA: One of my friends, Marisol, from LA. She lives out here and is throwing a thing. (She smiles, pauses, and then jumps in her seat.) I should take you—it will be fun. Do you want to go?

KELLY (shaking her head): I don't want to intrude.

MARISSA (reaches out and pats Kelly on the shoulder): You won't be. You will be coming with me.

KELLY (frowns): Who will be there?

MARISSA: Most of Marisol's friends from school and home who are out here. About 30 of them (pauses). Why?

KELLY (frowns): What kind of people will be there? I mean, will I stand out? I won't know anyone.

MARISSA: What kind of people? What do you mean? (speaks loudly) Regular people. Most will probably be Latino, but they are just like you and me. (firmly asks) Is that a problem?

KELLY (pauses and softly responds): Yeah, I don't know. I think I probably will just study all weekend.

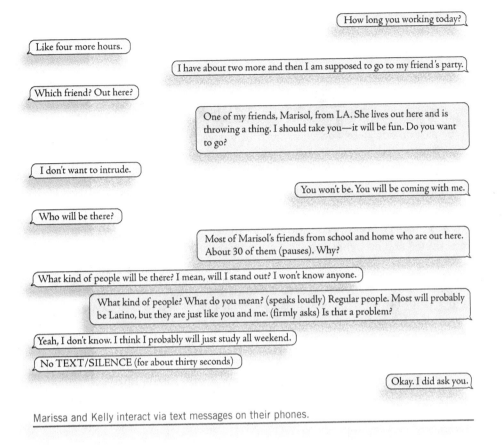

How long you working today?

Like four more hours.

I have about two more and then I am supposed to go to my friend's party.

Which friend? Out here?

One of my friends, Marisol, from LA. She lives out here and is throwing a thing. I should take you—it will be fun. Do you want to go?

I don't want to intrude.

You won't be. You will be coming with me.

Who will be there?

Most of Marisol's friends from school and home who are out here. About 30 of them (pauses). Why?

What kind of people will be there? I mean, will I stand out? I won't know anyone.

What kind of people? What do you mean? (speaks loudly) Regular people. Most will probably be Latino, but they are just like you and me. (firmly asks) Is that a problem?

Yeah, I don't know. I think I probably will just study all weekend.

No TEXT/SILENCE (for about thirty seconds)

Okay. I did ask you.

Marissa and Kelly interact via text messages on their phones.

SILENCE (for about thirty seconds)

MARISSA: (looking at her watch) Okay. I did ask you.

We would then concentrate on the communication behaviors of each of these interlocutors, the messages they send to one another, the intended meanings inscribed into those messages and the interpretations made of those messages, the type of communication medium (face to face, telephone, e-mail or instant messaging), and the immediate setting (the location of the actual conversation). By underscoring these main elements of communication episodes, we presume as many of the traditional communication models do, that these elements convey the full meaning of the interaction. While these aspects are important, they represent only one of many layers of meaning involved in communication encounters and, more specifically, with regard to intercultural communication encounters. Following Stuart Hall (1980a), there are several other and less obvious layers that affect the intercultural interaction between Marissa and Kelly (as well as their other interactions and nature of their relationship), namely the **historical context** and the **sociopolitical context**.

The Historical Context Framing Intercultural Communication Encounters

The connection between historical context and intercultural communication encounters is not obvious. The notion of historical context refers to those past events, moments, crises, perceptions, and experiences that have affected specific cultural groups. Such happenings from the past do not merely disappear as time passes. Instead, these factors remain and circulate within the collective memories of specific groups, or the collection of painful, conflicted, and triumphant experiences and representations that have occurred in the history of a cultural group (as discussed in more detail in chapter 6) (Lipsitz, 1990; Whelan, 2016). When a cultural group undergoes similar experiences as those in the past with the government, society, or other cultural groups, images and memories of its historical past are re-activated and brought to the surface as a primary lens through which to interpret current happenings. How the past always plays into the present, illustrates the tricky and far-reaching effects of historical context on communication encounters between culturally different groups. This can be seen in the previous interaction as Kelly appears hesitant to socialize with Marissa and her friends for fear of a lack of acceptance that may be triggered from her own historical experiences (and that of her family) with other groups.

Because of the slipperiness of the historical past, we ought to consider several ways in which the historical context touches on and frames our intercultural communication encounters and relationships. Here is a description of some historical factors that situate our intercultural relations and encounters:

Perception of Cultural Background Over Time

Individuals negotiate a relationship with their own cultural identities and groups over time. Our views of our cultural backgrounds may run consistently throughout childhood and into adulthood, or these may shift based on different life stages (for example, not engaging in cultural identity practices throughout adolescence and then, in adulthood, showing a great interest in one's cultural identity, or being fully enculturated into one's cultural identity throughout childhood and then withdrawing from it later to "fit in" more). Because we may see, understand, and feel differently toward our cultural identities over time, our perceptions of our cultural identities become **historical frames** (or lenses shaped by the past) that inform our emotions, motivations, and views of others before, during, and after interactions (Irwin-Zarecka, 2017). The extent to which we identify with our cultural group and have positive experiences with such a group, unduly influences how we feel toward that identity. This, in turn, plays into how we feel about others trying to appeal to a presumed cultural identity. For example, how an interlocutor negotiates such a relationship and perceives her or his identity also factors in to how receptive he or she will be when being approached and/or spoken to by another interlocutor based on presumed cultural group membership. In reflecting on her interactions with Marissa, Kelly thinks it is "odd" that Marissa approached her with "Black talk" and assumed that she was really into all things that are considered "Black" (music, clothing style, political views).

Kelly shared that this made her feel hesitant about interacting with Marissa because she did not consider herself to be "that Black" and "yet some girl is talking to [her] because she thinks [she] [is] Black and that [she] feels Black." Such a disconcerting experience caused Kelly to withdraw from many interactions initiated by Marissa. Thus, how one perceives and or makes sense of his or her cultural identity is a very private and sacred process, while also being touched on by the far reach of our historicized self-perceptions. Our historical frames of self-perceptions therefore intermingle with current and future interactions and relationships that we have of others.

Our own past experiences with other cultural groups are also not forgotten; instead, these are reserved in our historical memories in terms of the emotions felt and perceptions created of others during those moments. The extent to which an individual has had positive experiences with other cultural groups and, most notably, the cultural group of the interlocutor, may result in that individual being extremely motivated to engage in interactions with members of this group and in feeling more of a connection with that person. On the other hand, if the experiences were distant or outwardly negative, the individual may either work hard to avoid members of that cultural group (or of all culturally different groups) or draw inward, which may reinforce negative sentiments toward that group due to past experiences. Though past experiences with other cultural groups become major factors in shaping intercultural interactions, the relationship between past experiences with cultural groups and an individual's views, perceptions, feelings, and communication styles and approaches is unpredictable.

For instance, most of the interactions that Marissa has had with Blacks/African Americans were not "friendly" and "very tense." Due to living in a neighborhood of Latino and African American residents who competed over jobs and political control of the city, Marissa admitted that she would try hard to "avoid Blacks" and not engage them in interaction. When she met Kelly at work, Marissa explained that she decided to befriend Kelly to "break away" from her past negative experiences with Blacks/African Americans. Meaning, that in this case, it seems that past negative experiences actually pushed open a space for Marissa to alternatively and actively try to interact with a culturally different person (and from her view, a member of the cultural group with which she has had negative experiences). Past negative experiences with a cultural group, then, in this guiding example, helped to create, for Marissa, the positive desire and path to view and approach Kelly differently than her other encounters with Blacks/African Americans. Positive experiences one has with other cultural groups and the cultural group of the interlocutor may lead to continued positive experiences, but not always. Past memories and experiences with culturally different groups become the "X" factors, activating a range of possible trajectories (from enthusiasm/strong desire to interact and connect to ambivalent distance, and to avoidance and complete rejection of) to perceive of and act in current and future interactions. Asking one another about past experiences and how these have affected us over time, may reveal great insight into how and why intercultural encounters and relationships occur (or do not occur) in the way they do.

Family Experiences With the Cultural Group

The experiences that our family members (immediate and extended family) have had with the cultural group of the other interlocutor, play a major role in shaping our initial perceptions and feelings about that cultural group and its members. We love our family members and also trust that their experiences and knowledge are important and "truthful." As a result, we may, throughout childhood and into the beginning stage of adulthood, invoke our family's perceptions of other cultural groups as useful information for our own interactions. Thus, stories that family members have had with a member of a specific cultural group, as well as their judgments about the "true" nature of that group, are circulated within a family and taken as the "last word"; after all, your own loved one would not tell you lies or spiteful prejudgments or lead you astray. For instance, in the case of Marissa, her family members would always make comments that depicted Blacks/African Americans as angry, hostile, and not trustworthy. Her father had had several experiences when he first moved into the neighborhood of icy confrontations between Black/African American families who felt that Latinos were encroaching on their territories. This affected Marissa in that she always played back these stories in her mind when she would interact with Blacks/African Americans. She reflects, "I would not interact with that group, go near them, and was actually both scared and suspicious of all Blacks/African Americans." One's experience stands as powerful and deeply felt evidence (especially if the knowledge or story about the cultural group member is negative) that when passed down through family generations, sets into place certain perceptions, feelings, and stances other family members have when interacting with members of that group. Thus, past experience is a

We are influenced by our own family members' experiences with other cultural groups, and oftentimes these experiences shape our impressions and perceptions.

potent force that touches on both the present and future in that one's past experiences with cultural groups can influence the perceptions and actions of other relatives who may not have had those experiences or that type of contact with the group (as in the case of Marissa's family members' experiences and how these impacted Marissa who did not initially have these experiences herself). Our family's past, whether or not it actually happened to us, can be very present and at work in present-day intercultural interactions. What seems odd here, is that past family experiences with other cultural groups end up becoming a self-fulfilling prophecy for intercultural interactions, meaning that these experiences constitute a difficult-to-break cycle that configures later generational members' own perceptions, attitudes, and communication approaches toward other cultural group members. What happened a long time ago, therefore, becomes a very present influence on our mindsets, views, and communication approaches with culturally different others.

Historical Myths of the Cultural Group

We also carry the historical myths, images, and stereotypes that we hear of with regard to our own cultural groups and other cultural groups. In society, cultural groups are characterized by the government, media, and popular thought in a specific way over time. Historical myths are explanations about the past that may derive from stereotypes and false information. For example, the myth and image of Black men as aggressive, sexual predators who prey on White women was circulated during the 18th and 19th centuries (or the period of US enslavement of African Americans) and continues to this day (Sailes,

Historical myths about the past—like the one about a young George Washington who cut down his father's cherry tree—enter into our own understandings and perceptions of cultural groups—especially myths about cultural groups from the past.

2017). Likewise, Latino/as have been characterized throughout the media, newspaper coverage, governmental discourse, and popular culture as always being undocumented (illegal) "aliens" who are living the American dream undetected (Tukachinsky, Mastro, & Yarchi, 2017). Another continually reproduced stereotype that we see in media, governmental reports, and popular culture is that Asian immigrants and Asian Americans have inbred loyalty to their Asian homelands and are not trustworthy citizens to the US (Lee & Zhou, 2015). These larger myths, whose origins can never be fully traced, are circulated among and in part, absorbed by individuals and their perceptions of other cultural groups. Think about stories that were told about other cultural groups at family dinners and occasions—the stories about racially, ethnically, culturally different persons—and how your parents, grandparents, or relatives may have told you how another group really is. These stories are likely to be extracted from historical myths, images, and stereotypes of cultural groups that have been persistently reproduced and passed down over time from generation to generation. These historical myths, images, and stereotypes enter into our intercultural interactions in that these representations are already part of our frame of reference, memories, and perceptions (even if we do not fully believe in these images).

For instance, Marissa explains that her parents always told her to be wary of Black men because they "only wanted one thing" from women and that Black people in general were always angry and hostile and feel entitled to more opportunities without working for them. Marissa also admits that these stories and stereotypes were often verbalized during private family dinners and conversations and that, over time, these images would always come to mind when she would see or interact with Blacks. She described her encounters with Kelly:

"When I first started talking to Kelly at work, I was so surprised that she was not at all "angry" or "hostile," as I had thought she would be. She did not seem bitter at the world or that she was owed something. Kelly was very nice to me and that made me open up more with her. And I keep talking to her … because she is not like the stories I had heard about Blacks."

Here, Marissa demonstrates how historical myths, narratives, and stereotypes become a part of our perceptions and initial expectations when encountering a culturally different person. She refers to her "surprise" that Kelly did not act in the way that family stories had narrated. Marissa points out that Kelly's unique behavior (and behavioral difference from the stereotype of Blacks) made her want to interact her with more. Thus, a historical myth serves as Marissa's baseline measure from which to perceive, evaluate, and act toward Kelly. The fact that Kelly, a Black woman, did not act in accordance with a historical stereotype and then, because of this, Marissa positively perceived Kelly and continued interacting with her, demonstrates that the historical myth shapes the initial perception, interaction behavior, and the intent to continue contact. Though Marissa ended up continuing a friendship with Kelly, the historical myth or stereotype remains intact and may be even more strongly reinforced while Kelly is exalted for her unique behavior. Historical myths, images, and stereotypes reach far into our perceptions and expectations of other cultural groups and unknowingly "sneak" into our intercultural interactions as the continual reproduction of these images and stories naturalizes them as "truths" and "facts."

Past Cultural Relations Between/Among the Cultural Groups

The type of racial, ethnic, and cultural relations that have transpired in the past between and among the cultural groups of the interlocutors and/or relational members involved, can set a particular tone for the exchange (and future ones) and affect how interlocutors come to understand and view one another. How the groups of the interlocutors involved, got along in the past, and communicated with one another over time are important considerations in analyzing how they are positioned in relation to one another. In keeping with the example of Marissa and Kelly's beginning friendship, the extent to which Latinos in the United States interacted with and related to African Americans in the past may shape the conditions around how Marissa and Kelly came to meet, interact, and perceive one another. A history of conflict, economic and political competition, cooperation, alliances or solidarity, or ambivalence and avoidance between the cultural groups of the interlocutors involved, undoubtedly informs how those interactions take place and are perceived. In past racial and ethnic relations in the US, African Americans and Latinos often came together in the civil rights struggles in the 1960s and protested side by side for equal and fair treatment (Chang & Leong, 2017). However, as economic hard times fell over the U.S. in the 1980s (with foreign investment pouring into the country) and the increased immigration of Latinos from Mexico, Central America, and Latin America, African Americans and Latinos were placed in a competitive position for jobs, affordable housing, political power (with key decision-making positions in local government) and establishment of their own communities. As such, these groups, in areas such as New York, San Francisco, Los Angeles, and Florida, engaged in competitive, hostile, and antagonistic encounters with one another. Such a history of race relations then affects the encounters between Marissa and Kelly in that each may feel uncomfortable interacting with a member of a cultural group that has had difficult relations with her own. Preconceived notions of the other cultural group and how members act are shaped by past cultural relations between groups and can propel how Marissa and Kelly view one another before, during, and after interactions (and before they even began interacting).

Society's Historical Treatment of the Cultural Groups

Larger society (in terms of the government, court system, law enforcement, educational and public institutions, media, and popular views) treats and depicts cultural groups in different ways. For example, in the case of Marissa and Kelly, the historical treatment of their cultural groups is noticeably different. The US government and society have historically oppressed African Americans because of their skin color (which is deemed as reflecting their inferior nature) from the long history of slavery and the continued framing of this group as "dangerous" and "angry criminals" and/or "lazy," "unskilled" individuals who want a "free payout." There are also numerous reports that document the high number of racial profiling incidents by law enforcement toward African Americans (Legewie, 2016). The economic organization of US society and the hierarchy of jobs also has further displaced African Americans to lower-tier/low-wage jobs and placed them in dilapidated, urban areas to live. Mexican Americans have also endured harsh treatment by the US government and society.

With this in mind, Kelly and Marissa may act in a particular way toward one another in response to how historically their groups have been treated in the past by society. Kelly explains how she initially felt about interacting with Marissa: "I just assumed that she would see me as Black. That's the way it is always done. Society always see Blacks as just 'Blacks' and usually the associations are not positive—not our personalities or what drives us as individuals, but only how Blacks are. So, I guess you could say I was not that anxious to start conversations up. It's hard for me to do that with other cultures." Thus, Kelly alludes to the over-simplistic historical perception of Blacks as "always just Black" and that individuals qualities are not the focus. Such a historical view of Blacks then de-motivates her into interacting with other cultural group members such as Marissa. Again, a cultural group's treatment by society over time enters into perceptions and can often guide behavior. In addition, the historical treatment of a specific cultural group often shapes cultural group members' views of their own identities and their value or worth in society. Such historically informed self-perceptions may put individuals on guard when interacting with culturally different persons and possibly feel "defensive" about their cultural backgrounds due to the past historical treatment of their group by society. For example, Marissa reflects on feeling "defensive" when interacting with Kelly and other Blacks/African Americans. She states:

> You know, I see it all the time. The way people treat us—Mexicanos—they look down on us like we are always dirty, poor, and desperate to be here in the US. That's always how people have treated my parents and other Mexican Americans, even in the 1960s. I made the decision a long time ago that I would not be treated that way. If someone does, I tell them off. The bad thing is that, yeah, it does put a wall up around me when I talk to people. But, even with Kelly, I had that wall up. I was so sure she would treat me how everyone else treats Mexicans.

Here, Marissa reveals that the negative historical treatment of Mexican Americans has toughened her up and compelled her to put a defensive wall up to guard against malicious comments. The unfortunate result of this is that Marissa goes into interactions with others, like Kelly, with a hardened expectation that she will be discriminated against and negatively perceived, which causes her be on the defensive first and not be as open to the interlocutor or gain new insights from the interaction itself. In addition, how cultural group members have been treated in the past frames how those members view other groups, especially those who have historically competed with and/or fought with their own group. Once again, "history" becomes the elusive third party in the interactions and relationship between Marissa and Kelly; history always has an unseen presence in our intercultural interactions and relationships.

The Sociopolitical Context Framing Intercultural Communication Encounters

In addition to the surrounding historical context, our intercultural communication encounters are impacted by the larger sociopolitical context. A sociopolitical context refers to the contemporary landscape of power in which the government, legal system, economy, institutions, and media act toward cultural groups in disproportionate ways. For example, the government may issue legislation that adversely affects, restricts, and/or privileges some groups over others in terms of tax breaks, minority contracts and hiring, affirmative action policies, and immigration limits, among others. The legal system may also make critical Supreme Court judgments on issues such as affirmative action, desegregation programs in schools, discrimination laws, hate crimes, and the "legality" of same-sex marriage, which may restrict the movements of (and what is deemed as acceptable behavior for) certain cultural groups over others. In a similar vein, the fluctuating economy, which is regulated by the government and legal and political institutions, creates conditions around minimum wage, cost of living, housing prices, and criteria for home/business loans. These economic elements all differentially impact cultural groups and shape the kind of lifestyle they can lead, with some groups being relegated to the dilapidated areas (making minimum wage) and others to middle class suburbs with soaring property taxes and decreased tax breaks (not to mention those groups that historically and consistently live in affluence and decadence). Thus, through their authority, the government, legal system, and the economy all shape the contemporary conditions for everyday living, survival, and happiness for cultural groups. Through these forces, the sociopolitical context differentially positions cultural groups in relation to one another and thus, also places interlocutors in specific relations with one another. There are several ways in which the sociopolitical context plays into our intercultural communication encounters, as discussed in the following section.

Experiences With the Cultural Group

Our intercultural communication encounters are not just affected by external forces and parties; they are impacted by individuals within the cultural communities to which we belong. Cultures are constituted by members who come together to define, maintain, and reinforce what it means to be in that cultural group. Such a group dynamic is political in that certain individuals and power interests are able to govern and shape cultural membership and criteria for cultural authenticity. The way we view our own cultural identities also influence how we act in and what we think about intercultural communication encounters. How an individual views his or her cultural identity and the specific experiences he or she has had with his or her cultural group plays a role in shaping the importance he or she attaches to that identity. If his or her experiences have been positive with his or her cultural group and he or she feels accepted by that group, the interlocutor is more likely to positively associate with his or her cultural background and thus may share that background in his or her relationships. The interlocutor may also expect and prefer communication attempts by other interlocutors that affirm his or her cultural background. However, if the interlocutor has had negative and distant relations with his or her cultural group and/or is not accepted by the cultural group, he or she may refuse to talk about his or her cultural background in interactions and may even avoid the idea of culture, ethnicity, or race altogether. The interlocutor would reject any appeals made by others toward his or her cultural background, for these may conjure up painful memories. Thus, our social experiences influence the amount of power and valuation that we assign to our cultural identities, which in turn play into how we approach others and conduct ourselves in intercultural communication encounters, and how the preferences we have for how individuals should approach and relate to us.

In our guiding example, Marissa's strong connection to her cultural identity (and the fact that she feels accepted by that cultural group) powerfully shapes how she interacts with Kelly because she does so as a "Mexican American" who is wary and hesitant about interacting with Blacks/African Americans (and possibly engaging in hostile confrontations as in her past experiences). In addition, Kelly's felt distance between her cultural community and herself also frames how she interacts with Marissa in that she does not want to be approached as a Black/African American, a cultural identity to which she does not have a strong connection. When Marissa does, in fact, slant her behavior toward Kelly based on the presumption that she is and perceives herself to be Black/African American, Kelly is displeased at first and feels less liking and motivation to speak with Marissa. How our cultural groups judge and accept us as cultural members shapes how we see ourselves and then plays into how we view and interact with culturally different persons.

Current View of the Cultural Group

In specific sociopolitical moments, society and public opinion cast a view and judgment of cultural groups. Some groups are deemed favorable, unique, and socially important, while others are characterized as socially unacceptable. Asian Americans, for example, have been represented by politicians and media as hard-working, highly educated, and social climbers (all seemingly positive characterizations) and as foreign, unassimilable, and not loyal to the US. These representations stand as US society's larger view of Asian Americans and how they are deemed as important to our economy but as less than ideal American citizens. Currently, Latinos are experiencing a mixed view as well. They have been depicted in the media as mostly poor and determined workers who pursue the American dream and are willing to tackle lower-tier jobs. However, historically, Latinos have been framed as an ongoing national problem with too many Latinos entering our borders illegally. The construction of Latinos as swarming the country and depleting our political, social, and economic resources reveals the US society's view of Latinos as a mostly troubling and dangerous (poach-like) group. The views of Asian Americans and Latinos may therefore squelch the desire of some to interact with members of this group.

In addition to historical myths and representations, we unconsciously invoke societal views and judgments of cultural groups into our own perceptions. This can go the other way as well. With Asian Americans being "positively" designated as the "model minority," or a group who achieves the American dream with economic success and educational achievement, many individuals may be open to interacting with this group because of society's semi-approval of this group's work ethic and assimilation. What others—even in the most general sense—think about cultural groups, undeniably informs our own judgments and views of other cultures, especially since we often aim to surround ourselves with socially acceptable people. Marissa echoes this notion in her discussion of how she rarely interacts with Blacks/African Americans because they are "the lowest group in our society; everybody see its that way" and one with "too many negative attributes." Her view is shaped by past experiences as well as societal messages that circulate about Blacks/African Americans.

Societal views of specific cultural groups enter into our interactions. Cultural groups such as Latino/as are deemed as chasing the "American Dream" even though this cultural group is not seen as truly belonging to the U.S.

On another level, when we interact with members of this group, the societal views of these groups may prematurely slant individuals' perceptions, judgments, and expectations of those group members. When interacting with a Latino, one may perceive that person in accordance with the larger societal view of that group. He or she may constantly presume in the back of his or her mind about how the Latino interlocutor came to this country and grew up and what his or her lifestyle is like. Kelly reiterates this point when she explains that she just "assumed that Marissa and her family came from Mexico or somewhere like that and that they work hard jobs." She goes on to say, "I guess I kind of do assume that Latinos are the lowly ones—that they are illegal aliens. This didn't stop me from talking to Marissa. But it did make me think I already knew everything about her." Thus, societal views are relied on as automatic and credible forms of knowledge prior to or in spite of actual interactions with cultural members.

Economic Positioning of the Cultural Groups

The issue of economics (how much money we have, our socioeconomic status and economic worth) seems so distant from intercultural interaction. However, there is indeed a link between the two. Cultural groups occupy different rungs on the economic ladder of society and are positioned differently in terms of socioeconomic status, material wealth and capital, and level of financial self-sufficiency (Goldberg, 2016). Scholars argue that African Americans, Latinos, Pacific Islanders, and Southeast Asians live within the lower tiers of the economy while Asian Americans, Whites/European Americans, and some Middle Eastern groups occupy the top levels. The difference between our own economic placement and that of our intercultural interlocutor may, in part, determine whether actual interaction occurs and the nature of that interaction. As discussed in chapter 1, we will mostly interact with members of cultural groups that occupy the same economic rung as our own group. With increasing economic segregation of neighborhoods, schools, universities, and companies, individuals are exposed to a limited range of other culturally different groups. For example, Whites/European Americans and Asian Americans (Chinese and Asian Indian) often live within the same affluent and gated residential communities or sprawling upper middle class suburbs. Other Asian Americans (Filipinos, Vietnamese, Chinese, Cambodian, Hmong) and Pacific Islanders (Samoans and Tongans) often reside in areas shared with Blacks/African Americans and Latinos. It is likely then that if intercultural interaction is to occur, it will be so between the racial or ethnic groups that live and work within the same communities, meaning that it may be difficult to be exposed to and interact with individuals outside of your own economic class, especially because most areas of life (home, school, work, leisure, and community) are contained within economic classed-areas. Interactions with culturally different persons outside of one's economic class may therefore be more in the form of service transactions, in which a member of a specific economic class is hiring or paying a member of a different economic class to perform a service (cleaning one's home, gardening, childcare) or provide a product (retail stores, fast food chains, restaurant service). Service transactions may be brief and specific to the context, and may not involve a great deal of actual communication or sharing of personal information. Even groups who occupy the same economic class do not just automatically get along or reach cultural understanding; in fact, these groups are more likely to compete and push away similarly classed groups who are perceived as economic and social threats to their own amount of wealth and capital. Thus, the economic positioning of cultural groups helps to determine who we interact with in the first place, and the type of interaction (whether it is service related or social and leisure-like) that will likely occur. In Marissa's case, she narrates how she lived near and among many Black/African American communities and felt that these were tense, awkward, difficult, and hostile because of economic competition over affordable housing, jobs, and school admissions. Kelly, who grew up as one of the "few Black families" in an all-White/European American affluent neighborhood, never had any interactions with Latinos except service workers (their housekeeper and gardener), and these interactions were brief and stunted. Thus, the different economic classes of Marissa and Kelly expose them to specific cultural groups and establish the nature of those interactions with those members while also placing them in unequal positions from which to relate and interact with one another.

In terms of the nature of interactions among individuals of similar economic classes, intercultural interactions may involve mutual respect and understanding as "neighbors" who share commonalities in goals and lifestyle because of similar economic status. But, these interactions may also be plagued by hostile economic competition as groups in the same area may vie for increased economic, social, and political power. Conversely, groups that share economic status and common interests, such as home security, quality neighborhood schools, political struggles, and tax breaks, may actually engage in cooperative and collaborative communication encounters in which each works in unison with the other. These encounters become temporary positive alliances shaped by economic interests and common goals.

The Position of the Cultural Groups in Society

Another sociopolitical factor that affects intercultural encounters is the larger racial order and positioning of cultural groups in society. According to scholar Claire Kim (2000), US society is not merely a vertical hierarchy but is racially ordered as a field constructed of at least two axes (i.e., superior/inferior, insider/foreigner). She argues that this racial order "stands at the intersection of the discursive-ideational and social-structural realms; it is a discursively constructed, shared cognitive map that serves as a blueprint for who should get what in American society" (Kim, 2000, p. 10). Thus, a racial order places each cultural group in specific relations to one another based on the ordering of racial categories and meanings and the differential distribution of rights and resources to specific groups. For instance, Kim argues that there exists a current racial order with Whites at the top, then Asian Americans in the middle, and Blacks and Latinos at the bottom of a triangular hierarchy. Such positioning impacts how cultural groups interact and view one another. Encounters between a White/European American and a Black/African American envelop an awkward separation between the groups based on racial ordering. The Blacks/African American interlocutor may feel that the other interlocutor has gained more economic and educational opportunities and overall valuation by US society. The White/European American interlocutor may perceive the other interlocutor to be in a different economic and social class—a lower one—but also to be "privileged" over him or her with affirmative action and minority scholarship and hiring programs. The racial order's positioning of cultural groups relative to one another shapes the impetus for interaction and how that interaction will transpire. Resentment over not getting what is due to them while others are clearly getting more, may cause some cultural groups to spurn other groups and make premature judgments, which sets the tone for communication exchanges.

These sociopolitical factors play into our intercultural communication relations with other groups.

Thus, when two culturally different speakers interact in a communication episode, scholars have typically viewed the messages and meanings expressed between the speakers in relation to the conversational moment and assume that the speakers occupy equal positions relative to one another. By re-conceptualizing communication and intercultural communication in this way, our attention should be re-directed toward the immediate communication act *and* the under-the-surface layers of meaning in such an act created by the following: the historical and sociopolitical context(s) between the speakers and their respective groups/communities (even if the speakers themselves were not part of every group action), the power differences (economic and social) between the speakers and their groups (and how these groups are situated in relation to other groups in that specific sociopolitical context), and the representations of each speaker's group that have circulated in society. Hence, communication is an invisible matrix that is shaped by power interests and history, and, in turn, "links" speakers, groups, and meanings into already-configured specific power relations (Hall, 1980a, 1985).

Communication From a Power-Based Perspective

Historical and political contexts "stitch" interlocutors into place. The historical and sociopolitical factors previously described, place us into certain communication positions from which to perceive, interpret, and act in intercultural encounters. Communication position refers to the specific vantage point from which to view and approach culturally different interlocutors. This vantage point is established by historical factors such as past relations between interlocutors' cultural groups, as well as sociopolitical factors, such as the current societal view of the interlocutors' cultural groups and the racial order and economic placement of those groups. Such a vantage point includes how one's motivation and willingness to interact with a culturally different person in the first place is historically and socio-politically shaped. The fact that the initial desire and impetus *to communicate* across difference and one's own comfort zone determines if communication occurs at all, illustrates how contextual factors—the historical and sociopolitical—directly impact intercultural communication. The communication position we are placed in, as shaped by our past experiences and surrounding historical and sociopolitical contexts, directly impacts how we act toward and view interlocutors and intercultural interactions as a whole.

The speaking or communication positions of each interlocutor intermingle, collide, and shape the ensuing interaction and the nature of the relationship between and among the interlocutors and their respective cultures. It is also important to remember that the intercultural interactions we have make an indelible imprint not only on the immediate interaction and our perceptions of the other interlocutor, but also on subsequent interactions with other members of that cultural group. Because the cultural markers of gender, race, ethnicity, sexual orientation, age, and national and regional identity, among others, become primary lenses through which to view our intercultural encounters, it makes sense that we unconsciously and consciously apply our impressions and evaluations of our past intercultural encounters to future ones. In a haphazard way, past encounters intermingle with and collide against one another as we see others as connected to markers of difference and thus, an encounter with a member of a specific cultural group will affect how we see that person and *all* other members of the group that we have yet to meet. Cultural group members therefore do not need to have interacted with you in order for you to apply your impressions of cultures to other interactions you may have in the future with those cultures. Such impressions can become fixed as permanent frameworks for acting toward cultural groups.

Re-thinking communication and intercultural communication from a critical intercultural communication approach provides us with a nuanced view of our intercultural relationships and the larger embedded forces of power.

Summary

Looking at communication from a critical intercultural communication approach provides an altogether new view. Communication is no longer seen as a neutral channel between two people in the immediate moment. Instead, it is an exchange that is affected by the historical contexts and sociopolitical contexts that surround each interlocutor and his or her cultural groups.

Keywords

Communication

Communication position

Historical context

Historical frames

Historical myth

Sociopolitical context

Traditional model of communication

Questions and Activities

REFLECTION activity:
Think of an intercultural friendship or relationship that you have. Diagram an interaction about that relationship from the traditional communication model and reflect on what aspects of that relationship get the most attention. Then, diagram an interaction from the critical intercultural communication approach and the historical and sociopolitical context layers. What aspects of that relationship are drawn out through this approach? How is this different from the first diagram that you drew?

DISCUSSION activity:
Discuss other structural/societal layers that should be considered in the critical intercultural communication approach when looking at intercultural relationships. Does this chapter neglect any other layers that should be highlighted?

Chapter 4

Ideology and Intercultural Communication

Learning Objectives

- To understand how ideology is created from and reproduced through power
- To explore how ideology frames the way we view other cultures and the world, thereby shaping intercultural encounters
- To reflect upon major intercultural ideologies that we face on a daily basis

Introduction: Kenji and the Japanese Way of Life

As his alarm clock sounded off at 5:00 a.m., Kenji got up, sighed, and felt a sense of dread at starting another 60- to 75-hour work week. Kenji, 35, had lived his entire life in Kyoto, Japan. He grew up modestly as both his parents were local school teachers, and, thus, he and his two sisters were expected to financially help out the family as they entered adulthood. For the last 10 years, Kenji had worked at Fujitsu, a successful electronic company and global brand based in Japan. He seemed mostly satisfied with his job, but it frustrated him that business operations moved so slowly because at Japanese companies like Fujitsu, the larger group had to thoughtfully reach consensus on all business decisions (e.g., what products to create, how to market

these products). In addition, his company refused to take any type of risk in introducing innovative products that were not guaranteed to make lucrative profits. He found himself asking, "Why does it have to be this way?" and "Is this all there is?"

Lately, Kenji seemed to always be complaining to his parents that he had good ideas to help his department increase its revenue but that his supervisor always ignored his comments. Kenji had been told repeatedly that the "group" (the entire company) must "work together" on any new directions and ideas. No one person could just lead the charge; it was much too forward and competitive for Japan. It was, simply put, not the Japanese way. Kenji's parents always reminded him that to stand out so

Kenji experiences and struggles with the ideologies of his home country, Japan.

boldly is to go against the very basis of Japanese culture. Kenji had heard this his entire life; he had lived in a family in which the best interests of the family always came first. For example, Kenji had an opportunity in college to study abroad in Australia, but this opportunity conflicted with his family's need for him to stay and contribute what he earned as a shop clerk to the family income. Kenji's parents reminded him that there was something to gain: If he adhered to the rules of groupwork and cooperation in his job, Kenji would gain lifetime employment and financial security. There was indeed a gain but also a very real personal cost to Kenji.

The schools that Kenji went to throughout his life always discouraged "individuality," such as wearing free dress to school or clothes other than the mandated uniforms, or boasting one about one's own test scores to classmates. One of Kenji's teachers in high school always reiterated to his class that being a good member of society (or specifically Japanese society) required that individual sacrifices be made for the good of the group and for the good of the country. His teacher, Yamagata-sensei (Mr. Yamagata), would repeatedly say,

"You must always look at the greater picture and how your actions affect everyone else's." This message was reinforced, not just at home and in school, but all over the Japanese culture. Local and national newspapers featured stories that highlighted "team work," "national loyalty," and cooperation in neighborhoods, schools, and communities. Until the mid-1980s, there were no laws that privileged an individual's right to equal treatment or redress from discrimination, again indicating how much Japanese society values the group over the individual.

Likewise, the entire Japanese government and economy have long been maintained by the collectivistic values that Kenji and his fellow societal members are told to live by everyday. The economy is strengthened by the corporations and industries that people like Kenji work for and that thrive off of employees' loyalty, hard work, and team efforts (as opposed to individual success, career promotion and mobility, and competition, which would make for a fleeting and unstable workforce). And, families like Kenji's are important to Japan; Japanese families adhere to the prevailing social roles and rules. By doing so, these Japanese families provide the economic backbone of the country and, on a daily basis, reproduce the Japanese world view of group interdependence and cooperation, and, at the same time, the status quo social arrangement of power in Japan.

_____

Understanding Cultural Views as Ideological

In this featured narrative, Kenji finds himself reflecting on the cultural system in which he has been raised and questioning the nature of that system. Asking difficult questions such as "Why does it have to be this way?" and "Why are we like this?" stand as powerful moments in which a cultural member experiences the limits and boundaries of her or his culture. Kenji therefore examines what most accept as a presumed natural truth: one's cultural view (the way in which a culture sees itself, the world, and acts in accordance with such a view). Kenji's personal story highlights, in particular, how cultural views and traditions are, in fact, socially constructed, meaning that these cultural views and ways of life come to exist through a group's, a community's, or a nation's adherence to and reproduction of the cultural view (the "Japanese way"). But, this is not all that is required to make a cultural view stick and powerfully manifest itself into the souls of a culture. The other essential factor is power. That is, cultural views are created, reproduced, and made real on a daily basis by larger power structures, such as a nation's governmental administration, a court of law, an entire religion, a culture's economic markets, a country's set of media outlets (television, radio, film, music, and internet offerings), and educational curricula and values. Each of these power entities helps to recreate a cultural world view. This idea that cultural views are socially created by means of power demonstrates that cultures and their world views and traditions are *ideological* in nature.

This chapter will explain this notion of culture as ideological. Such a perspective may change how you have ever understood culture in relation to power. Do you see culture as a preordained, "automatic," and natural entity? Or, might culture be a system of beliefs and values that requires "work" to exist—the "work" of members' buy-in and the structural reinforcement of such a view across different venues (governmental, institutional, legal, media, economic, and educational)?

Defining Cultural Views as Ideologies

There is a guilty comfort in knowing a culture's way of viewing the world, in having that supposed certainty in understanding a cultural group different from our own. In relation to the previous example, it may seem that we already know Kenji and the Japanese culture. Kenji acts in this way because it is the Japanese culture. Here, we tend to think that Kenji is that way, that the Japanese culture is that way. Or at least this is what it seems to us.

There is great appeal to this type of certainty with regard to this cultural knowledge when navigating through issues of intercultural communication in an unstable world filled with complexities and uncertainties. Having information about a cultural group that seems certain, known, and predictable makes us feel as if we can "nail down" and "put our finger" on the huge, unwieldy nature of culture. In learning about other cultures, a common source of knowledge is the world view, or the set of cultural patterns that frame a culture's way of seeing and behaving in the world, its core orientation toward humanity, nature, life, death, and other philosophical issues of the world (Samovar, Porter, McDaniel, & Roy, 2015).

World views and cultural patterns therefore stand as the most sought-after pieces of information about intercultural communication in the modern world. For instance, business executives flock to intercultural trainings in order to learn about the rules of Asian and European clients in order to secure more business. University students register for intercultural communication courses with the hopes of gaining knowledge about how cultural groups "are" as they seek out careers in the global world. Elementary, middle, and high school teachers in multicultural societies such as Canada, Australia, and the US participate in trainings to learn diverse cultures. Recently, health care practitioners have employed psychologists to help them understand how patients come with different cultural perspectives about the body, sickness and treatment, and dying. In the United States' War on Terror, anthropologists have been employed as "security anthropologists" to collect and share information with the US military about the world views and cultural practices of the Iraqis (Gonzalez, 2004).

Indeed, we seek out knowledge about cultural world views. Ideology then carries an enormous amount of power and reach into how we view other groups, act toward them, and understand our intercultural world.

Definitions and Forms

Ideology refers to a set of meanings that structure a cultural group's view of the world (Thompson, 1990). Simply put, ideology makes up how a culture sees itself and its relation to the rest of the world. The key difference here, though, is that ideology not only constitutes a cultural world view, it does so in line with specific power interests, namely a national government, a political party, an economic structure, or a religious institution, among others. Ideology is therefore not innocent or neutral; it always speaks from the vantage point of a specific power position (Hall, 1986; Thompson, 2013). According to critical media scholar John B. Thompson (2013), ideology refers to "the ways in which meaning serves to establish and sustain relations of domination" (p. 56). Put another way, all societal structures, groups, and individuals create and circulate an ideology or world view that mostly benefits their own needs and priorities. For example, consider how many individuals and countries believe that politicians (president, prime minister, cabinet) and authority figures (high-ranking military officials, religious leaders, scientists, and teachers and professors) have our best interests in mind (in terms of national security, everyday safety, and economic survival), and thus, in turn, exercise a "trusting" and sometimes tacit acceptance of decisions made by those in power. Such a view of authority is not automatic; it does not just appear as if by magic. This view is created, expressed, circulated, and reinforced by those very power figures and represents a form of ideology.

More specifically, ideology is an instrument of power because it becomes attached to the private and personalized area of selfhood and identity. That is, we identify with an ideology because it represents what we perceive to be real and true. Ideology shapes the real conditions of people's lives and constitutes the world views by which people live and experience the world (Barker, 2003). The notion that authority figures work with our best interests in mind stands as a world view that many of us internalize and use as a guideline to go about our lives with trust and "faith" in the powers that be.

As another example, consider the view that every human is entitled to freedom and the ability to make most of her or his life decisions (where to live, what to do, who to love or marry, where to go). For many of us, this view is key for living out our lives and conceptualizing the value of human agency, or the ability to make choices and take action. For Western nations, citizens greatly value and invest in the notion of democratic freedoms—that individuals should decide for themselves in a fair election process how they should be governed and by whom and that they have basic rights to express their opinions and views about issues and speak out against any social injustices. This view, however, can quickly slip into becoming an ideology when it is used as a justification to impose "democratic rule" on non-Western nations. For instance, the US government has historically moved into war-torn countries with regimes of power (Vietnam, North Korea, Iraq, among others) that are deemed "dictatorial" and "oppressive" to their citizens and has aggressively pushed military forces into these nations with the primary goal of "liberation" and creating contexts of democratic freedom. The irony is that an ideological view that espouses human freedom and choice, on one hand, becomes an unwieldy tool of power that can be employed by Western governments to "force" democracy onto nations with deeply established historical and religious conflicts.

In daily public discussion, Westerners also invoke this ideology to justify their home country's military action over an oppressive government as necessary to bring about truth, justice, and human freedom. How can a view that elevates the importance of human freedom in the same breath be used to justify the takeover of another nation? This is exactly the tricky nature and operation of ideology. Many feel compelled to take ideology this far because it stands as the core, resonating material by which they make sense of their worlds, and it is real to them. But, again, these systems of meaning are ideological because they operate from a specific position of power, reinforcing only their own interests (and their own "truth") and hiding other interests.

Different Forms of Ideologies

Ideologies represent specific power-vested world views of cultural groups. It is also important to note that there are different types of ideologies present within cultural societies: dominant ideology, negotiated ideology, oppositional ideology, and hegemony.

Dominant Ideology

One key type of ideology is known as dominant ideology, or a world view that reproduces, maintains, and justifies the status quo and hierarchical power relations within a people. Thus, because it is born of power, ideology stands as the world view of a dominant group(s) who hold(s) the most power and influence among a nation and its people. As the major world view presented to the public, dominant ideology can often "provide the symbolic glue ... which unifies the social order and binds individuals to it" (Thompson, 2013, p. 90). By spreading a world view that directly privileges a minority of people in a society (i.e., a nation's leader, political cabinet, the wealthy, religious and intellectual authorities), dominant ideology serves to benefit and advance the interests of a larger social force or structure or institution of power.

Louis Althusser, a French Marxist theorist born in 1918, developed an important theory that primarily explained this notion of ideology as a form of dominant power. Given the time in which he lived, when governments, such as Germany and Italy, ruled by martial law and imposed authoritative and dictatorial regimes, it is no surprise that Althusser (1969, 1971) possessed a somewhat bleak outlook on power and how it shapes society. Specifically, Althusser argued that individuals' sense of reality was powerfully shaped by larger forces of power such as the government, military, economy, and law. Althusser (1969, 1971) believed that domination was secured primarily through the social (or the social conditioning of people). He was intrigued by the ways in which the public's view of the world were socially controlled by powerholders through the concept known as ideology. Althusser held the view that

Society is much like a "Matrix" in that dominant forces shape society and our "realities."

although we typically think of physical suppression (holding someone down with physical force) as the ultimate form of power, the most insidious and dangerous form of power is to hold someone down using her or his mind.

The popular Hollywood film, *The Matrix*, is a useful example of how Louis Althusser understood dominant ideology:

> MORPHEUS (TO NEO): How do you know the world that you see and live in is the "real world"? How do you know that we are not living in the "Matrix"?

In *The Matrix*, the story revolves around a man named Neo (Keanu Reeves), a computer programmer and hacker in a metropolitan city in 1999. Neo, however, begins to inquire about a rumored group of social renegades working under the leadership of a man named Morpheus (Laurence Fishburne). Through a chaotic series of events, Neo meets Morpheus and his renegade counterparts who form an underground group of critics who the know the "real truth" about the human society and the "secret" of the "Matrix."

Morpheus reveals to Neo that the world he knows is really a tragic society run by ideology. The human race and society are dominated by a powerful race of machines who took control. Machines rule over humans by placing them in "pods" and using them as energy sources (e.g., the heat from their bodies) for the machine race. Humans are thus "slaves" created for the sole purpose of serving machines. So, humans are not walking around on public streets in everyday life. No, they are lined up in pod stalls with plug connections placed in their brains, necks, and body parts.

Humans, though, are not fully aware of this reality. Instead, they are hooked into a mental computer program known as the "Matrix," which simulates an everyday "reality" that they think they are living in, while masking the actual dark world of machine domination. After this discovery, Neo utters that he would rather have not learned about the Matrix reality. He struggles with the reality that has been shown to him and the notion that human life is merely about pure (physical and mental) domination. Louis Althusser's theory of power can be further understood in relation to *The Matrix*.

Domination is achieved through ideology

Ideology can be defined as a set of ideas and meanings that structure an individual's or group's reality in the name of power. This concept of ideology is similar to the notion of consciousness, or a state of mind, not the way things "truly are" but what people perceive to be true. Such a version of reality is imposed on individuals by social force and manipulation. For example, Neo and all humans are victims of an ideology of human freedom and free will. They believe this ideology to be true, which frames their reality. Humans like Neo, believe in the reality that the Matrix projects and simulates, thereby enabling larger power forces—the machines—to dominate without a trace. Most humans (except Neo's group) in the Matrix world do not ever question the conditions of their own existence or the possibility that they are oppressed, for that is not the reality that they experience. They only experience the dominant ideology of the Matrix: humans are free.

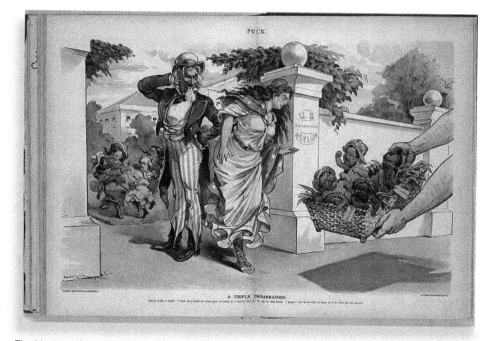

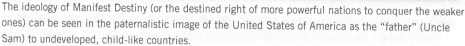

The ideology of Manifest Destiny (or the destined right of more powerful nations to conquer the weaker ones) can be seen in the paternalistic image of the United States of America as the "father" (Uncle Sam) to undeveloped, child-like countries.

As another example, dominant nations in past centuries have employed ideology to colonize indigenous peoples. For instance, the British empire colonized African and Asian (India and Hong Kong) kingdoms by shaping the ideological view that modern industrialized Anglo nations were more "civilized" and "superior" than "dark, heathen," "undeveloped" (and "savage"-like) nations. The ideology of Manifest Destiny (or the destined right of more powerful nations to conquer the weaker ones) reconfigured the modern world with the colonization of former sovereign nations, such as Africa, Puerto Rico, Philippines, Hawai'i, India, Hong Kong, among many others. This colonialist ideology of racial superiority plagued nations that did not possess the military or financial strength to ward off intruders. Even worse, indigenous peoples often internalized the ideology of Anglo superiority in a destructive process of internal colonialism and saw themselves as being grossly "inferior." Many natives attempted to be just like their colonizers, abandoning their languages and cultural traditions and engaging in a cultural self-hatred. It is this internalization of Anglo superiority that sedimented colonialist takeovers as native peoples submitted to such an ideological view. Ideology, backed by colonial physical force and governmental and economic power, therefore forges a tight-locked "reality" for marginalized groups.

Consider, as yet another example of ideology, the idea that English is and should be the global language. This view presumes that English is (by natural evolution) the most superior of languages, as evidenced by its adoption in many countries as far away as Ghana and Japan and as close as the US. In addition, proponents argue that English is *the* global language in that it can connect all cultures and nations into one symbol system. Such an ideology, however, hides the ways in which global capitalism and Western colonialism have imposed American English on many third world countries. This ideological viewpoint suggests that English is widespread due to the individual and group choices of people. Nowhere in this ideology is there a hint that English is indeed a global language but by *force* (*not individual choice*) and economic or corporate colonization, as led by the US. The global English idea advances the dominant interests of US culture and Western capitalistic corporate power. Politicians, students, teachers, business executives, and even citizens of colonized nations argue in support of this ideology, which demonstrates the seductive nature of dominant-framed ideas.

Ideology Is a Representation

Ideology is a representation of the imaginary relationship of individuals to their real conditions of existence. Meaning, ideology is indeed a representation of the imaginary relationship of individuals to their real conditions of existence. If, indeed, ideology is a world view of how "reality" is to be understood, then ideology stands as the "mental" or "imagined" relationship between individuals and the surrounding world. What becomes "real" is not based on the actual physical context outside of us, but rather our individual and personally felt (yet structured) interpretation of the world. Here "imaginary" is not fantastical or dream-like; it connotes a mental perception that stands as real. The Matrix, a computer simulation of reality for Neo and all humans, is internalized as the mental or imagined projection of reality, or one that "is" a happily mundane picture of everyday life (i.e., people going to work, driving their cars, walking on the streets, making their own choices, and living a "normal" existence). To Althusser, ideology represents the most dangerous power of them all: the social control and manipulation of the mind.

Ideology Is "False"

Ideology stands as a "false" set of ideas perpetuated by dominant forces and absorbed by societal members. Althusser (1969, 1971) explained that ideology was no innocent creation; it was a social viewpoint created and reproduced by those in power. Thus, the individuals, groups, and structures that develop and circulate such viewpoints are named "dominant" (and their viewpoints are named "dominant ideologies"). Keep in mind that dominant forces can advance several dominant ideologies at once in order to socially control people. Ideology represents a vital tool for bringing about the conditions and effects of domination. Specifically, dominant powers give rise to a set of ideas and perceptions accepted by everyday people, which perpetuates (and even increases) the authority of the ruling class. In this regard, these ideas are created out of a false and misleading purpose. According to Althusser, individuals who believe in and act on such ideologies are therefore immersed into a "false" consciousness, or a lack of awareness or knowing of the dominant interests embedded in ideologies. We, as individuals who invoke ideologies, are labeled "dupes" or manipulated individuals who unknowingly become the puppets and mouthpieces of dominant interests.

In *The Matrix*, the machine race manipulates the "reality" of humans and deceives Neo and all humans into thinking that they are free agents in an open world. When humans accept this false ideology, they become dupes and are unwittingly invoking a reality that masks their own domination and suppresses their need for resistance (because humans believe that they are free in the world and thus do not need to resist anything at all). Think about the power of the Matrix: It structures the eternal submission of humans to power and crushes any chance of resistance. Humans will not recognize the state of their own domination for it would require them admitting that they are not in control of their own lives, which stands as an unbelievable premise for most

The ideology of divine birthright (the notion that only a few by birthright are destined to be rulers while the masses should be ruled) represents a dominant viewpoint that continually guarantees monarchical authority.

individuals today. Think about this: What would you say if I told you that your world is nothing but a hoax? Would you dismiss the idea based on the notion that we all have free will in a free world because the actuality of the idea may be too frightening to consider?

Take, as another example, the cases of monarchical rule in kingdoms or countries such as Great Britain, Spain, Japan, Jordan, and even as close as Hawai'i. With these cases in mind, I ask the question: How does a small class of monarchical rulers assume control and divine rule over a nation of millions of citizens? The ideology of divine birthright and royal blood (the notion that only a few by birthright are destined to be rulers while all others—the masses—should be ruled) is a dominant viewpoint that continually guarantees monarchical authority. Divine rule then stands as a false set of ideas that becomes a false consciousness for national citizens who are ruled over. These citizens bow to and uphold the monarchical traditions for it is the "natural order of things" or a "national and cultural tradition" and thus never question the conditions on which such rule has been created. Rhetorical scholar Barry Brummett (2014) explains that the ideology of monarchical rule is based on a flimsy idea that blatantly allows for social domination by the elite.

The Superstructure and Ideology

For Althusser, the superstructure consisted of two agencies that maintain power and reproduce ideology. Like theorist Karl Marx, Louis Althusser (1969, 1971)

Repressive status apparatuses (RSAs) can be seen all around us and function to enforce, control, and maintain social order under the guise of "protection."

believed that dominant forces created a superstructure that was composed of social institutions and ideas. However, he primarily focused on the institutions and conceptualized the center of dominance as deriving from the state. The state represents the status quo or ruling and dominant interests of a society's government or nation and includes several structures that together, create, enforce, and reproduce ideology. More specifically, Althusser described the superstructure as operating through two types of agencies of the state: repressive state apparatuses (RSAs) and ideological state apparatuses (ISAs).

The first type of agency is known as the **repressive state apparatus (RSA)** and included entities such as the police, military, prisons, and court systems. These repressive state apparatuses enforce a dominant ideology in everyday life, especially when it is threatened by deviant or resistive action. RSAs thus work through the constraining power of repression and coercion. Throughout *The Matrix*, for instance, the police and the "black suits" represent the RSAs that attempt to thwart the social resistance moves of Morpheus, Neo, and the crew. When any one, such as Neo, tries to dismantle the dominant ideology of the Matrix, the black suits and law enforcement chase that person down and work to destroy her or him so that the ideologically constructed reality can be safeguarded. Repressive state apparatuses (RSAs) exist

Religious institutions stand as institutional state apparatuses (ISAs) that function to create and reproduce dominant relations of power through seemingly innocent notions of faith, salvation, and religious viewpoints.

to protect and enforce dominant ideologies using physical, governmental, and legal forms of coercion.

Today, the police and law enforcement, as RSAs, enforce the ideology of peaceful and orderly citizen-like behavior. They do so by inciting individuals who violate "peaceful order" rules by protesting against oppressive corporate employers in public spaces (which is also a way in which dominant powers can crush resistance groups) and the homeless who supposedly "loiter" and "degrade" the clean, peaceful public image of our streets. Any threat to the ideology of public safety, orderly conduct, and national security (even those threats that are harmless in nature and resistive to the state) is swiftly and mercilessly realigned back to the status quo through the repressive power of law enforcement, which possesses the power to fine, arrest, and imprison individuals. Note the commanding presence of SWAT teams and military round-ups during protests and marches; individuals who are merely holding protest signs or blocking entrances without physically harming anyone are sometimes hurt by police canes, sprayed with stinging gas and pepper spray, and held down with brutal force. Such repression occurs in order to perpetuate the ideology of status quo orderly citizen conduct as well as to make social protest and resistance unlawful and illegal.

The second type of agency underscored by Althusser is the **ideological state apparatus (ISA)**. Several examples of ISAs are educational institutions, churches or religious institutions, family, media, and popular culture. These apparatuses create and reproduce dominant viewpoints more subtly through social, everyday institutions and practices and not by force or repression, like in the case of the RSAs. These structures also recreate, justify, and legitimize relations of power, status quo ruling interests, and the attitudes and behaviors of dominant groups. ISAs, therefore, naturalize and normalize specific viewpoints by reinforcing them in everyday institutions and seemingly innocent activities, such as church and family.

For instance, religious institutions are often deemed as innocent and neutral, yet religious leaders promise salvation to those who abide by sacred codes and beliefs. One of the most widely touted "sacred" tenets of many religions is for individuals to engage in eternal heterosexual matrimony with another member and produce a family of followers, thereby strengthening the religious community and spreading one's faith. Heterosexual (or heterosexist) marriage is also framed as being the necessary precursor to the procreation of children. Religious members invoke such a viewpoint and justify it as being "true," "good," and "natural." In this sense, churches and religious institutions promote the dominant ideology of heterosexual marriage and family via the promise of salvation and goodness. Such a framed reality is reproduced and internalized through seemingly benevolent and compassionate religious principles and communities. The church or religious institution is an ISA that often escapes careful scrutiny, criticism, or questioning because it is an entity that purportedly affirms and centers members and is deemed as good and true.

Schools also function as powerful ISAs. As institutions of learning where people "open their minds," schools serve the function of instilling knowledge and expanding individuals' perceptions. But, through the focus on knowledge and learning, schools also function to shape youth and adults into "good citizens" and future workers for the nation-state. For instance, as young children, we all learn the national songs and symbols of our countries; it just seems to be natural information about where we are from. But, by instilling these symbols, songs, and even standards for national language competency (or the ability to speak, read, and write in one's home language), individuals are being shaped into "citizens" of a country who will promote and extend the mission and well-being for that country and possibly even sacrifice and die for the nation. In addition to making citizens, schools also ideologically function to make students into workers. Here, students are given the mindset that their education will lead to a good, steady job. In the US, for example, students understand high school and especially college as primary sites to prepare them for attaining a high-paying job. Rather than the focus being on learning and understanding a variety of subjects and topics for social critique, American universities have instead emphasized the preparation of young adults for work in the industrial economy and corporate world.

Because ISAs represent the social and everyday forums of our lives—schools, family, churches, media, and popular culture—Althusser (1971) argued that ISAs stand as some of the most dangerous vehicles for circulating and reinforcing dominant ideologies. Given their everyday and supposed "harmless" nature, ISAs are rarely questioned and often taken for granted, which guarantees the undetected reproduction of dominant views.

While Althusser's explanation of ideology is useful, especially with regard to its focus on dominant powers, it also has its limitations. The notion that humans are always oppressed by dominant structures with little to no chance of resistance seems rather bleak. What are the options? Are we forever at the mercy of structures of power and of the powerful? What does this mean for us, our lives, and our future? Can we transcend the social, political, and economic conditions set forth by dominant structures? These questions bring to the foreground the notion that individuals have the capacity to act, make decisions, and protest the surrounding societal structures of power, or what is known as human agency. **Human agency** refers to the "socially determined capability to act and make a difference" (Barker, 2003). Noted critical discourse scholar Michel Foucault (1980) theorized human agency in terms of "micropolitics," or the ways in which small groups of people with multiple voices and interests contest the social and discursive practices that dominate society. Thus, scholars like Michel Foucault and Stuart Hall strongly assert that power cannot completely squash our human agency but that human agency is always connected to and framed by ideologies and power forces (Foucault, 1980; Hall 1986).

It is this notion of human agency that other scholars and thinkers have highlighted as being essential to the operation of ideology in society, which are reflected in two specific types: negotiated ideology and oppositional ideology.

Negotiated Ideology

Unlike Althusser, other theorists, such as Terry Eagleton (2014) and John Fiske (1992) understand ideology to be world views driven by power forces but in ways that cannot fully suppress human agency and creativity. Literary scholar Terry Eagleton (2014) argues that individuals cannot be brainwashed into believing in dominant ideology; he values the notion of human agency too much to accept Althusser's notion of false consciousness. For individuals to invest in dominant ideologies that benefit the powers that be, they must be able to connect with some aspects of that dominant ideology. Eagleton (2014) explains that dominant ideologies "must engage significantly with the wants and desires that people already have" and must be "real enough" to resonate with their identities and experiences (p. 22). While dominant groups and structures certainly engage in deception and manipulation of the larger public, these are not the only strategies of power used by dominant forces. Instead, Eagleton (2014) contends that individuals who invoke and accept dominant ideology are not always deluded into some unconscious "false" state of mind; instead, these individuals may be perfectly aware of the power moves in play and be more than willing to accept these. This does not mean they are dupes, but rather is because the current prevailing system, though unjust and oppressive, is still the best alternative to other more severe forms of oppression (e.g., martial law, facism). Moreover, individuals may give into dominant ideology through a negotiated ideology position because it serves their social and economic needs and interests or because it reflects a system that is improving itself for the future.

One particular type of ideology discussed in this way is **negotiated ideology**. According to John Fiske (1992), negotiated ideology is one through which an individual accepts the dominant ideology but inflects it to her or his own unique experiences and identity. Here, an individual "negotiates" the meaning between a dominant ideology or power-based world view and her or his social position. For example, in more patriarchal countries, when women accept their culture's dominant ideology that men are superior to women socially and politically and yet, at the same time, call attention to the importance that women make in the domestically, private sphere of that culture (taking care of children, nurturing a family, and helping the male head of household) succeeds. Immigrants who settle in the United States in particular may accept the American dominant ideology of meritocracy or the world view that anyone is able to access economic success and achievement in the culture through hard work and discipline, while also identifying the key factors for success (connections, networking; moving to certain parts of the country that are more open to immigrant arrivals) that worked for their immigrant friends. Thus, immigrants actively negotiate a dominant ideology that they face in their host country with the actual experiences and positions of immigrants like themselves. In these examples, note that individuals are invoking part of the dominant ideology and then inflecting it to their own social experiences and placement. There is no explicit rejection of the dominant ideology at the outset.

Oppositional Ideology

Stuart Hall argues that we are not fully trapped within a dominant ideology (Barker, 2003; Hall, 1986). Ideology is dynamic and represents the constraining and enabling aspects of power. Ideologies are also sites of productive tension, contradiction, and conflict in which dominant ideologies can be inverted, challenged, and redeployed to serve counter interests. Just because dominant ideologies derive from dominant structures does not mean that they cannot be deflected or resisted.

In this vein, at the opposite end of the spectrum from dominant ideology is another type of ideology: oppositional ideology. **Oppositional ideology** is a world view that directly challenges, refuses, and rejects the dominant ideology or world view of a culture or society (Fiske, 1992). One can see oppositional ideology in the case of a female member of a traditional, patriarchal culture that outright rejects her family's expectation that she will marry an appropriate male and instead pursues a career in business overseas. Another case in which a male member of a culture may dismiss his culture's dominant ideology that he must marry within his ethnic group and religious membership by marrying someone of another ethnic and religious background reflects an example of an oppositional ideology. This ideology that goes against the grain of dominant meanings and world views can occur in a variety of ways: private and public criticism, public and massive protest, collective political action and mobilization consciousness-raising, and strategic performance and imitation. Cultural members can remake dominant ideologies by opposing these forms and engaging in direct challenge through private critique or illustrative behavior and action.

Hegemony

A more contemporary understanding of ideology as a power-constituted world view, but without the sense of individuals' false and duped submission to structures and groups in power, is the theory of **hegemony**. Noted scholar Antonio Gramsci (1971) found the concept of hegemony to be more useful in terms of the role of power in our lives and in framing our view of the world. He refers to hegemony as the persistent reproduction of authoritative meanings and practices. His major explanation of hegemony is that while societies engage in coercive control, or the control of people through direct force or threat, much of today's power dynamics across countries and culture is done through consensual control, or the voluntary (consensual) acceptance of the world view of a dominant group by subordinate classes. That is, cultural members today genuinely and willingly invoke and embrace the ideas, values, and leadership of a dominant group "not because they are ideologically indoctrinated but because they have reasons of their own" (Strinati, 2004, p. 166). These reasons may be in terms of accepting a dominant world view (one that may actually go against their own power interests and what benefits them) because a "concession" has been granted or a "deal" has been made, usually in terms of economic benefits or gains (wage increases, welfare provisions, prevention of tax increases, economic prestige or status, the image of equality).

Hegemony can be seen in two key examples. For instance, in 1994, California state residents passed an initiative, Proposition 187, that eliminated state-supported health and social services, including access to public education, to illegal or undocumented aliens and their children. Surprisingly, a significant percentage of California's Asians (57%), many of whom are immigrants themselves or who come from immigrant families, voted in favor of Proposition 187; this was true for 31% of Latino voters as well (Chang, 2001). Why would a cultural group (especially one that has immigrant ties) vote for a state proposition that eliminates any state support for undocumented immigrant populations? Public opinion and polling experts found in follow-up interviews with Asian voters that this group willingly submitted to the dominant ideology that unnaturalized and undocumented immigrants deplete resources from more legitimate native residents and legitimated citizens (who have been naturalized) because it reflected badly on their own cultural group or immigrant status. Likewise, they felt that because many of them "earned" citizenship in the legally appropriate and sanctioned ways that other immigrants should do the same. By having the marker of undocumented or illegal aliens out in the state discourse, Asian voters responded by favoring a measure that would eliminate this marker and preserve their own hard-earned economic and social status as citizens. Thus, Asian voters (and according to these interviews, many Latino voters as well) made a concession to work against a segment of their own cultural group or immigrant population in order to maintain and/or strengthen their own social position in US society.

Another key example is that many gay men and lesbians serve in active duty (including the guard and reserve). Keep this in mind when also considering that the US military has historically had a strict "Don't Ask, Don't Tell" policy [federal law Pub.L. 103-160 (10 U.S.C. § 654)] through which "homosexuals" or anyone who "demonstrate(s) a propensity or intent to engage in homosexual acts" is prohibited from serving in the US military because it "would create an unacceptable risk to the high standards of morale, good order and discipline, and unit cohesion that are the essence of military capability." This act also prohibits any homosexual or bisexual person from disclosing her or his sexual orientation or from speaking about any homosexual relationships while serving in the US armed forces. Given this policy, one might ask: Why would a gay male or lesbian willingly enter an arena that formally opposes and rejects his or her sexual identity and personhood?

While the issue is complex, hegemony may work partially here, in that gay males and lesbians may enter and devote years of service to the US military, knowing full well of the military ban against their community, identity, and committed relationships. They may dutifully uphold the dominant US ideologies of patriotism, male-dominated public service, and freedom, all of which (ironically) run counter to the very notions built into those dominant values of free expression and enactment of one's private life, public identity, and civil rights as a marginalized group. Gay men and lesbians may consent to living a "different life" within the military for economic gain (veteran benefits, G.I. Bill, especially for gay men whose income falls below other men) as well as social acceptance as equals worthy of inclusion and fair treatment who can prove themselves to be honorable individuals devoting their lives to their country (Shilts, 2014).

Ideologies That Surround Culture

There are several ideologies that shape and surround our cultures and identities that may go unnoticed.

Nationalism

Because a major category of culture around the world exists politically, historically, and economically in terms of a nation, it is no wonder that **nationalism** represents a powerful ideology that naturalizes the superiority of a culture's beliefs, practices, and priorities. The nation-state "is a political concept that refers to an administrative apparatus deemed to have sovereignty over a specific space or territory within the nation-state system" (Barker, 2003, p. 64). You may think of nation in terms of the one into which you were born. This nation may seem quite large, very formalized (via a governmental structure), and with physical boundaries. But nation also refers to an ideological construction. According to Benedict Anderson (2016), the nation is an "imagined community" by people, in which a national identity is constructed through symbols and rituals. Such an imagined community reinforces the authority of a specific political system and set of power relations. Thus, nations are all at once symbolic, socially constructed, and material. Anderson (2016) explains:

> [A nation] is *imagined* because the members of even the smallest nation will never know most of their fellow members, meet them, or even hear of them, yet in the minds of each lives the images of their communion. ... The nation is imagined as *limited* because even the largest of them, encompassing, perhaps a billion living beings, has finite, if elastic boundaries, beyond which lie other nations. ... Finally,

Nations are constructed through ritual and symbols, such as flags, into larger "imagined communities."

> it is imagined as a *community* because, regardless of the actual inequality and exploitation that may prevail in each, the nation is always conceived as a deep, horizontal comradeship. Ultimately, it is this fraternity that makes it possible, over the past two centuries, for so many millions of people, not so much to kill, as willingly to die for such limited imaginings (Anderson, 2016, pp. 15–16).

Nationalistic ideologies can also be justified through universalization, or its representation as fulfilling the needs and interests of all, that all members are tied and bound to (and unified in) a particular nation (Thompson, 2013). The specific injustices and oppressions exacted on groups within a nation are glossed over and not named in this universalization process. In the UK, Paul Gilory (1987) explains how Black citizens were never incorporated or included into the image of Great Britain or the Union Jack; instead, their jarring experience as Afro Caribbean persons in England has been antithetical to the universalized national experience of Great Britain.

Consider the construction of Americanness through a national identity built on freedom and liberty. Images of 1776 and the Revolutionary War as the nation's major struggle to gain freedom from an oppressive nation constitute the American spirit and the very fabric of what America is: free, progressive, and democratic. The collective national identity that is formed in the US, however, obscures the negative, contradictory actions and histories that make up the nation. Our focus is on the unifying thread of freedom; to not act American (or in accordance with what is deemed as American behavior—speaking English; engaging in a Christian religion; paying tribute and loyalty to US institutions of government, law, and military) is to forgo one's right to or desire for a life of freedom and liberty. This tight connection between a dominant nationalistic ideology and one's belonging to a larger collective makes it understandable as to why nationalistic ideologies take hold.

We must remember though that individuals respond differently to the nationalistic ideologies and cultural patterns put before them. Some may adopt these views as their own, even though it works against their own economic and social interests. Others may try to rewrite and remake these ideologies in negotiated and oppositional ways to speak to other groups excluded from these ideological purviews. For instance, in today's society, gay and lesbian rights groups have argued that the US Constitution applies to all free people in the country. They have argued that equal rights mandates, afforded to all citizens, women, and minorities, are applicable and transferable to them as well. For instance, for the last 50 years, gay and lesbian activists have argued for marriage equality for their communities in line with all other citizens of the country. Thus, they do not contest the dominant nationalistic view in terms of what a "citizen" is but rather argue that they be included into that very notion—that as taxpaying citizens, they should be afforded the same rights as others with regard to marriage rights and health insurance benefits for partners. Here, one can see the "negotiated ideology" at play; a group seeks to take (and not directly challenge) the dominant ideology and apply it to its own experiences and identities within the specific terms of the current law. Other gay, lesbian, and transgender groups have gone further, demanding the rewriting of federal and state marriage acts away from "a man and woman" to generally identify "any persons." Creative protests and staged demonstrations represent some of the vehicles that these communities use to create oppositional ideologies to dominant nationalistic ideologies around citizenship and marriage. Even though a federal law recognizes same-sex marriages, there is still social rejection (i.e., identity shaming, denial of rights of services as with the baker who denied the gay wedding cake for a same-sex couple) for gay, lesbian, and transgender groups and because of this, they tirelessly protest and challenge society's treatment of them.

Finally, many ethnic and national groups do not always work in line with dominant nationalistic ideologies. Indeed, some engage in **strategic nationalism** through which nationalistic appeals are used to redress a colonialist past and restore power that was taken away by an oppressor nation. Frantz Fanon (1961) highlights how indigenous African Algerians had to rise, take a stand, and create counter-nationalism to the oppressive, dominant French nationalistic regime that took over that land. What Fanon demonstrates is that nationalisms are not all created equal and/or not positioned in exactly the same way; some nationalisms are used to bind a disenfranchised and oppressed group against a larger, dominant power. This specific example of strategic nationalism is an oppositional ideology against a dominant nationalistic ideology.

Cultural Patterns

Cultural patterns also stand as powerful dominant ideologies in that these represent systems of knowledge about cultural groups that were created and reproduced within contexts of power. Perhaps the most popular information about cultural patterns comes from well-known psychologist Geert Hofstede who, since the 1970s, has studied key cultural patterns that distinguish cultures from one another. In his famous work, *Culture's Consequences*, Hofstede (2003) highlights five major dimensions (individualism, collectivism, uncertainty avoidance, power distance, masculinity-femininity) that thread across all cultures, from his extensive survey of thousands of IBM (a multinational company) employees from all over the world.

While Hofstede's work on cultural patterns has provided valuable information, one could argue that this body of knowledge has, over time, become a dominant knowledge base, one born of dominant ideologies about cultures. Because Hofstede's work was based on different national employees' survey responses in a multinational corporation, one could argue that his conclusions about cultural patterns were already framed on a nationalistic model. Hofstede therefore presumed that all IBM employees would view their own world in terms of the national framework through which they were raised. This privileging of nation-framed and -based behavior in individuals illustrates that Hofstede's well-cited cultural pattern research is already infused with dominant nationalistic ideologies. Hofstede was studying (although unintentionally) what we had already learned earlier in the chapter: that cultural behaviors are manifestations and reflections of nationalistic power forces.

Re-envisioning cultural patterns as indications of dominant ideologies is important because we rely on cultural patterns as immediate explanations of how a culture is. Likewise, through knowledge about culture patterns, we oftentimes presume that the behavior of certain individuals is determined, fixed (and automatic), and bounded by the culture to which he or she belongs.

(Low Power Distance——————————————————High Power Distance).

Individualistic Cultures	Collectivistic Cultures
Self-oriented	Group-oriented
"I" is paramount	"We" is paramount
Immediate relations and family are important	Circles/layers of family (beyond the immediate) are important
Privacy is valued	Concern for the larger in-group is valued.

Geert Hofstede's Cultural Dimensions (or Cultural Patterns) have heavily influenced how people in the business and education sectors understand other cultures. However, cultural patterns can also be understood as dominant ideologies or systems of knowledge about cultural groups that were created and reproduced within unspoken contexts of power.

Through cultural patterns' research, specific national cultures are represented as being a particular way. Collectivistic cultures are deemed as group-oriented but also as passive when compared to individualistic cultures who come off as active, intentional, risk taking, and courageous. Cultures that are deemed collectivistic are characterized as being driven by group loyalty in almost a guaranteed, automated manner; cultural members take on the semblance of robots moving to the "beat" of the group (the nation-state) and without any individual voice or desire. Individualistic cultures come off much stronger; they are characterized as commanding in presence, voice, and action (although the representation does make it appear as if their relational bonds are scarce and superficial).

Within this individualistic-collectivism cultural pattern, a specific dichotomy takes center stage: individual (individualism) versus culture (collectivism). Interestingly enough, this polarity serves as a hegemonic mirror for dominant nation-state positions. For instance, the cultural—that of Japan, Korea, China, and Colombia—is always marked as different, as exotic, and as primitive, thereby reflecting, by its difference with the opposing term, the power of the standard, un-marked, normalized individual who is beyond anything cultural. What happens here is that this representation always privileges the Westernized "individual" (and individualism) (via Western, European nations) over the exotic, strange "culture" (and collectivism) (via Asian and Latin American cultures). Thus, the cultural pattern of individualism-collectivism, through a featured binary opposition, operates as a dominant ideological apparatus that highlights the Western liberal ideologies of free will, equality, and choice surrounding the individualism position, at the negation of an othered, exoticized culture (e.g., Japan, Korea, Africa, and Black cultures).

Because these cultural patterns position and represent cultural groups in unequal ways, these patterns can be viewed as dominant ideologies. The unequal positioning of cultural groups benefits the dominant Western nations (the first world power block) (or the **Global North**) in the global order and advances the notion that the West is superior, free, progressive, and futuristic, while the third World (or two-thirds of the world) (now often discussed as the **Global South**) appear sto be archaic, primordial, and pre-modern.

Meritocracy

Another dominant ideology that surrounds culture, especially in the US, is meritocracy. **Meritocracy** refers to a specific social system through which an individual's talent, ability, and work effort determine success, wealth, position, and social status. Such an idea has become a cornerstone of US thinking; Americans exist in a system through which they can attain success and wealth through the key factors of ability, talent, and hard work. This notion of meritocracy has been connected to America's immigrant roots through the well-touted promise of the American Dream. The American Dream can be defined as the promise that all citizens and most residents of the United States can pursue their goals in life through hard work and free choice (Johnson, 2014). Influenced by 19th century American writer Horatio Alger (1985), the American Dream has taken hold and become this larger-than-life mythic narrative in which impoverished immigrants who come to America to build a better life, after time and in long pursuit of the American Dream, achieve economic success.

However, absent from this narrative are any references to the difficulties caused by prejudices ethnic minorities have experienced in establishing their own businesses in America. This omission implies that all immigrants can succeed and that economic success indeed can be achieved through determination, commitment, and a solid family environment. This myth then functions to uphold and preserve the conservative American ideals of free enterprise and local success without government assistance and obfuscates the inequalities due to prejudice that ethnic immigrants continually face (Hamamoto, 1994). A meritocracy uses and capitalizes off American Dream examples and self-made millionaires to confirm the working of the current ideological system.

The suggestion is that if ethnic and immigrant groups can succeed, the American system of individualistic capitalism truly works for everyone. Thus, the ideology of meritocracy stands as dominant world view in that it legitimizes and preserves a hegemonic social order while appearing completely workable and accessible. Such an ideology is also challenged by ethnic, women's, and gay and lesbian civil rights groups since the 1960s who argue that power inequalities comprise US society.

Summary

Ideologies therefore represent specific world views, or meanings, that are shaped and reproduced by specific power forces. There are several types of dominant ideologies (or ideas that are created by ruling interests) that circulate in our culture and we accept, negotiate with, and resist dominant ideologies in our lives.

Keywords

Dominant ideology

False consciousness

Hegemony

Human agency

Ideological state apparatus (ISA)

Ideology

Meritocracy

Nationalism

Negotiated ideology

Oppositional ideology

Repressive state apparatus (RSA)

Strategic nationalism

Questions and Activities

REFLECTION activity: Re-examining your culture, your way of life:

Answer the following questions:

+ Have you ever raised questions, like Kenji does, about your own culture and why things are the way they are? Have you ever wondered if this is what your culture or life is meant to be and if there is more? Write down which questions you have raised in this regard and how often you have posed such questions.

+ If you have not asked these questions before, ask yourself why that is the case. Why do we not ask these questions more often? What would happen if we were to continually raise these questions as Kenji does?

DISCUSSION activity: Examples of dominant ideologies:

Read the listed examples of dominant ideology. Think about who benefits from society's acceptance of these ideologies.

+ The more education you have, the better.

+ The more expensive the high school and/or university, the better the education (and the better you will do in life if you attend).

+ We are respectful of all cultures.

+ Men make better leaders than women.

+ Every individual, regardless of gender, socioeconomic class, race, ethnicity, religion, or nationality, can achieve the American Dream and be successful in this country.

+ Everyone wants to get married and have children.

+ We are not controlled by the government; I am in control of my own life!

+ It's better not to know everything the government does. We should trust in it to do the right thing.

+ We are far better off than we used to be.

+ The legal and governmental system works if you obey and abide by its rules. It is a fair and neutral system.

Chapter 5

Speaking for Others and Intercultural Communication

Learning Objectives

> To understand how we all speak from a social location

> To explore the consequences of speaking about and for others

> To reflect on the responsibility of representing cultural groups

Introduction: Lina and Joel Speaking for Their Cultures

Lina, a university student from China who is participating in a study abroad program in the US, specifically in the state of Texas, is constantly asked by her professors and American peers to describe "what China is really like." She is stunned by how many times she is asked to explain the "true nature" of her country and to confirm if the following is true: "The lives of the Chinese are determined for them by the government," that boys are highly valued while girls are easily discarded, and that "everything is cheap" in China. Lina has grown tired of dispelling myths and feels a great amount of pressure to "correctly" represent the complexities (the strengths and shortcomings) of her country.

Joel, a Native American college student living in a metropolitan area of Denver, also feels great pressure to represent his own culture (the Sioux) to his classmates. He

must prepare a half-hour formal presentation about his culture for his class. But this task is not so straightforward. Joel attends a small, faith-based college with a predominantly White/European American student body. Most of his peers, therefore, have never interacted with a Native American and have only come to know what a "Native American" is from Hollywood film and popular culture portrayals. He must represent his culture to an audience that may have specific expectations and perceptions of his community. Joel also considers this assignment to be critically important because he may very well stand as the only contact his classmates may ever have with a Native American. His explanation, words, images, and demeanor will indeed carry great weight.

These examples of Lina and Joel illustrate the importance of representing cultures and speaking on behalf of cultures as a member or non-member and can be framed as dilemmas of cultural representation. The issue of cultural representation is central to the study and practice of intercultural communication because you will often be asked to speak for your own cultural group or country in some contexts and to speak for other cultural groups in others. This may take place in a casual intercultural conversation, a class discussion about world politics or cultures, or a business meeting in your job role. We all participate in the representation of cultures and thus must understand key aspects of this practice and several considerations and implications that arise from cultural representation. As you explore critical intercultural communication in this book, it is imperative that you understand the issues around cultural representation. Just by studying intercultural communication, you are studying one particular version or representation of how cultures are and how to make sense of them. You too will be asked in class assignments to portray and describe your own cultural group and that of others, and thus will be engaging in the work and politics of cultural representation. It is therefore advantageous to understand the issues and politics of cultural representation so as to be more mindful and thoughtful of the implications of speaking in a specific moment for, about, or with a cultural group.

This chapter will feature a framework of representing cultures that is informed by Michel Foucault (1972, 1973, 1978a, 1978b), feminist scholar Linda Alcoff (1995), and cultural studies scholar Stuart Hall (1997b). Through this framework, we will uncover several aspects, considerations, and roles that we may take up in our lives in representing cultures.

What Is Cultural Representation?

When you hear the word "representation," you may immediately associate this with the term or concept of a representative. In our system of government (local, state, and national), we elect politicians or leaders to "represent" or "stand in our place" and work for our interests. This is the key principle of representation; it refers to an entity that stands in the place of and speaks for something or someone else. Standing in for something else is the essence of cultural representation; it refers to the production of a message, image, or meaning that re-presents or re-says who or what a culture is (Brummett, 2014). So, when an individual or group speaks about, depicts, and/or explains what a culture is about, he or she is re-presenting cultures and re-articulating who and what these cultural groups are. This could be done in casual conversation, a formal presentation, an international conference summit, a newspaper article, a Hollywood film, or a mainstream hip-hop music video (Hall, 1997b). The work of cultural representation is all around us. Let's first explore a theoretical framework that helps to articulate key aspects of cultural representation.

Cultural Representation as Discourse: A Framework

In his book, *Representation: Cultural Representations and Signifying Practices,* Stuart Hall (1997b) defines representation itself as "the production of meaning through language" (p. 16). While the specific process of representation indeed involves giving meaning to

Music videos, among other forms, re-present cultural groups in specific and powerful ways.

things through language, this process is much larger. According to French philosopher and critic Michel Foucault, representation exists in a much larger world of discourse. **Discourse** refers to "a group of statements which provide a language for talking about—a way of representing the knowledge about—a particular topic at a particular historical moment ..." (Hall, 1992, p. 291).

For example, one historical discourse that has dominated the United States has been around one particular major event: the September 11th attacks on the World Trade Center and the Pentagon through the hijacking of four major commercial airplanes. A discourse has emerged around this major event that killed and injured thousands of Americans. In the United States, it is referred to as 9/11 and it invokes several terms and images all at once as a discourse. Individuals understand 9/11 as a terrorist attack and the phrase "War on Terror or Terrorism" (the US administration's campaign at fighting back against terrorist threats or enemies entered the mainstream vernacular. Citizens were encouraged to remember 9/11 and fight terrorism (report any unusual behavior or individuals) for the sake of national security. (Even my usage of "September 11th attacks" is a depiction or portrayal of this event from a specific view.) Likewise, a patriot (as in the U.S.A. Patriot Act, which enabled law enforcement agencies to search telephone, e-mail communications, medical, financial, and other records for suspicious activity, conduct more foreign intelligence gathering within the United States, and empower law enforcement and immigration authorities to detain and deport immigrants suspected of terrorism-related acts) was understood as an individual who worked for the safety and freedom of his or her nation, even if that meant giving up his or her individual and civil rights to privacy and free speech. These notions of 9/11, terrorist, the War on Terror, and patriot formed a larger discourse that provided a commonly understood language for Americans to make sense of what happened on September 11th, as well as of relations between the United States and nations in the Middle East and the US invasion of Iraq.

Discourse in this sense provides an understanding of a cultural group and shared and reproduced meanings within a specific period. Foucault explained that a discourse, like that of 9/11, constructs and frames the topic itself from the outset. It "defines and produces the objects of our knowledge. It governs the way that a topic can be meaningfully talked about and reasoned about. It also influences how ideas are put into practice and used to regulate the conduct of others" (Hall, 1997b, p. 44). The 9/11 discourse frames the events in a tight victim (US)—aggressor (terrorist/Middle East) polarity and shapes all subsequent statements, utterances, or responses around the poles of this victim-victimizer/aggressor relation. What has resulted is the constriction of free speech and discourse of alternative points of views around 9/11. Conservative political groups and politicians have targeted university professors and campuses for speaking out against the United States' military action on Iraq or even the larger history that led to the targeting of the US for 9/11. Critical pedagogy scholars Henry Giroux (2006) and Sophia McClennen (2006) examine how the rights of academic freedom on university campuses to present all perspectives on a topic (and even ones critical of the governmental status quo) have been compromised and targeted in the 9/11 aftermath to create an academic environment that condones and supports American patriotism and national rhetoric. This larger discourse has framed what 9/11 is about, what it is not, what is acceptable behavior and speech, and what is not; it defines itself at the same time that it delimits what it is not. Discourse shapes how we understand and come to know a topic; it delimits what can be said or thought about a topic and how we are to behave around a topic or issue such as 9/11. The discourse of 9/11, made up of specific words, statements, narratives, images, myths, and perceptions, creates a system of knowledge in a specific historical and political moment.

To summarize, Foucault helps us understand cultural representation in terms of discourse and how a discourse does the following:

- Frames how a cultural issue or group is discussed and understood

- Shapes what is acceptable and what is not; it rules out, limits, and restricts other ways of talking about a cultural issue or group

- Defines how we are to conduct ourselves in relation to the cultural issue or group or constructing knowledge about it

- Delimits what can be said or thought about a cultural issue or group

- Sets into place the "who" of a cultural group or a topic and how we come to know, see, and act toward that group

- Creates institutional practices and policies toward a cultural issue or topic (as in laws, policies, rules of behavior and conduct)

- Extends and circulates across a range of contexts, institutional sites, and settings within a society
- Is created within a specific historical and political moment

Cultural representations are powerful discourses that we all engage in, and these often take on a life of their own and can grow to carry enormous truth value and authority for individuals. When a discourse about Native American Indians was presented in the 1950s to the larger society and public from anthropologists through journal articles and field reports, it had a major influence on how Native Americans were viewed, understood, and known by the public, which continues today. This reach of influence and narrative authority is what Foucault refers to as a **discursive formation**. A discursive formation occurs when a discourse (or a set of words, statements, utterances, images, memories, and myths) takes on such great narrative authority or truth value that it dominates the range of knowledge and understanding on a cultural issue, topic, or group. In this way, what Foucault also refers to as an "episteme," a discursive formation becomes *the* definitive statement about a cultural issue or group, that is the ultimate kind of cultural representation, which constructs and defines all conclusions about a phenomenom.

While cultural representation as discourse is a major part of the theoretical framework of focus, it is important to uncover the key aspects and considerations of cultural representation. Key aspects of cultural representation and speaking about, for, and with cultural groups can best be understood in terms of Michel Foucault's notion of **discursive context** and feminist philosopher Linda Alcoff's (1995) research on speaking about, for, and with others.

Discursive Context

The work of representing cultures needs to be analyzed and considered within a dis-cursive context. Discursive context refers to the tight-knit, interlocked relationship between representation and power. Representations are created within fields of power with different consequences for different cultural groups. These differential consequences and treatments of cultural groups through representation could be due to the depictions themselves. Certain groups, such as Whites/European Americans and heterosexual "straight" persons, are depicted and portrayed in positive, affirming ways, while others, such as Blacks/African Americans and lesbian, gay, and transgender persons, are framed in negative, disconfirming ways. Another factor could be the visibility of cultural groups and/or the speakers or representatives themselves; some groups have more vocal, visible, and positive representatives or speakers on their behalf while others do not enjoy such privileges. The medium of representation can also create power differences among cultural groups; some groups enjoy more mainstream televisual, filmic, mediated, and research coverage (East Asians, such as Japanese and Chinese) than others (Southeast Asians, such as Cambodians, Hmong, among others). In addition to these elements, a discursive context creates a field of different power relations with cultural representation in terms of who is speaking, who is spoken of, who listens, and who will be impacted by the act of representation.

A discursive context of cultural representation can create power differences among cultural groups by way of several key aspects. In this next section, each of these factors will be delineated with examples and insight from both Foucault and Alcoff.

Key Aspects of a Discursive Context

There are several key aspects of a discursive context that we must be mindful of when examining, engaging in, and consuming cultural representation, all of which occur on a daily basis. These aspects derive from the work of Foucault and Alcoff.

The Act of Speaking

Representing cultures can be viewed in terms of acts of speaking, in that a cultural group or issue is being articulated, portrayed, and discussed in specific terms by a speaker and to someone else (or to a group or audience). The speaking itself could be in the form of spoken words, conversation, public speeches and arguments, legal policies and mandates, visual images, and/or mediated texts. To represent one's self, culture, or group and that of others seems to be so commonplace and routine in daily life. However, the ability to represent one's self, culture, or group and that of others does not come easily for most. It requires the space and authority to be able to project one's voice or representation; a high-ranking politician, for example, will have more space, authority, and means to represent other groups and individuals than a university student. Likewise, a female mid-level manager will not have as much access to other individuals of power to articulate or represent her group's interests (and those of others) than a higher-level, male vice president or CEO. Note that one's position, gender role in a particular society, and socioeconomic class, among other factors, will shape an individual's differential access to cultural representation that will have impact and influence on others. Thus, the act of speaking is not an act equally shared by all members of a society; anthropologists who have historical ties to museums and university collections and esteemed credibility across the world will have more means and channels to represent Native American culture than actual Native American tribes. Ironically, just because one is a cultural member of a group, does not mean that that member will be able to widely and influentially represent her or his culture to others. Our ability and position to represent culture is indeed differential based on a number of aspects discussed in this section. All this highlights how the very act of speaking is politically and historically situated.

Because the act of speaking is politically and historically situated, the question, "Why does one speak in a particular situation or context?" becomes important. The specific motives for an individual speaking on behalf of her or his own culture and a different culture should be considered. The motive could revolve around wanting to share information and educating decision makers, leaders, and teachers about a group that is not understood or known. But, it also could be to convince an audience to pass a specific piece of legislation that will help a cultural group or stop a preference given to such a group. An act of speaking could focus on negatively portraying a cultural group to advance a different group's interests. The motives could differ widely and thus, investigating why an individual is speaking about a cultural issue or group is vital.

Probing the why behind an act of speaking will also help to understand why the cultural group of focus may not be included in the act of speaking. To speak is an act of empowerment for a cultural group member; to be able to give voice to one's experience and share that and participate in the public construction and perception of her or his group can be self-determining and even liberating. For an oppressed group member to be able to voice her or his marginalization is a defining and critical moment in the step toward emancipation and de-colonization (Mendoza, 2002; Minh-Ha, 2009, 2014). Thus, we need to ask: Why is an individual engaging in this act of speaking? If applicable, why is a cultural member not doing the actual speaking for her or his own group? In fact, there could be viable reasons as to why a cultural member is not part of the act of speaking. For instance, it might be the case that there are potential physical threats against and retaliatory ramifications for a cultural member to speak about her or his group in either a positive or negative way. The targeted audience may also be in a different

The act of speaking could be in the form of presenting to an audience, writing an essay or book, and/or creating a mediated form.

linguistic and national context, which may make it necessary to have someone from that culture to engage in the act of speaking for full persuasive power. With many possible reasons, one must examine why a cultural group member is not included in the act of speaking because of the important agency and liberation potential imbued in speaking acts, especially in Western societies and the global society.

Social Location

A speaker's social location is another key aspect in the discursive context of cultural representation. Social location speaks to the notion that we all have different identities, backgrounds, and group affiliations and thus are "placed" differently in relation to one another with regard to our backgrounds. Specifically, social location refers to the power positionality and placement of an individual in a society in terms of key demographics such as gender, race, ethnicity, socioeconomic class, sexual orientation, nationality, regional origin, and language, among others. Based on how we are individually placed or located in society, we are treated differently in terms of voicing our perspectives. For example, oftentimes, in male-dominated societies, a male is taken more seriously when discussing specific topics (politics, business, news) in the workplace or in the classroom. However, in other societies and contexts, a female's point of view and voice are deemed more credible than those of a male's; for instance, in a legal hearing having to do with the custody rights of a child, the mother's perspective is given more weight than that of the father. When academic theorists from indigenous and historically marginalized backgrounds write manuscripts that explicitly acknowledge their political perspectives and backgrounds, it is looked down on as inappropriately biased and/or polemical. However, when European male scholars do the same, their manuscripts are regarded as "major contributions" and "groundbreaking theories." Thus, one's social location can delineate the reach or influence of the perspective being articulated and even shape the meaning and interpretation of the message.

This notion of social location also converges with feminist standpoint theory, which asserts that our social group memberships affect our positionalities and how we view the world and interact with others (Allen, 2017; Hill Collins, 2000; Harding, 2004; Hartsock, 1983). Feminist standpoint theory also explains that because our social identities and group members exist in a hierarchy, our inequalities create differences in our social locations. These social locations shape unique standpoints for individuals in terms of how they view others, speak to, about, and for others, and how these acts of speaking are understood and evaluated. Because of social location and feminist standpoint theory, even what we say by ourselves and about ourselves in our situated locations and standpoints has implications for others around us.

One's social location or standpoint will be framed differently depending on the positionality of that individual in relation to that of the cultural group or issue she or he is discussing. In this section, different positionalities and relations of speaking are explored.

Speaking as a Native Member (Inside)

It is more often the case that you will be asked to speak for your own cultural group (whether that is in terms of nationality, race, ethnicity, religion, gender, or sexual orientation, among others). Typically, we are asked to represent our own cultural group when traveling to another country or when situated in contexts where you stand as one of the few representatives of that group. For instance, when you are traveling abroad, you may notice that individuals will ask you about your own country; this is to confirm or validate their understanding or sense-making of your country. You may even feel a bit awkward in that you are asked to speak about formal governmental policy or a historical decision made by your country's leaders even though you are just a university student or possibly in disagreement with such decisions. In specific settings, your social location as a representative of your group becomes paramount and central. Other times, you may be in a classroom or institutional setting when your cultural group is highlighted as a topic of discussion; the instructor or facilitator may ask you to speak about how your cultural group really is. Your positionality as a native member of your cultural group can therefore be invoked across many settings in your life.

Speaking for your own group is not as straightforward as it appears. Some may presume that if they are members of a group that they have unlimited license and authority to speak to their own group without recourse or challenge. On the contrary, your social location can be varied in different ways from most others in your cultural group.

Consider the social location of a Hawaiian female, Laurie, who was born and raised in North Carolina. Though she is an indigenous Native Hawaiian, Laurie is a mainland or diasporic Hawaiian who genealogically and ancestrally hails from Hawai'i but is not born of the native homeland. This impacts her voice as a Hawaiian and her ability to speak for Hawaiians as a whole. When individuals in her community in North Carolina ask Laurie about Hawaiians, she is tentative about what she says because how she represents her cultural group may have serious implications for those Hawaiians at home. Laurie explains, "They are surprised that I am born in North Carolina and wonder how I got to be there. Then I have to tell them that while there are lots of Hawaiians on the mainland, there are Hawaiians in Hawai'i who struggle for land rights and cultural recognition. Just because I am more more of an urban mainland Hawaiian does not mean that Hawaiians are dying out or that we have gotten our due. I have to be careful about saying that or else it hurts my people, my ohana (family) in Hawai'i." As Laurie illustrates, speaking for her cultural group is complicated by her unique positionality within that cultural group. How one speaks as a native member must always take into consideration how that native member is situated in relation to the cultural group at large in a context.

Similar to Laurie, John, a 35-year-old African American male from Chicago struggles with speaking on behalf of his African American community. He was born and raised in Jamaica and emigrated to the United States when he was 20 years old. While he identifies as an African American, John understands when other members in his community challenge his views and perspectives on the community because he did not have to grow up and form his self-esteem in a racist America with a legacy of slavery. As a principal of an elementary school, John works hard to promote the African American community he values but faces many questions from cultural members about the authenticity of his words and experiences.

Speaking as a "native" involves situating one's identity (and experiences and background) in relation to the cultural group and in relation to the politics of authenticity in that group. The politics of authenticity refer to a group's perceptions of what makes someone a "true" cultural member of its group. What makes someone "authentic" over another person can never fully be resolved, but it does create another layer of the role of speaking for one's group. When a native member who is deemed as "not authentic" represents or speaks for her or his cultural group, that group may protest and challenge that representation, especially when speaking to an external audience. A cultural representation from a native member with a divergent and even privileged background can in fact be the source of conflict within a cultural group. Speaking for one's group is not without its considerations, risks, and pitfalls from within that group.

But while a native representation of his or her culture is more complex than we typically think, it is important for us to understand that "native" members and those from historically marginalized and oppressed backgrounds can indeed speak for themselves. Famed critical scholar Gayatri Spivak (1988) argues that the "subaltern can speak." She explains that native members should absolutely speak for themselves. This, Spivak argues, is especially crucial given that historically and structurally, a "native" or "subaltern" group may have been silenced or restrained from speaking or creating representations and may have been excluded from participating in media or the academy to proffer knowledge and information about him- or herself. Why not enable and empower native members to participate in their own cultural representations as they have distinctive insider experiences, insights, and perspectives to share about that cultural group?

To recognize the power and unique role of native members in acts of cultural representations is *not*, at the same time, to presume that native member voices necessarily carry an immediate or purer sense of truth than other non-native perspectives. For instance, does a Chinese female cultural member in Australia who has grown up and been identified as a Chinese in that country for all her life have a more truthful and liberal version of "what it means to be Chinese" than a non-Chinese researcher who has been studying Chinese communities in Australia for many years? No, according to Spivak; however, claims of truth must be situated and relationally determined. There is no pure version of truth from any perspective. At the same time, though, living as a member of a historically, structurally, and socially disadvantaged group carries a great deal of negative consequences and burdens for that individual than for an outsider. The experience (positive and negative) of living as a native member in a dominant society may create a more comprehensive, multi-faceted view of what it means to be Chinese in a particular society. Lived experience as a native member (as a Chinese) is different from outsider knowledge as a non-native member (as a non-Chinese researcher), thereby making a native representation of one's cultural group more insightful as opposed to being more truthful.

Speaking as a native member is constituted by more than an image of speaking about what we know and those we know. We do not only speak for ourselves; others (even other native members) are unduly affected by what we say and represent. A native's point of view, influenced by that native's social location in relation to other native members and the politics of authenticity within that group, is rich with insight but does not necessarily carry more truth or resistive potential than those of others.

Speaking as a Non-Native (Outsider)

If you are an outsider and in a position to speak on behalf of or for a cultural group of which you are not a member, there are several issues to consider. The first has to do with the impetus and motivation to speak for or about a cultural group. As discussed earlier, a non-native (outsider) must answer the following questions: "Why am I speaking for this cultural group? What do I gain from this act? What might the consequences be for this cultural group?" Answers to these questions may vary depending, again, on the social location of the outsider and her or his positionality in relation to the cultural group. An outsider may be in a highly visible position (as a high-ranking official, visible community leader, affluent business executive, or celebrity) that could be advantageously employed for a native group. Sometimes, to specific audiences, an outsider with influence can change public perception of a cultural group and one that has been historically misunderstood or forgotten. A non-native's access to power and resources may indeed help a cultural group,

Former President Barak Obama was often deemed as representing all African Americans and their experiences. In some ways, this increased the **cultural capital** (the social advantage or leverage one gains from a social relationship or association) of African Americans while also creating larger societal expectations that all African Americans can easily increase their socioeconomic and political mobility. This also carried limitations in terms of an outsider point of view in that Obama's viewpoints were taken as representing ALL African Americans.

and, thus, her or his position on the outside may make all the difference (and in more impactful ways than an insider who may struggle to get a place at the table to speak). You can see this in the United States with the public fascination on Hollywood celebrities. Several non-native celebrities, such as George Clooney, Angelina Jolie, and U2 singer Bono, have urged the public and elected officials to pay attention to important global causes such as the "lost boys in Sudan" or world AIDS and the suffering and cultural genocide in Rwanda. Their celebrity influence has become useful to set the American public's awareness on world issues and suffering nations, not originally on their national agenda of focus. Several of these celebrities have also met with our nation's leaders to push for political action and assistance to those nations.

Another example of a non-native's influence on representing a cultural group can be seen in famous American anthropologist Margaret Mead's (1971) popular account of Samoan culture in 1928, *Coming of Age in Samoa*, which was published in many reprint editions, in a variety of languages, and which made her famous. In this account based on field observations and interviews with Samoan youth, Mead concluded that the transition between childhood and adolescence in Samoa was a smooth one unlike what was seen at the time in the United States (e.g., emotional, psychological distress, anxiety, uncertainty, and confusion). Mead also described how young Samoan women deferred marriage for many years while enjoying casual sex and then, later on, married,

Celebrities such as Angelina Jolie have brought widespread attention and visibility to urgent global issues and in ways that native members (**cultural insider** or a person who belongs to and is accepted in a cultural group) could not given Hollywood celebrity culture.

settled down, and successfully reared their own children. Anthropologists and Samoans themselves have criticized Mead's account for romanticizing Samoan life and portraying Samoan adolescent sexuality in an offensive manner. What is interesting here is that Mead became famous for this work (the book is considered to be a classic for most anthropology courses in the world) and put ethnography and anthropology on the map in the United States. In addition, because of her work, academic standing, and subsequent popularity, Mead also put Samoan culture on the minds of American academics and students, as well as anthropologists, across the world. Her outsider (non-native) status and access to research visibility in the academy brought widespread attention to this small and, at the time of the 1920s, unknown Pacific Islander culture. At the same time, though, such attention specifically framed Samoan culture as a primitive and oversexualized group in a way that enabled her to promote a specific argument about American culture.

An outsider, however, can also wield harm if his or her information or depiction is negative, misleading, or not fully representative of the interests of the cultural group. This can be the case even if that non-native speaker has taken all the precautions, meaning, intent aside, that consequences can run deep for the cultural group being represented even with a speaker's benevolence and good will intact. For example, many contemporary non-native or outsider documentary filmmakers and anthropologists have worked hard to make films and conduct research that involve and include native persons in the creation and construction process as collaborators rather than as informants from the colonialist and dominant filmmaking and ethnographies of the past. Here, native members are not only

COMING OF AGE
IN SAMOA

>>>>>>>>>>>>>> <<<<<<<<<<<<<<

*A Psychological Study of Primitive
Youth for Western Civilisation*

By

MARGARET MEAD

Assistant Curator of Ethnology
American Museum of
Natural History

Foreword by Franz Boas
Professor of Anthropology, Columbia University

>>>>>>>>>>>>>> <<<<<<<<<<<<<<

WILLIAM MORROW & COMPANY
NEW YORK   MCMXXVIII

In her popular account, *Coming of Age in Samoa* (1971), famous American anthropologist Margaret Mead provided a "glimpse" into the Samoan culture and forever re-presented the cultural community from an outsider point of view.

included more (in terms of their voices and experiences) but also portrayed in a more positive and sympathetic light. Though different from the past forms of representation, some argue that non-native filmmakers and anthropologists employ a radically different approach to cultural representation that it is still harmful and negative. According to Maya scholars Edward Fischer and R. McKenna Brown (1996), "Westerners' attempts at empowerment of indigenous peoples, however, are inherently delicate situations, because, while well-intentioned, they often appear to the intended beneficiaries as simply the old colonialism in a new guise" (p. 3). Well-intentioned cultural representations can therefore be accused of standing as "gentler" forms of colonialist oppression and as paternalistic (though kinder) vehicles of control over a cultural group.

A second consideration is that speaking for and about others can spill into one another. It is difficult to discern between an act of speaking for and an act of speaking about since the consequences for that group may be the same. An example is that an individual may be asked to share knowledge and information about a cultural group and not realize that speaking about can serve as a substitute for that cultural group to represent itself, thereby simultaneously making that act one that is speaking for such a group. Think about how an advertising executive may be asked to find research about an Asian community, one for whom her firm is trying to market a product, and must formally present this to the vice presidents in that firm. The research or knowledge that she finds and then summarizes for her bosses will be used exclusively by those VPs to make key business decisions on marketing and designing advertising campaigns for that group. That cultural group may not be included in these conversations given the quick timelines and expensive costs for creating advertising campaigns. Given the particulars of this context, then, that advertising executive's representation *about* that Asian community will stand in place of and become a representation *for* that group. The two distinctions blend and blur into one another, making representation a tricky practice that requires a mindfulness and healthy questioning process of all the issues presented in this chapter.

You may think that speaking as a non-native outsider seems too rife with risks and damaging consequences, that it is not worth the effort, that it is, in fact, better to not represent other cultural groups of which you are not a part to be safe, fair, and intercul-turally considerate. This is also known by Linda Alcoff (1995) as the "retreat response," or a retreat from all practices of speaking "for it asserts that an individual can only know her own narrow individual experience and her 'own truth' and thus that she can never make claims beyond this" (p. 107). The notion that it is better *not* to speak because it is safer and exempts us from making mistakes and worse, disempower a cultural group that we want to help and usher in another form of domination on that group, may be even more problematic than speaking carelessly about a cultural group. Certainly, this is an understandable reaction; however, Alcoff argues that the choice to opt out of speaking for others may actually be, in and of itself, an enactment of privilege and a luxury that others do not have. Remember, having a voice to use for one's own group and other groups who may not be invited to the table, is critical.

So, the impulse to retreat is not the best alternative to mindfully and carefully speak for or with others. Instead, there needs to be more focus on *what can* be done:

- Carefully understanding one's social location in relation to a specific cultural group (and even if you are a member of that group)
- Thoughtfully examining the context around a cultural group or issue to know if a non-native, outsider positionality can be responsibly employed for that group's political gain and advantage
- Engaging in dialogues with the cultural group at hand so that speaking with and across groups occurs, making the speaking and representational context one of dialogue, connection, and mutual participation.

When understanding the role of speaking within these considerations, we can work to build alliances and speak opportunities through our social locations.

Even though Linda Alcoff (1995) said, "[H]ow what is said gets heard depends on who says it and who says it will affect the style and language in which it is stated," social location does not completely determine the message or the cultural representation. An individual's social location has great influence but does not lock into place how that representation will be invoked or the kind of impact it will make. There are other intervening factors to keep in mind, such as the audience, the history of representations for that cultural group, and the political moment, which are covered in the next sections.

Speaking With an Audience in Mind

When representing or speaking about another culture, one must be mindful of who is the audience or who is on the receiving end of the representation. Those individuals who constitute the audience could shape how a representation is designed and/or the reach of impact the representation has on that group. In addition to the who, it is important to trace the specific relations between the speaker's social location and those of the audience in a particular context. These situated relations will help highlight issues that need to be considered before, during, and after one engages in acts of cultural representation.

Native to Native

As discussed earlier, native members of cultural groups who end up in positions of speaking for their group do not necessarily have an easier time or any kind of immunity from harming others in acts of cultural representation. In fact, it may be more difficult and painstaking to speak about a group, especially when the audience consists of other native members. For example, a Cambodian social worker may be speaking to a group of Cambodian members about issues he sees in the Cambodian community. Through this representation, the Cambodian social worker may refer to issues of gender relations, traditions, values, and controversial issues such as Cambodian gay and lesbian sexuality and intracultural prejudice. This may lead to a positive reaction from the community, especially if the information coincides and confirms the past and present experiences of the other Cambodian members. Or, there could be a more chilly response from these members given the speaker's social location or background and/or the kind of information presented about the group. If the information highlights a negative aspect of the culture (such as the prejudice that Cambodians have toward racially mixed Cambodians) and or one that other members do not want to discuss or acknowledge (e.g., the growing number of gay Cambodian youth who feel rejected by their families and communities and experience depression and anxiety), then that speaker may be discounted. Thus, the social locational aspects of the audience and recipients of a cultural representation matter in terms of age and generation, gender, time of emigration, sexuality, religion, ethnic composition, socioeconomic status, and education level, among other factors. These aspects, in line with those of the speaker's social location, will often frame the tone of the interaction between speaker and audience and the impact (positive or negative) of the cultural representation on that group. Differences in social location do not always mean negative or divergent interactions between speaker and audience; instead, having a Cambodian social worker who was born and raised in the US speak to a group of Cambodians who emigrated in adulthood may serve an exciting informational exchange. Native members may indeed welcome hearing information and/or reading the perspective of a speaker from their own group but with a slightly different social location and positionality in relation to them. A native-to-native relation between speaker and audience raises different issues and complexities than a native-to-non-native relation.

Native to Non-Native

When a native speaker is speaking to a non-native audience about her or his cultural group, other issues arise. The same Cambodian social worker could instead be speaking to a group of non-native members (African Americans, Latino/as, and White/European Americans, separate or all together). The information presented may take on a different connotation for a group of members outside of the cultural group of focus. Such information may be the first point of contact that outside audience members have about Cambodians and thus will carry great weight because of the topical content and that such content comes from a Cambodian him- or herself. Likewise, audience members may carry a pre-formed view of Cambodians based on the media, or worse, a stereotype that then can be confirmed if it coincides with what a Cambodian speaker presents. For a native member to present information that resonates with or confirms a stereotype or an exoticized view of a group is to put into motion a powerful authenticating effect of prejudgments and stereotypes about that group. A native speaker can have that effect because a native voice authorizes and validates a stereotype that may be tentatively held, and it seems counter-intuitive that a cultural group would represent false information about itself. This may explain why native members become concerned over misleading or distorted representations made by their own members.

We will speak to our own cultural group members (within culture) in different ways than we will speak to individuals outside of our own culture.

In addition, the native-to-non-native relation may influence what information a speaker decides to present to an outside group. An African American woman will speak differently to a group of African American members than she will to a group of Asian Americans. In the former situation, she may use certain commonly understood terms or ways of speaking that are valued in that group and speak about issues that are mutually understood and affirmed. This same African American female speaker will behave differently with a group of Asian Americans; she may need to provide background information and key terms to develop understanding of her community as well as dispel myths or stereotypes about her group. Depending on the purpose of the representation (to inform, educate, change an opinion, or get public support for a community issue), the speaker may need to, for the sake of understanding, present information that generalizes aspects of her community (as opposed to drawing out all the particularities of the group). This could be done to make the information more accessible and coherent. Taking license to generalize or categorize his or her own group comes with some risks. Representations from a native speaker may run deep and count as more truthful than any other accounts and thus, generalizations may mislead or distort how outside groups see a particular cultural group or issue. A native speaker needs to be mindful of this possible consequence and carefully craft messages that are accessible but that also push audience members to find out more information, ask questions, and not draw definitive conclusions across contexts and individual members.

Non-Native (in Position of Power) to the General Public

Non-native speakers, especially those in positions of power, such as elected officials, business figures, and diplomats, find themselves more often in positions to speak about a cultural group or issue to a larger general, non-native public than native members of the cultural group of focus. Given the greater access they have to larger audiences, non-native speakers who represent or share information about other cultural groups must be mindful in how the ways they speaking about and for cultural groups of whom they are not members. On one hand, given their social locations and potential positions of power, these non-native speakers have a responsibility to exert as much positive influence as they can on a larger public, in terms of educating an audience about a group or issue, dismantling a long-held, inaccurate view of a cultural group, or advocating for public support on behalf of this cultural group. Such positive influence should be discussed and collaborated between the non-native speaker and actual native members of the cultural group. Nothing is more powerful, in some cases, than a White/European American male CEO to argue for the mentoring, development, and hiring of minority female and male CEOs in corporate America to the larger business community and philanthropic interests (made of mostly other older, affluent White/European American males). Thus, having a non-native speaker or figure push and advocate for change and action on behalf or in the interests of a cultural group may actually create more immediate change than if a native speaker did so. Herein there is the issue that this situation is demeaning to minority groups, because the White hero is positioned as helping "saving the day" for people of color. However, if non-native speakers work with cultural groups as allies, or individuals committed to helping and advocating for one another, then a non-native speaker can help leverage her or his privilege or social location to help other groups, as determined through collaboration and discussion with members of that group (DeTurk, 2007, 2011). In this way, speaking does not have to be reduced to just identity politics but can involve coalition building and alliances across social locations and situated privilege and interests, depending on the context and speaker-audience relations. That is, non-native speakers can work toward helping cultural groups through their social locations, visibility, and network of influence. All of this is more ideal and opportune to the notion of non-native speakers not engaging in cultural representations (which is unrealistic as it happens often) and/or in speaking for and about other groups in careless and non-collaborative ways.

History of Representations for the Cultural Group of Focus

Another intervening factor to keep in mind in acts of speaking and cultural representations has to do with the history of representations for the cultural group of focus. Cultural groups, for instance, may experience a specific kind of history of images, depictions, and portrayals of their group by the media, government, and public information. In European and US media, several scholars have examined how India and Asian Indians are usually represented as poor, subservient, and desiring of Westernization across newspaper, literature, and filmic representations. Followers of Islam and Islamic nations have been depicted consistently in Western media and journalistic accounts as misogynistic, violent, and radicalist for over 20 years (Trevino, Kanso, & Nelson, 2010). Representations of homosexuality in Western societies take on sinful, diseased, and immoral connotations in moral, legal, medical and psychiatric discourses, practices, and institutional apparatuses of the late 19th century, according to Michel Foucault (1978a, 1978b). Given the patterns of these representations across media, contexts, and countries in a specific period, Foucault would frame such histories of representations as "discursive formations" that can take on a life of their own and powerfully stand as indisputable truths to all. These "regimes of truth" can be very difficult to dismantle, challenge, and break down given the accumulated power and deeply embedded and historically naturalized pattern of representations affixed to a group. One way to see this is that Asian American images or portrayals in the media will always be framed in terms of the forever foreign, unassimilable depiction, on the one hand, or the commonly remembered tropes of the Asian kung-fu master, Asian subservient female, unfeeling, de-sexualized Asian, and the evil Asian male villain, on the other. Even if alternative films attempt to challenge such image patterns, the ways through which individuals come to understand, critique, or research these films is by calling up and applying these patterns. Here, then, the history of representations as a discursive formation always frames and locks a cultural group into a set pattern of meanings and images; patterns that dominate the ways in which we see, think about, and discuss any subsequent representation. Hence, a discursive formation or history of representations for a group can be quite powerful.

This history of representations for a cultural group needs to be considered when speaking about, for, and with a group, especially when a non-native speaker is representing a group to a native group or a larger audience. Non-native speakers must be sensitive to the ways in which a cultural group has been historically represented so that she or he does not merely recall images or information that call up painful historical stereotypes or frame the group in a historically inaccurate manner. To continually frame African or indigenous students in France, the United States, or Canada as "at risk" or "low performing" students is to recall educational stereotypes that have mischaracterized specific ethnic groups in negative ways. For an educator or expert to present a similar tone or set of images to one of these groups may shut down the possibility of dialogue or sharing across groups and their social locations given the history of representations. Similarly, when a non-native speaker does the same thing but to a

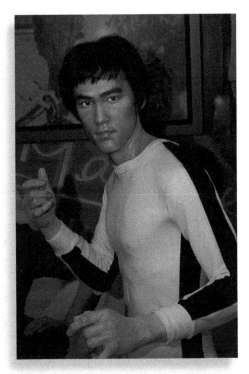

Asian Americans are always connected to the larger history of representations around Asian Americans. For example, Asian American males are either portrayed as Kung Fu masters (or martial arts experts), one-dimensional villains, or asexualized characters.

larger non-native audience, there could be a domino effect of spreading, unleashing, and reactivating a history of misleading and negative representations to the larger public who may take such information, not only as familiar, but as truthful and real. We must think about the likely and possible effects of acts of speaking on the discursive context and the cultural group at hand and the lingering effects of cultural representations.

Political Moment

The time period or historical moment in which an act of cultural representation occurs will undoubtedly shape how that representation is viewed and its sphere of influence. Michel Foucault (1978b) asserted that discursive formations of cultural representations and acts of speaking are specific to the surrounding historical and political moment. An example of this can be seen in the controversy over Black Lives Matter. Black Lives Matter represents a social movement that developed in 2013 as a resistive protest against the systemic violence and racism against Blacks in America. The movement gained momentum in response to the killings of Trayvon Martin, Michael Brown, Eric Garner, Black queer and trans people, and many others. When Black Lives Matter became a hashtag throughout social media and formed into a larger campaign, many individuals responded with a #AllLivesMatter hashtag, which appeared to erase the importance of Black rights and the racial focus of the movement. In this moment, when individuals who

In the specific historical and political moment of the Black Lives Matter movement, a social media message or hashtag in response to Black Lives Matter was tightly fixed to a specific set of racial politics.

were not Black used the #AllLives Matter hashtag (whether as a way to communicate the importance of unity across racial lines or as a way to tout a colorblind focus), they were perceived as racist and anti-Black. In this specific historical and political moment, a social media message or hashtag in response to Black Lives Matter was tightly fixed to a specific set of racial politics.

Reflexivity and Responsibility

Lastly, taking all the factors discussed in this chapter together, there needs to be an intentional effort on every individual's (native and non-native, insider and outsider, member and ally) part to be reflexive about speaking for and about and representing a cultural group or issue. To be reflexive is to be careful, mindful, and aware or conscious of all the factors (the key factors of a discursive context) that enter into the practice of cultural representation such as the following:

- The act of speaking
- The social location of speakers
- The audience in mind (and the specific speaker-audience relations)
- The history of representations for that cultural group
- The political moment surrounding the act of speaking

Moreover, as societal members, we must *all* continually pay attention the following:

- Social location
- Discursive context
- Who is listening
- Immediate setting and context
- Implications of what is said
- Connection to other images
- Messages
- History of message on a group
- Power relations, now and future

Summary

This chapter highlights the ways in which a larger politics of cultural representation frames how to learn, understand, and interact with other cultures. The conditions and contexts of speaking, as well as our own positionalities, powerfully shape how cultural groups are characterized. Speaking for and about others carries a significant impact on those represented cultures. We should understand the politics of cultural representation so as to be more mindful of the implications of speaking in a specific moment for, about, and with a cultural group.

Keywords

Allies

Discourse

Discursive context

Discursive formation

Representation

Social location

Speaking as a native (inside)

Speaking as a non-native (outsider)

Questions and Activities

REFLECTION activity: Examining dilemmas of cultural representation:
Consider the following true stories and excerpts from Alcoff, 1995, p. 97:

- "Anne Cameron, a very gifted white Canadian author, writes several first person accounts of the lives of Native Canadian women. At the 1988 International Feminist Book Fair in Montreal, a group of Native Canadian writers ask Cameron to, in their words, 'move over' on the grounds that her writings are disempowering for indigenous authors. She agrees."

- "At a recent symposium at my university, a prestigious theorist was invited to lecture on the political problems of postmodernism. The audience, which includes many white women and people of oppressed nationalities and races, waits in eager anticipation for his contribution to this important discussion. To the audience's disappointment, he introduces his lecture by explaining that he cannot cover the assigned topic because as a white male he does not feel that he can speak for the feminist and postcolonial perspectives that have launched the critical interrogation of postmodernism's politics. Instead, he lectures on architecture."

Upon reading these examples, answer the following questions:

- What is the dilemma of cultural representation in each of the stories?
- What are the similarities and differences among the stories?
- What do you think of the final outcomes of the stories?

DISCUSSION activity:
Discuss the following in class:

- Is there ever a situation or specific context when speaking for others can be positive and useful for groups? Or, is speaking for others always a dangerous thing to do?
- Should we just *not* speak at all for others, even when other cultural groups are in need of advocacy and alliances? How might this "non-movement/non-action" be even more dangerous?

Chapter 6

Identity Layers and Intercultural Communication

Learning Objectives

> To understand the interconnected layers of identity (the social/structural and the personal)

> To examine how identity is connected to power and specific larger structures

> To reflect upon how our identity positions disadvantage and or privilege us

Introduction: Len's Identity

Len is a young advertising agency professional who just graduated from college. He currently lives in his hometown of Toronto, Canada. He identifies himself as a "Canadian," a 20-something millennial. When individuals see and meet Len, they immediately identify him as Asian and when hearing his last name (Wong), denote him as Chinese. Others walking past Len on the street see him as an Asian man and possible as someone from Asia or a foreigner; someone not necessarily from Canada itself, his actual home country. He does not speak the language of his parents—Mandarin—and has never been to China, the ancestral homeland of his family; in fact, he is fluent in Spanish and travels quite a bit to Costa Rica and Guatemala.

Lately, Len has been noticing how acquaintances and business colleagues compliment him on the fact that he does not seem to speak with an accent. He finds that comment to be odd, given that he was born and raised in Canada. Local Canadian newspapers and Canadians themselves have described Asians in Canada (like Len and his family) as immigrants who are not real Canadians. Len also notes the local, national, and US-based and Hollywood-mediated depictions of Asians as foreigners and as specific character types (quiet, submissive, passive men; foreign immigrants; seductive, geisha-like women; karate-yielding, kung-fu martial arts experts). He insists, on a daily basis, that he is Canadian and does not understand why others and even the media cannot accept that.

Len is especially bothered by the images projected by the Canadian government of who Canadians are. Those images historically depicted European or White Canadian males and not the diverse groups that have made Canada their home: Chinese, Filipinos, Indians, and many more. For Len, he was a Canadian and had always been. Why wasn't he being recognized as such?

Being recognized is important in a different way for Len. His great uncle from Beijing, China, always visited his family's home in Toronto. But whenever he did, he always told Len that he was not really Chinese. To be Chinese was to be in the homeland and living in the Chinese way. Len was bothered by his great uncle's view. Even though he identified strongly with his Canadian-ness, Len also saw himself as Chinese and, ultimately, as Chinese-Canadian. He did not like how his own family judged his Chinese belonging while external forces judged his Canadian belonging. Len was grappling with layers of identity, as explained by a critical intercultural communication approach.

On a daily basis, then, Len is confronted with the layers of identity (social/structural and personal) in terms of how he sees himself. He also is judged against the looming expectations (from society and even from within his own family) around his authenticity or claim to an identity group membership.

What this example of Len demonstrates is the important and multi-layered arena of identity. Typically, when we think about identity, we immediately assume that it is a personal and private choice, that you are in charge of selecting, declaring, and owning your own identity—whatever that identity consists of in terms of the social roles you occupy (daughter, son, sister, brother, mother, father), traits you emulate (trustworthy, loyal), and/or types of group memberships that you have (in terms of faith, race, ethnicity, sexuality, gender, socioeconomic class, and educational status, among others)). But, as Len experiences on a daily basis, identity ushers in more than one's own personal choice about who she or he is and what constitutes her or his selfhood.

From a critical intercultural communication perspective, identity stands as a multi-layered arena of defining who we are but through two specific key layers: A) our personal view or declaration of our own identity (the personal layer), and B) others' framings of our identities or of who we are (the social/structural layer). In addition, it is not just the people around us in the social world that ascribe and assign our identities; social (societal) structures (the government, law, education, health care, media) do this as well in the social/structural layer. For instance, Len identifies himself as a Canadian and invests a great deal of who he is in this notion. However, he cannot merely rest on this identification as he interfaces with other individuals who want to see and identify him as an Asian foreigner (even noted as Chinese) with an accent. Len also hits against the notion that some identities (like Canadian, in this example) are marked by specific notions of what is authentic and real; local Canadian discourse implies that "true" or "real" Canadians are not Asians in that country. Len must therefore navigate his own personal identification as a Canadian with what others around him see (in the physical and cultural sense), presume, and imagine him to be and in terms of their understandings and definitions of cultural authenticity; he must also carefully steer through a similar process with larger structures of power (such as governmental, legal, institutional, and mediated spheres) that misrecognize and identify him as Asian or foreign. Thus, as revealed in this narrative introduction, identity is not a one-dimensional, smooth concept that is under the complete control of Len or any of us. Rather, identity is, as Mendoza, Halualani, & Drzewiecka (2003) argue, the dynamic construction of who we are, as mediated by structures and conditions of power and social groups (the social/

structural layer) and our remakings of who we are in response or relation to these structures (the personal layer).

This chapter highlights the connection between identity and power in terms of two key layers: a) the **structural** framings of our identities (**the social/structural layer**), and b) our **personal** and group constructions of identity in response, reaction, and relation to these structural framings (**the personal layer**). Likewise, we will discuss how identity is very much politicized (or that identity carries implications and consequences of power) and historicized (or that identity is situated in a specific historical period and time) and what this means for who we are and how we claim who we are to others.

What Is Identity?: Identity and Power

When you think of the concept of identity, you may immediately understand this to mean how you see and view and define yourself. You may also refer to identity as the aspects of you that you find most important, whether that includes a role or position you occupy (a teacher, an athlete, a musician), a familial or personal connection and role (a daughter, a son, a mother, a father, a sister, a friend), and/or one of your group memberships (in terms of ethnicity, race, gender, sexuality, education level, socioeconomic status, religion or faith, nationality, region, or language). Many also associate identity as encompassing how they want others to view them. Most people understand identity (who we are) to be something we choose for ourselves and something that is in our complete control and purview.

While we each, in part, construct our identities, identity stands as more of an interchange between a) the structural and historical conditions and framings of who are (which are often activated and reinforced by structures of power such as governmental apparatuses, the legal system, educational institutions, and the media and popular culture, among others) and b) our personal and group constructions of identity in response, reaction, or relation to these structural framings. This interchange is important to unpack because it provides a more comprehensive understanding of the role power plays in identity and the process of identification. For instance, consider the example of the struggle over the authoritative voice for a culture and political or legal recognition to rights and land in terms of several different indigenous groups—the Miwok tribe, Samoans, the Maori peoples, the Chamoru from Guam, the Seri people, the Nisqually people, and the Aleut. In the *Storytellers of the Pacific* documentary, members of the Miwok tribe foreground how national documentation by the Bureau of Indian Affairs and other US agencies shape legal, societal, and personal concepts of who they are as "unknown/Non-white" and thus, without rights as a group (Pacific Islanders in Communications & Lucas, 1996). Also, a member of the aboriginal peoples of Australia tells of a national domestic procedure that affected aboriginal identity in that the Australian government mandated the removal of thousands of aboriginal children and placed them into adoption arrangements with Australian White citizens.

Thus, identity stands as an interchange between the structural and the personal. This interchange can include, for example, a specific historical context (in terms of key events,

Identity

How do we understand identity? We typically see identity as concept about who we are and what constitutes our selves.

crises, population decline), waves or forms of colonization (e.g., political conquest, economic trade and business, military occupation, missionary cleansing, tourist commodification), economic formations, legal recognitions, government agencies created to "be Native," narrative constructions of "who we once were," and material claims to land, territory, and self-determination. These layers, interrelated and contradictory at times, underscore how identity among different cultures involves much more than cultural groups' own selected framings of who they are.

Structural Framings of Identity (Social/Structural Layer)

Our identities and who we are involves more than just our thoughts and desires of who we want to be and our individual agency and free will to make this happen. Instead, our identities are shaped within the larger matrix of social power or historical forces. Indeed, identity constitutes and is constituted by surrounding historical conditions and structures of power. This concept refers to the first part of the interchange between the structural and the personal that anchors this chapter: the structural framings of identity (the social/structural layer), or identities for and in the name of individuals. Such a unique view of identity has been circulated and discussed by a field of research known as cultural studies.

Cultural studies represents an interdisciplinary, multinational field of study that examines the ways in which culture and societies are shaped by power and context (see Hall, 1980b, 1989). Identity stands as a cornerstone of cultural studies and how it understands how individuals make sense of their worlds. We see our "selves" in relation to social groups and contexts.

But, the connection between the structural and the personal may not be as obvious. British Cultural Studies focused on this connection by examining the ways in which the British governmental, political, and economic structures have framed cultural meanings, identities, and social actions through policy, laws, economics, and the media in the British context. This area of study also uncovers how individuals and communities in England respond, react, and remake their own identities and cultural behaviors in relation to these larger power shifts. For example, the British punk scene thrived in the 1970s as a way to reject mainstream national culture and governmental oversight. British youth (and youth all over the world) used such music and other pop culture phenomena to exert their voices and express who they are in response to structures of power (During, 2004; Grossberg, 2014).

There are many different forms of cultural studies, depending on the specific sociopolitical context (e.g., British cultural studies, American cultural studies, Black British cultural studies, Asian, Asian American cultural studies, Pacific cultural studies, African American cultural studies, Latino/a cultural studies, Queer cultural studies, and feminist cultural studies, among others). In cultural studies, identity is theorized beyond the who

I am as a cultural form powerfully shaped by structures of power and ideologies in several spheres (e.g., governmental, legal, economic, educational, media, and social spheres).

Another example of this social/structural layer of identity can be seen in how national governments, courts of law, and educational institutions all create official definitions of racial, ethnic, indigenous, and native groups; minorities; and underrepresented cultural groups in specific sociopolitical periods. These official definitions and racial or ethnic classifications delimit what these terms mean and who is and is not included within these groups (Goldberg, 2016). Moreover, these definitions carry enormous weight as they are legislated and mandated by official authorities who can widely disseminate, sanction, and enforce these on society. Critical race scholar David Theo Goldberg (2016) argues that the US census categories have greatly impacted how cultural groups see and identify themselves and how they want to be seen by others. In the year 2000, national multiracial organizations lobbied the US census body to create a distinctive category entitled "Multiracial" to better capture those individuals who belong to more than one racial group. In this very act, these organizations attest to the heavy influence the national census has on shaping, recording, and presenting cultural identities in the United States. It is not merely a survey to fill out; it is part of a structure that identifies groups and its members.

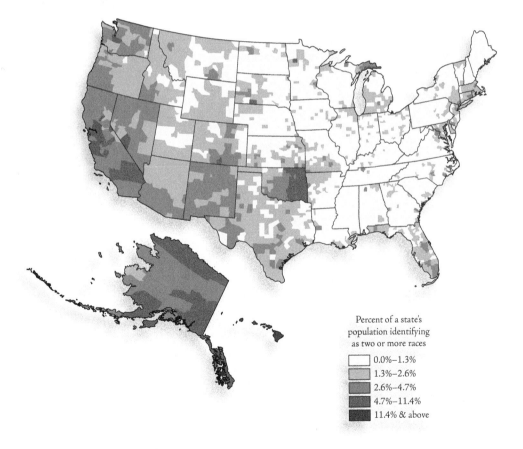

Percent of a state's
population identifying
as two or more races

☐ 0.0%–1.3%
▨ 1.3%–2.6%
▨ 2.6%–4.7%
▨ 4.7%–11.4%
■ 11.4% & above

NOTE: Please answer BOTH Question 5 about Hispanic origin and Question 6 about race. For this census, Hispanic origins are not races.

5. **Is this person of Hispanic, Latino, or Spanish origin?**

☐ **No,** not of Hispanic, Latino, or Spanish origin
☐ **Yes,** Mexican, Mexican Am., Chicano
☐ **Yes,** Puerto Rican
☐ **Yes,** Cuban
☐ **Yes,** another Hispanic, Latino, or Spanish origin — *Print origin, for example, Argentinean, Colombian, Dominican, Nicaraguan, Salvadoran, Spaniard, and so on.* ↗

[_____]

6. **What is this person's race?** *Mark* ☒ *one or more boxes.*

☐ White
☐ Black, African Am., or Negro
☐ American Indian or Alaska Native — *Print name of enrolled or principal tribe.* ↗

[_____]

☐ Asian Indian   ☐ Japanese   ☐ Native Hawaiian
☐ Chinese   ☐ Korean   ☐ Guamanian or Chamorro
☐ Filipino   ☐ Vietnamese   ☐ Samoan
☐ Other Asian — *Print race, for example, Hmong, Laotian, Thai, Pakistani, Cambodian, and so on.* ↗   ☐ Other Pacific Islander — *Print race, for example, Fijian, Tongan, and so on.* ↗

[_____]

☐ Some other race — *Print race.* ↗

[_____]

Through its racial/ethnic classifications, the US Census has delimited how cultural groups see and identify themselves.

Thus, identities are constructed by multiple parties—cultural groups, individuals, and societal structures of power.

The social/structural layer therefore explains that our identities are organized in line with historically specific conditions and structures of power. Identities are created in specific historical moments (in certain historical periods, after specific events) and by powerful structures (e.g., the government, economic base, court system, educational and social institutions, and media). Because of the structural power behind identity constructions, certain identity framings gain more widespread attention, popularity, and prominence among larger society, cultural groups, and individuals themselves than others and are also taken up by cultural groups as authentic reflections of their own identities (Halualani, 2002). Cultural studies scholars emphasize this very point: that there is a disproportionate amount of power and influence among structures, groups, and individuals in creating, circulating, and reproducing identities. Structures of power and dominant parties in power (such as national leaders, rulers, religious authorities, and official historians) naturalize certain identity versions as real and credible, which privilege their interests and achieve their aims. This is referred to by scholars as the ideological construction of identity through which a set of ideas, representations, and meanings is framed as constituting the essence of a particular group but done so in the name of power (and in a way that benefits larger structural interests and not the group constituted). These identity constructions that are created by historical and power forces are seductively shaped to speak to and resonate with cultural groups.

An example of this can be seen in the work of critical intercultural scholar Thomas Nakayama (1994). He insightfully discusses how identities for and in the name of Asian Americans are continually constructed through history and power relations. He traces identity positions of Oriental and Asian American and how each serves different political interests. According to Nakayama, Oriental signifies a larger ideological tradition known as "Orientalism" (Said, 1978). According to postcolonial studies scholar Edward Said, Orientalism is an ideology that exalts the superiority of the West over the East. Simply put, this view constructs Europe, the West, as the familiar valorized "us," and the East as the "strange" Orient, as the degraded, marginalized "them." Thus, by extension, Asian Americans who appear physically and "racially" different from Westerners are subjected as "Oriental" others. Such a classification pervades American popular culture, television, and film. Thus, Oriental is an identity construction created for, about, and in the name of Asian Americans, while Asian American is a re-made identification (as discussed in the next section), created and invoked by many diverse Asian Pacific groups so as to politically mobilize and resist forever foreign representations.

Nakayama explains that identity can be conceptualized as an identity position imposed on a specific cultural group. With regard to Asian Americans, this occurs through (dis)orientation. (Dis)orientation is a dialectical process of identity formation that consists of two parts. The first part is constituted by the historical experiences and identities of Asian Americans. The second part, or the "Orient-ation" aspect involves the socially created condition that Asians can never be Americans. Thus, the former constructs an Asian American identity based on Asian American histories, and the latter dismantles such an identity to one of Orientalism, which is based on European colonial histories. Herein we see how the Oriental construct "writes over" the identities of the author and all Asian Americans, placing them somewhere other than where they think they are. Nakayama, like other Asian Americans, experiences his identity through the historical and political framing of Asianness in the Western world as an Oriental. Because his family members, all of whom were American citizens, were detained in the Japanese-American internment camps during World War II, this scholar must continually wrestle with the structural framing of the Asian foreigner identity by the US government and media and prove his Americanness.

Yet another example of the social/structural layer of identity can be seen in the US census race and ethnicity check boxes. US census categories provide the options for how one should fill out their racial or ethnic background. Where do these categories come from? David Theo Goldberg (2016) argues that these categories derive from the governmental classification of race via governmental structures and the legal system.

Identity constructions are never neutral or equivalent to one another. For example, native Hawaiian identity is advanced by differently located power interests such as colonial forces from the past (i.e., Britain and the United States), federal and state administrations, courts of law, newspaper media, organizations devoted to serving native Hawaiians, and Hawaiians themselves. Hawaiians (like most other cultural groups) have been subject to a series of identity constructions created by various power interests that portray them in a persistent way over time (Halualani, 2002). For instance, as evident in explorer journals and missionary notes, from the 1800s through the 1900s, British and American explorers cast Hawaiians as an "undeveloped," "heathen," and "dying race" not meant to survive in modern times. In the early 1900s, Hawaiians were also identified by the colonialist US administration (who illegally occupied Hawai'i in 1893) in terms of a dying (and practically extinct) race whose identity was based on blood percentages (or blood quantum) with few pure-blooded Hawaiians left. Subsequently, US federal and local state mandates (which are upheld by federal and state courts of law) set into stone, through the Hawaiian Homes Commission Act (HHCA) that individuals of Hawaiian descent were strictly those with 50% or more of Hawaiian blood (Parker, 1996). Because of this legally sanctioned definition, Hawaiians who seek land, benefits, and services reserved for Hawaiians, must go through a rigorous identity ritual (as set forth by the Department of Hawaiian Homelands, DHHL) of proving their 50% blood amount with formal or official written records and documents in English, such as birth or death certificates and census records (Halualani, 2002).

In the 1990s and to this day, national and local newspaper coverage has continually depicted Hawaiians as being outspoken political activists who seek independence from the US government and demand sovereignty as a Hawaiian nation (Schachter, 2015). Such coverage has therefore necessarily framed Hawaiian-ness as an extremely politicized and contentious identity, which has become popular and trendy for many Hawaiians to invoke. As I discovered in interviews conducted with Hawaiians in the late 1990s, many Hawaiians in Hawai'i and on the mainland seem to make sense of their ethnic identity in support of and/or very much in defiance of its representation as an overtly political identity. Organizations created to serve and aid native Hawaiians, such as the Office of Hawaiian Affairs (OHA), Department of Hawaiian Homelands (DHHL), and Alu Like, have also connoted Hawaiian identity in line with federal, state, and legal definitions of Hawaiian-ness based on blood quantum (with a minimum requirement of 50% proven Hawaiian blood). Thus, certain images and signified meanings of Hawaiian identity have been naturalized over time through the historical establishment and gained authority of various structures of power (colonial/neocolonial administrations, federal and local governmental apparatuses and courts of law, and popular media) and power interests. As such, these identity constructions have framed the conditions through which Hawaiian identity is perceived, understood, and invoked by Hawaiians themselves. As highlighted in this social/structural layer of identity, historical-political identity encodings, therefore,

For Native Hawaiians, identity has been structurally and historically framed in terms of various constructions such as an "undeveloped," "dying race," and blood quantum that must be proved through formal documentation.

may frame the terms through which an individual comes to understand her or his cultural identity.

This notion of identity as structurally framed (the social/structural layer) resonates with Marx's popular explanation of social life: "that people make history but in conditions not of their own making" (Grossberg, 1996b, p. 151). This perspective of identity highlights how we all stand as unfixed yet marked social subjects. The idea here is that who we are is constituted by many overlapping structures of power: the arenas of law, economic forces, governance and regulation, and historical memory. While seemingly autonomous, these different structures work in line and in conjunction with one another, powerfully establishing conditions for particular identity positions for us to take up and invest in.

In this section, we have explored how our identities (for and in the name of) are created, constituted, and shaped by structures of power. Given this, it is important to highlight, then, that **identities are politicized** or permeated with power implications and consequences. Our identities are political in that each construction is created and spoken from different positionalities (through structures of power, by communities themselves) and in response to past and present discourses of identity. As with cultural groups such as Asian Americans and Hawaiians, among others, identity constructions work for different power interests and carry varied political effects.

Personal/Group Constructions of Identity (Personal Layer)

Identity constructions created by different structural power interests influence how we personally perceive, understand, and experience our own identities meaning that many of us feel compelled to identify with these constructed positions provided to us and that these positions become designs for living, ultimately shaping the ways in which we conceptualize ourselves, others, and our real experiences. According to critical theorists Louis Althusser (1971) and Antonio Gramsci (1971), social meanings, such as identity constructions that are created and reproduced by historical forces and structures of power, become indistinguishable versions of reality and truth for different individuals. This is done in a way that historically persistent and seemingly real identity constructions, created by external power forces, gain currency within a cultural group because of their continuous reproduction in the media and throughout society and/or the scientific or governmental authority behind such constructions.

The identities shaped by historical and power forces (as discussed in the previous section), therefore, enter into and embed an individual's or cultural group member's private subjective experience and how he or she sees him- or herself. Individuals make sense of their identity in support of, in negotiation with, and or in defiance of the identity constructions circulated by structures of power. According to cultural studies, the historical and political constructions of cultural identity provide the range of meanings and representations through which an individual wades through in search for one's cultural self. This concept, then, is the other part of the interchange between the structural and the personal that anchors this chapter: *the personal and group constructions of identity in response, reaction, and relation to the structural framings (personal layer)*, or identities by and in relation to individuals.

As explained by critical and cultural studies scholars, we should rethink identity positions as structurally framed and powerful but not fully guaranteed (or sealed). Richard Johnson insightfully poses the question: "What are the different ways in which subjective [identity] forms are inhabited?" He highlights how identities, while framed by larger structures of power, are *not* fully complete or guaranteed to be in line with those structures. Our identities are not doomed to or dominated by structures of power. Instead, we as individuals have the capacity to remake our identities while in conditions of power around us. Thus, the everyday communicative practices of identity—via our experiences, memories, and interactions in the social world—demonstrate how individuals can remake and potentially resist the structural framings of who they are. These identity practices reveal how misrecognized or misidentified cultural groups can re-assemble who they are in complicated, creative, and oppositional ways to the identity constructions reproduced by structures of power.

One key example of the personal layer of identity lies in the re-appropriation or taking back of oppressive labels, names, and identities by historically marginalized cultural groups. For example, several gay and lesbian rights movement groups have worked hard to re-appropriate, invoke, and remake the historically derogatory terms "queer" and "dyke." These terms have stood as harmful linguistic, conceptual, and philosophical weapons of domination wielded against gay and lesbian persons for generations. According to Anten

(2006), "[T]he reappropriation of former slurs is an integral part of the fostering of individual and group identity, recapturing the right of self-definition, of forging and naming one's own existence" (p. 1). When a structure of power (a governmental body, a court of law, an educational institution, a television show) exercises the awesome power of naming and constituting a group (with an identity), it can wreak havoc onto a cultural group who suffers from a historical and structural misrecognition for years (and these misrecognitions can be hard to break). The performative and often controversial act of reclaiming a word, a term, or an image—one that, in another historical moment, was dominant and oppressive—can be an exercise of strategic resistive power on the part of that effected cultural group. They can re-appropriate that identity label and work to remake it under new conditions and circumstances while trying to imbue it with its own agency and influence.

As another example, distinguished scholar and sociologist Mary Waters (1990) contributes an influential theory about the complex subjective and sense-making processes that underlie one specific type of identity for cultural groups: ethnic identity. She argues that ethnic identity is much more than a predetermined and predictable construct. Instead, "ethnicity is a variable with a range of meanings attached to it" and "the degree of importance attached to those meanings by individuals" (Waters, 1990, p. 93), meaning that individuals do not experience or claim their ethnic identities in the same way (even for those within the same racial or ethnic group). Waters explains that ethnicity is a complex and shifting construct in that people selectively choose to identify with certain aspects of their ethnic identity or even a specific ethnic identity from their multiethnic background. In what

LGBTQ+ movements have reclaiming derogatory labels and terms used against them and redefined what these mean in terms of strength and agency for their identity.

she calls "situational ethnicity," ethnicity operates oftentimes as an option voluntarily taken up by individuals in a specific context for a specific reason and based on a number of factors, including (but not limited to) family histories, parental influence, knowledge about ancestors, physical appearance, cultural practices, societal acceptance of one's ethnic identity, and the surrounding historical and polit-

Latinx

Latinx is term that was created to speak to, represent, and include all genders.

ical context. Thus, for individuals, ethnic identity involves a personal and often private process of deciding what aspect of what ethnicity is important and those others that are not, from context to context and over time. It is this deeply situated subjective process of invoking and claiming an ethnic identity over others (and in a certain form over another) that Mary Waters (1990) underscores.

In her qualitative investigation of White ethnic identity via in-depth interviews, Waters (1990) concludes that her interviews with third- and fourth-generation White Americans reveal a complex and multi-layered subjective process through which individuals attach meaning to their ethnic identities, make sense of and understand their identities, and make contextualized decisions about how to project and report their ethnicities. This process, Waters argues, is likely to be different and unique for each ethnic group given its historical context, the structures of power that shape that identity, the length of time that the ethnic group, as a whole, has been in the United States, the larger society's attitudes toward and treatment of the ethnic group, and the degree of importance attached to the ethnic identity of a group.

Additionally, in 2015, Latino/a communities in the United States that were comprised of mostly college students and academics, created a new term—Latinx—to better represent the Latino/a community in terms of all genders. Historically, the term "Latino," a male gender form, has been used to represent the entire community, thereby not reflecting members of all genders. (Alternatively, "Latino/a" has been used to be more gender inclusive.) Thus, "Latinx" symbolizes an all-gender inclusive identity framing for this larger ethnic community and on its own terms. This represents a personal layer of identity or how a cultural group creates its identity in response to or rejection from dominant forms of their identity.

The Colliding Dynamic Between the Layers of Identity

Though identity is constituted by the social/structural layer and the personal layer, these layers often collide, mix, and clash in terms of power implications. For example, there are many instances when a structure of power shapes an identity for a cultural group that conflicts with the way in which that group frames and identifies itself (or when the social/structural layer clashes with the personal layer of identity). These moments can be understood as forms of misrecognition, or the erroneous naming or representation of a cultural group (Coombe, 1998). For example, when a media campaign or a public service announcement uses a specific language (Cantonese, Spanish) to appeal to a specific cultural group and that group does not identity with that language (preferring English or a different language), then misrecognition occurs. When a transgender person does not see his or her gender preferred pronoun of choice or gender identity designation on a health insurance, school, or job application, he or she is experiencing a moment of misrecognition, or that disconnect between how society sees that person and how he or she sees him- or herself. These moments of misrecognition capture how the social/structural layer of identity comes into direct conflict with the personal layer of identity, which reveals the complex nature of identity, according to the critical approach to intercultural communication.

In recent years, there were media reports that a genetic DNA test could prove or verify a person's Native American identity. Proving Native American identity allows for health benefits, land, and educational access. Historically, Native American persons have to prove their ancestral link in terms of blood quantum and tribal lineage to one of the United States' federally recognized tribes through the Bureau of Indian Affairs (BIA). This is done through a Certificate of Degree of Indian Blood (CDIB) and furnishing documentation that connects lineage to an Indian tribal role. This process of proving one's Native American identity represents a structural framing of identity. DNA test reports (as offered through companies such as 23andme, Family Tree DNA, and Ancestry.com) add to this structural framing of cultural identity through the use of science (and genetics) to provide indisputable evidence of cultural membership. The authority of science in combination with the governmental administration of Native identities demonstrates the power of larger structures in identifying who we are (and by which requirements) (McKay, 2016).

However, with this same example, some Native American members and communities have used these structural framings of Native identity to their advantage. They argue that the DNA tests (via the dominant structures of science and genetics) proves, without a doubt, that they are Native American. The dominant DNA or scientific framings of their identity, therefore, are remade into irrefutable (as science just is) forms of evidence of their Nativeness. Thus, the personal layer of identity can be seen here in the creative usage of dominant forms of identity to establish identity and serve their needs.

This example is rife with other complexities. The DNA test could open the door for measuring and prioritizing certain blood quantum percentages over others, thereby creating a more fixed hierarchy of inclusion and exclusion. Moreover, many could claim that they are Native even with small amounts of Native blood quantum. Or, Native members may receive negative DNA tests given the historical intermixing of cultural groups and Natives, and thus, may lose their identity status as Natives.

Identity Politics of Authenticity

While being shaped by historical and power forces, how we declare and claim identity also occurs within a larger hierarchy of whose cultural identity is deemed more authentic than another's, or what is referred to as an identity politics of authenticity (Anderson, 2006; Clifford, 1994; Lavie & Swedenberg, 1996). Identity politics greatly impacts how individuals understand, make sense of, and report their cultural identity because they are drawn toward selecting and reporting certain identity constructions that are in favor (and for some, in disfavor) within their cultural groups and ones that demonstrate genuine

Proving Native American identity has become more complex. Historically, Native American persons have to prove their identity through blood quantum and tribal lineage to one of the U.S. federally recognized tribes. Some Native Americans argue that the DNA tests (via the dominant structures of science and genetics) proves without a doubt that they are Native American.

cultural membership and loyalty. An identity's politics of authenticity is a larger set of politicized constructions of cultural membership that intermingle and oppose one another (Anderson, 1983; Hall, 1990). Identity constructions that are framed as authentic are articulated by different power interests and carry different political effects (Hall, 1990).

Authenticity

Authenticity, which in this context refers to the notion of what it means to be a true or real or native member of a group, is a theoretical concept (Hall, 1990). Cultural groups participate in the construction of their identities and definitions of authentic membership. These definitions, however, are politically charged in that they are created within specific historical contexts and social conditions and from specific positionalities. Thus, what it means to be an authentic Chinese in the United States today is different from what it meant 10 or 20 years ago because of the increase in Chinese immigration from Taiwan, Hong Kong, and China and because of the political shifts in power between these sites (Wong Lau, 1998). The challenge then lies in uncovering different identity constructions of authenticity and tracing the political consequences these carry for members of a cultural group. Who is included and/or excluded in terms of generation, age, language, place of birth, and geographic residency in ethnic group's identity constructions? What types of ethnic identities are used to connect cultural members and exclude others?

Consider how relations among the generations in a culture are always impacted by identity issues with regard to authenticity. In answering the question, "Who is more authentic?" there are different responses depending on the generation and the nature of identity at play. For example, the earlier (or first, second, third) generations most often take up the position of being the most culturally authentic. Such a power position derives from the fact that earlier generations are usually born and raised in the cultural or ancestral homeland (e.g., Polish being born and raised in Poland). In addition, these earlier generations usually practice the cultural traditions and speak the native language—they engage in the key markers of that cultural identity.

So, practicing cultural behaviors becomes attached as a criterion of authenticity, here. Later generations and ones that have migrated to multiple sites of settlement (Polish to Turkey, Canada, Australia, the United States) would be deemed as less authentic than the earlier generations because they may not have been born or raised in the authentic homeland. Likewise, the later generations may not engage in cultural traditions or practices (religious, traditions, dance or diet) or speak the language. Thus, the criteria for authentic membership privilege the original (or originating) homelands and cultural practices and behaviors from the past. Later generations often internalize such criteria and judge themselves harshly as cultural inferiors, imposters, or as assimilated. Such authenticity criteria then create negative self-images for later generations and demeans their own (albeit) different relationship to their culture and identity. However, later generations may argue that they are truly cultural members but in a different way than their parents or grandparents.

Thus, cultural groups never claim and/or make sense of their identities in a vacuum; instead they do so in response to and in relation to their group counterparts' identity constructions and decisions, as well as the larger set of identity politics of authenticity that circulates within their group. Specific to Native Hawaiians, research has revealed that they make sense of who they are in relation to how other Hawaiians see themselves and the larger set of identity politics of authenticity that circulate among Hawaiians. For example, many Hawaiians define true Hawaiianness based on behavioral criteria such as actively engaging in cultural practices such as *hula* (Hawaiian dance), *ho'opono'pono* (Hawaiian rituals of conflict resolutions), and speaking the Hawaiian language. Others have framed authentic Hawaiian identity as one that is more political in nature, meaning that true Hawaiians are those who believe in and fight for Hawaiian sovereignty or independence from the United States. Several Hawaiians have gone as far as to claim true Hawaiian identity as being one in which individuals of Hawaiian descent are born and raised and still reside in the homeland of Hawai'i (and definitely not on the mainland). Hawaiians internalize the externally imposed structural blood quantum requirements of the federal andstate governments and believe that genuine Hawaiians are those who can prove (with certified documents) that they possess 50% Hawaiian blood ancestry. Given the range of authentic identity constructions for Hawaiians, the process through which Hawaiians make sense of, understand, and claim their ethnic identities is multifaceted and entangled by identity politics.

With migrations of cultural groups all over the world, the notion of authenticity and what is traditional and modern have also shifted. Oftentimes, the ancestral homeland of a particular culture (China, Japan, Korea, Bulgaria, France, and Greece, among others) is always framed as the center of tradition, or the originator of cultural customs and rituals. However, as Wong Lau (1998) highlights, this distinction is dynamic and shifting. Due to the massive migration of a cultural group to multiple sites of settlement or what is referred to as a diaspora, when Greek cultural experts are needed to impart cultural knowledge of a ritual or

"Little Saigon" in San José stood as a controversy around Vietnamese American identity. While some wanted the name "Saigon Business District," the Vietnamese American community pushed for the use of the name "Little Saigon." The question was: Which term best represented the Vietnamese American business community?

dance onto younger Greek generations, those cultural experts are called from California as opposed to just Greece. Wong Lau (1998) explains that immigrants often preserve certain aspects of their cultural practices in their new site of settlement and construct their identities in memory of practices and histories from the homeland (or practices held in the home country at the time of immigration). In this way, in the United States, Asian immigrant groups with diasporic pasts struggle to define an authentic ethnic identity or a larger community centered on their specific social and political needs. Diasporic groups therefore face the pressure of authenticating their identities, maintaining links with homeland communities or sites, and reconstituting their identities to speak to a new context.

The identity politics of authenticity can also be seen in the naming controversy over San José's (California) Little Saigon. In 2008, there was a controversy over what to name an area of San José, California that featured 200 Vietnamese American retailers and businesses. After consulting with other council members, San José's councilwoman Madison Nguyen recommended the naming of this area "Saigon Business District." However, the Vietnamese American community pushed for the use of the name "Little Saigon"—which had been used to name other Vietnamese American community areas in California. The name "Little Saigon" carried an important cultural meaning for Vietnamese-American community members because this reminded them of their homeland before the communist takeover (especially for those who fled Vietnam after the fall of South Vietnam). Here, the controversy was over which term would best represent the Vietnamese American business community. Vietnamese American community members argued that their voices, votes, and demands for Little Saigon should be honored. Whose identity framing, then, is more authentic and true and should be honored?

Linguistic fluency is also another marker attached to one's cultural authenticity. Next to native language speakers, heritage speakers, or those raised in a home in which a non-majority language is spoken for most of the time, have been positively framed in the United States as responsible for extending cultural identity. Multicultural societies often privilege the cultural authenticity and credibility of heritage speakers over those who were not raised in such linguistic conditions (and are often later cultural generational members). So, if you are Korean American and do not speak Korean, you may be judged as culturally inferior to a Korean American who does. This is perceived even more negatively if you are a first-generation Korean American. Such a hierarchy based on one's linguistic background in relationship to his or her generational status in their site of settlement operates under specific presumptions of who is authentic and by what means.

Summary

Identity is constituted by two interlocked layers: the social/structural layer and the personal layer. These two layers are often in conflict and tension with one another. Our identities are framed by larger structures of power and we reshape our identities in response to these structural framings (either through rejection, response, and or re-creation). According to Stuart Hall (1997), identification (i.e., a practice that shapes a person's recognition of a common origin, a shared characteristic or belief, with another person, group, or entity) is better understood as a *process* revolving around "questions of using the resources of history, language and culture in the process of becoming rather than being: not 'who we are' or 'where we came from', so much as what we might become, how we have been represented and how that bears on how we might represent ourselves" (p. 4).

Authenticity

Identities as "politicized"

Identity

Identity politics

Misrecognition

Personal and group constructions
    of identity

Structural framings of identity (social/
    structural layer)

Questions and Activities

REFLECTION activity:

What is your identity? How do people and structures respond to your identity?

- Think about your identity or how you define yourself. How would you define who you are? Write your response (and this could include several components).

- Now write down how others have responded to or identified who you are in personal conversations that you have had. How do others around you respond to you? How do they (friends, acquaintances, co-workers, colleagues, and strangers) identify or view you?

- Record your observations in terms of the following: How does your national government or educational institution recognize you? What do these structures see you as?

- According to Collier and Thomas (1988), when those who are in intercultural interactions with you affirm and speak to the way that you see yourself (your "avowed" or declared identity, as in the personal layer), then your interaction will likely be deemed more positive and satisfying. Is there a match between how you see yourself and how others or structures see you? If there is a match, how do you think that is possible? If there is *not* a match, share reasons as to why you think this is the case.

REFLECTION activity:

The structural framings of your identities (for and in the name of) Follow the instructions.

- Write down at least one ethnic or cultural identity and one national identity. Separate each with a line.

- Next, write down the two identities you have that are most important to you. Write down reasons as to why these are most important.

- Write down the most controversial identity you have to the larger society or government (one that is the most threatening to these entities). Explain why.

- Write down the identity you feel is most accepted by the larger society or government. Explain why.

- Write down the identity you find most difficult to share with friends and acquaintances. Explain why.

- Write down the identity of yours that your family and loved ones most know and refer to. Explain.

- Write down the identity of yours that is most negatively represented by the media. Explain why.

- Write down the identity that will get you the furthest in terms of your goals (money, jobs, success, achievement). Explain why.

- Write down the identity that you think you will hold near to your heart for the rest of your life. Explain why.

- Write down the identity that you feel holds the most stakes and risks for your future. Explain why.

- Go back and read what you wrote. Answer the following questions: What do you notice about your responses? Do you feel torn between your many different identities? Are you negotiating between identities? What are some larger issues of identity raised?

- Your responses should demonstrate **how our identities are always mediated by others and larger structures of power around us.** Many structures of power and people are affected by our own identities and this may, in turn, influence which identity we highlight more than others, in specific contexts, and with certain groups.

DISCUSSION activity:

Discuss the following in class:

- To what extent can you tell if someone is a member of your cultural group? Is this clear and obvious?

- What are all the different ways in which you can tell someone is a member of your cultural or ethnic group. In your mind, what is necessary for one to be an authentic member of your cultural or ethnic group (e.g., knowledge of the group, language fluency, geographic residency in the country for at least 4 years)? Provide reasons and discuss.

- How did you learn or gain this criteria for membership? Is there one set of criteria for all members?

- What does it mean if we all have different criteria for cultural group membership? Who decides? What are the potential consequences for the cultural group and individual members?

Chapter 7

Historical Memory and Intercultural Communication

Learning Objectives

> To examine how history (and the narratives about the past) shape our intercultural encounters and relationships

> To understand the role of historical memory in our intercultural lives, relationships, and contexts and how what is remembered (and forgotten) as history is largely influenced by power

> To learn about how history represents the power to be able to authorize, create, and reproduce a version or memory of the past

Introduction: Lisa and Historical Memory

Lisa, a university student in Dallas, Texas, is at an important crossroads in her life. She is about to graduate from college and her relationship with Doug, also a graduating senior at her college, is getting serious. She and Doug have been making plans to get engaged to be married in the next year. However, their families have yet to meet one another. Lisa, a second- to third-generation Chinese American, has a traditional Chinese father and mother who were both born and raised in mainland China. She decides to talk to her parents during her next visit home to Houston. Lisa is quite anxious about this impending conversation because Doug is Japanese American. While Doug is a third-generation Japanese American

from California and considers himself to be American, Lisa's father has made negative comments about the Japanese ever since she was a child. Her father had always pointed out how cruel the Japanese were to the Chinese in his country and hometown (and to his own family) during the war. Lisa always thought her father would eventually change his mind as he interfaced with a number of different groups in the Houston suburb in which they lived since she was eight years old.

In the next month, Lisa approached her parents with her news of the wonderful relationship she has with Doug and how serious it is getting (toward marriage). Lisa's fears were confirmed. Her father remained silent and then replied, "This cannot be. He is Japanese.

We don't want them in our family. They are not family to us. They are not part of us. This cannot be." Lisa grew angry and lashed back, "Dad, that was so long ago. It's 2009. Doug is from the United States. His parents are from the United States. They weren't part of the war effort. Let it go. I love him."

Lisa waited for a response from her father. There was silence. She grew frustrated. Lisa blurted out, "Why don't you give him a chance? You focus too much on the past. He wasn't even around then."

Lisa's father waited and then responded, "You don't understand. Japan did terrible things to our home country. We were under their rule for years. They banned us from using our language, our traditions, our names. They took our identity from us. The Japanese—they did that. He's Japanese."

He then asked, "Why can't you find someone Korean so you can continue our culture?" Lisa shook her head. There was no way around the impact of history and what her family remembers (and wants to forget) about the past. She stormed out and drove back to school. She told Doug that they will have to either wait for her father to come around or that they will have to become engaged without her family's support.

This narrative highlights how history—a supposed past event, occurrence, memory, or experience—dynamically moves across time and is activated in different contexts and by different generations and carries major consequences for our present-day relationships and lives. It is indeed tempting to presume that history was "yesterday's business" and that those events and relations should not enter into or impact what is going on today. However, historical memory is a powerful collection of experiences, feelings, sentiments, relations, and perceptions (memories) that transcend time and space. Historical memory touches our lives in consequential and unexpected ways. This chapter will explain the role of historical memory in our intercultural lives, relationships, and contexts and how what is remembered as history is largely influenced by power: the power to be able to authorize, create, and reproduce a historical memory.

What Is History?

Oftentimes, when the concept of history comes up, we immediately think of something or some event that has happened in the past, a long time ago, and perhaps before our own time. From a Western-oriented perspective, history takes on this particular connotation as it is framed as distinctive break in time from today's activities and occurrences. Residents of the United States have typically thought of the historical past as irrelevant to today's state of affairs and even counterproductive to national progress. Countries in Europe, Asia, Latin America, and Africa have made history the cornerstone of their identities and legacies that continue to shape their current governmental, business, and social practices. For these countries and embedded cultures, history marks a continuous reality that links yesterday with today and tomorrow.

History as a Field of Power

Though it can be viewed in terms of different time-space dimensions and modalities, history can best be understood as a power-laden collection of events, images, experiences, sentiments, relations, and perceptions (memories) for a specific nation, culture, or group. This collection, however, is not neutral or objective; many presume that history and historical narratives are completely devoid of any bias or vantage point (akin to the notion that our high school history textbooks tell the complete and unfiltered truth). Quite the contrary, as critical scholars Terry Eagleton (2014), John Thompson (2013), and Stuart Hall (1996a), argue, history is shaped from a specific perspective or positionality of power. In the same vein as this book's other chapters, history indeed represents a field of power that is shaped by dominant structures and parties (e.g., governmental bodies, economic interests and corporate powers, media conglomerates, legal and educational institutions, reigning majority groups). While there are many types of histories and some are

We tend to think of "history" as the past, long ago, and/or information contained within archival books on a shelf.

articulated by marginalized or oppressed and resistive (to the dominant powers) groups (as discussed later in this chapter under the notion of collective memory), this section's focus on history frames History with a capital "H" to delineate its dominant construction and reproduction of the past for the majority or ruling power interest. History as a field of power, therefore, takes on the following characteristics:

History Derives From Power

History is always created from a position of power. A key misconception about the past (and its recording) is that History is always objective and unbiased, that there is some greater and purer truth about what really happened. Similar to stories, statements, and claims, a historical narrative is articulated from a specific vantage point and vested position. For example, when an individual travels abroad and is asked about a specific historical event (a world war, a civil uprising, a riot, the unification of several countries), that person will describe and explain that event with his or her own interpretation, words, and framing (aspects that derive from another biased source—a book, person, teacher, written or verbal account, and national point of view). There is no space outside of history through which an unfiltered or pure truth exists. Instead, as standpoint theorists Sandra Harding (2004), Nancy Hartstock (1983), and Patricia Hill Collins (2000) argue, we are all situated in specific social locations (national, gender, racial or ethnic, socioeconomic, regional, and sexualized, among others) that in turn frame how we see, understand, articulate, and re-tell what has happened in the past. In this way, then, all historical re-tellings, especially that of History, are created and spoken from a specific position of power. To understand this is to truly open our eyes about how representations of the past are mediated by our positionalities, identities, and power interests and that we have much to gain and lose by narrating specific versions of the past. These narrations can solidify a group or national identity and or vilify a group, nation, or religion as well as hide social injustices and atrocities or celebrate and romanticize a national myth, tradition, or group. For instance, historical accounts of the early American pioneers, settlers, and military forces in the West—out to settle the land and build a community—romanticize the work ethic, sanctity, and virtue of early American settlers while simultaneously understating the physical, political, and social decimation of Native American tribes and their way of life. One narrative can, all at once, celebrate and deny in one fell swoop.

History Advances Dominant Interests

The History that is created, is a version of the past that exclusively advances the interests of dominant (and status quo) structures and power interests. Meaning, the History that is created is a construction and specific vested version of the past that exclusively advances the interests of dominant (and status quo) structures and power interests. Because historical narratives derive from a specific positionality, it is important to note that History, or the most articulated version of the past in a particular country, is created and articulated from and by a dominant structure and power interest. By this, the version of the past that receives the most air time or play in a culture or country is typically that of History, the dominant perspective of what has happened. For example, in all its Historical accounts, China continuously stresses that Tibet, a once autonomous country, is part of China. China, as a dominant power structure, therefore, insists that they have owned Tibet (and that it is part of China) all the way back to the Chinese Tang Dynasty when a Chinese princess was offered to the Tibetan king to civilize the Tibetan people. This claim, however, is heavily refuted by the Tibetans who claim that they are a sovereign people with their own entitlement of human rights. As a dominant structure, China continues to reproduce a nationalist history of inclusion of and ownership over Tibet (politically, legally, culturally) in order to sediment and proclaim its nationalist authority over all deemed territories of China (Hong Kong, Taiwan, Tibet, and Macao, among others) (and prevent the possibility of ethnic and political separatism of these territories). To do so legitimates and exercises this country's role as a supreme ruler over everything deemed as China's territories. Whether in textbooks, verbal accounts of the past, or the larger public consciousness (in China and all over the world), this version of China-Tibet History comes from and advances a dominant governmental/national structure and power interest, that of China. History from a dominant position promotes and secures the existing status quo of ruling parties, groups, and interests. It does so by excluding and thus denying or effacing any other interpretations of the past that do not coincide with its own version, its own History. Such a power is daunting because it legitimates one group's account of the past on a continual basis (leading to a cycle of historical naturalization).

It Takes Work to (Re)Produce History

Much work and effort are taken to continually and subtly reproduce the dominant version of History and the embedded power interests. History from a dominant position comes into being because of its proximity to and origin from a reigning power—a power that provides media and cultural access to its own version of the past. A dominant structure or interest possesses the means and resources to reproduce History in major newspaper or other media outlets, textbooks across an entire educational system, displays and wordings in national museums, and verbal accounts and memories are passed on to the people of a territory, country, or community. This power is not afforded to other communities or groups with less means to reproduce their conflicting narratives and versions of history. Thus, History can become a dominant truth because of the surrounding power and resources that make it so; in some countries, other conflicting historical narratives can be suppressed by their removal or prohibi-

Tibetans refute the officially and widely reproduced narrative that Tibet is under the sovereign control of China. They see themselves as a sovereign people with their own rights and identity.

tion of certain accounts from reigning and dominant-aligned media outlets and social media (including YouTube, Vimeo, Facebook, Instragram, and Twitter). This, however, takes a great deal of work and vigilance on the part of dominant structures and interests to continually articulate History on all fronts. Such work is safeguarded by linking the promotion and investment in History to the ideology of national and cultural patriotism. To not accept these narratives is to be a cultural or national traitor; to reveal any other version is to be a heretic and naysayer of the culture. The focus shifts to the dissenting individual or party and not on the dominant structure who relentlessly defends History, which reveals the seductive nature of dominant structures in the production and reproduction of History.

History Mostly Speaks From a Male, White, and Upper-Class Voice

The dominant accounts of History are most often biased perspectives from reigning male, White, upper-class-oriented positionalities. Feminist scholars have long argued that accounts of the past are deemed as "his story" for a reason; they emanate from a patriarchal point of view. Male explorers, rulers, leaders, and movements across the world are documented in world histories; very few highlight the achievements and movements of women in this regard. This is largely due to the long-established presence of patriarchal power across the globe and how this larger colonial force (as male) has shaped histories throughout the world. This can be seen not only in the male leanings and bias in most cultures, but also in the privileging of male information for birth certificates, identity documents, and cultural and familial genealogies at the expense of unnamed and forgotten female relative names and information. Many individuals who go through the process of filling out their family genealogies notice how completion of family histories relies on knowing male surnames and birth dates at the expense of female names and dates. Critical scholar Anne McClintock (2013) takes this further by tracing how representations of history via maps, political cartoons, and product advertisements from the 1900s privilege the male perspective. Maps delineate explorers and places by male names only and ships and territories that are conquered are named after women. She argues that, in fact, it is

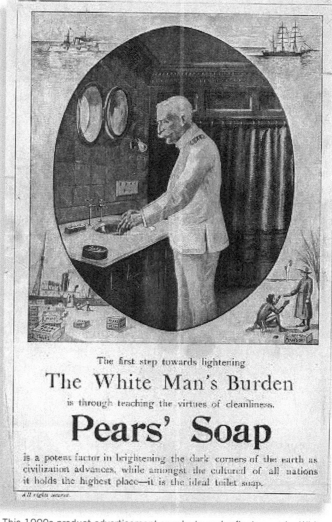

This 1900s product advertisement speaks to and reflects a male, White, and upper-class privileged account. It also projects the need to "clean" and "civilize" colonized/dark native groups.

not only the accounts of and about White males, but affluent White males in different societies that dominate the representations (McClintock, 2013). Because History derives from a dominant position, it articulates the voice and perspective (and bias) of those historically in power: males who are White/European and of upper socioeconomic standing. Thus, being exposed to History will mostly frame, for us, these dominant positions as the real and objective truths of what actually happened in the past.

Understanding History as a field of power is important to re-conceptualize History as a power-laden collection of memories about the past for a specific nation, culture, or group.

Historical Memory

How do structures and groups remember and forget the past? Indeed, while the creation and reproduction of History is always situated in power, the notion of memory stands as a key component for how History embeds our thoughts, perceptions, viewpoints, and identities.

Historical Memory

Historical memory (also termed as collective memory) refers to a remembrance of the past as shared by a group or nation (Olick, 2013). How we see and understand the past is largely a construction created, maintained, and circulated by a group or collective. Critical scholar Benedict Anderson (2006) explains historical and collective memory as important for the creation of a nation. Specifically, he argues that through historical memory, a nation forms itself as an imagined community, a nation that comes into being through a unified vision of who it is and where it came from. Think about the ways in which the country you come from (and the countries of your parents) delineate or narrate its historical past. Is it a seamless narrative of unity among all citizens? Does a tale of struggle over foreign influences prevail? Is there one deemed hero or glory period to be hailed by your culture? (questions for you to answer in the reflection activity for this chapter.) The answers to these questions will vary but reveal how what we know about our cultures, countries, and ourselves is largely memories created, crafted, and spread by a collective or group and one in context of a hierarchy of power.

As another example, in his national bestseller, *Lies My Teacher Told Me: Everything Your American History Textbook Got Wrong*, sociologist James M. Loewen (2008) argues that what Americans learn in their history classes and from their history textbooks are inaccuracies and slanted representations that promote the positive (and innocent) image of the US government. He contends that the image of America as benevolent, modern, progressive, and heroic dominate outdated historical narratives in textbooks and serve as a vehicle of nationalism, patriotism, and investment in the ideologies of meritocracy and opportunity that pervade the United States. Why is it, according to Loewen (2008), that American history textbooks do not discuss the following, as noted through historical documents and interviews:

- The United States dropped three times as many tons of explosives in Vietnam as it dropped in all theaters of World War II, including Hiroshima and Nagasaki.

- Woodrow Wilson, known as a progressive leader, was in fact a white supremacist who personally vetoed a clause on racial equality in the Covenant of the League of Nations.

- The first colony to legalize slavery was not Virginia but Massachusetts.

- Helen Keller was a radical socialist.

- People from other continents had reached the Americans many times before 1492 (the year of "discovery" by famed explorer Christopher Columbus).

Loewen (2008) argues that these details are not in the public consciousness of Americans because they were not part of the historical memory of who we are. Such remembrances are key to shaping our identities as a nation and people. While most Americans will not remember most historical facts well, the memories of America as a defender of freedom, independence, progress, and equality stay intact and persist in our mind and consciousness. This is the power of historical memory.

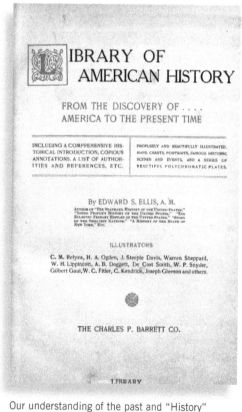

Our understanding of the past and "History" derives from what we were exposed to in history textbooks during our childhood years.

Historical or collective memories function as strong vehicles of power because they are based on perceptions or sentiments that transcend all demographics and communication forms to embed in our minds, hearts, and identities how we are as a people and as a nation. Thus, the real power comes from these memories personalizing history to us, to the collective we—how we are a people and not some nation as a separate, outside entity to ourselves. The personalization of memories and their attachment to our cultural, national, and religious identities make them hard to distinguish and critique or question. After all, our memories are sacred and true; they are also about us.

Historical memories of the past—especially brutal injustices against cultural groups—are not remembered and/or selectively forgotten. However, traces of that forgotten or eluded past do linger. Think about the controversy from the 2018 Winter Olympics in South Korea when an NBC commentator highlighted Korea's strength and how it was due to the "cultural and technological example" of Japan. South Korean viewers were horrified, given the long occupation of Korea by the Japanese from 1910 to 1945 (Qin, 2018). An apology petition circulated among thousands of South Koreans with the following words: "Any reasonable person familiar with the history of Japanese imperialism, and the atrocities it committed before and during WWII, would find such a statement deeply hurtful and outrageous."

It appeared then that not many fully knew of the historical occupation and colonization of Korea by Japan in the 20th century. Korea was annexed into the empire of Japan in 1910 after years of war and aggression and remained under the control of Japan until 1945 (Dudden, 2006). During those 35 years, many vestiges of Korean culture were intentionally stamped out by the Japanese government (Cumings, 1998). The Korean language was prohibited to be spoken. Only the Japanese language was to be used. Korean historical documents and histories were replaced with Japanese historical narratives. In fact, over 200,000 of Korean historical documents were burned by the Japanese empire, thereby literally extinguishing Korean historical memory. Koreans were also forced to work in Japan and its other colonies, which pushed them into harsh conditions, especially for Korean women who were socially and sexually enslaved. This historical memory (one that informs the reaction of Lisa's father toward her Japanese boyfriend) is one that is not fully known in larger public society (and even in the United States) but one that still lingers and hurts a cultural group.

The notion of which elements of historical memory are preserved and which fall to the wayside and are forgotten is tricky at best. In recent years, students and public citizens have protested the names of buildings and statues at universities in the United States (Chan, 2016). For example, in 2015, students at Princeton University demanded that it rename its Woodrow Wilson School of Public and International Affairs because Woodrow Wilson was known to be a vigorous racist in the South. Likewise, students at the University of North Carolina at Chapel Hill demanded that a building named after William Saunders—a Ku Klux Clan member since 1922—be renamed. At Yale University, law students argued for the stripping of the name of one of its residential undergraduate colleges—Calhoun College—which bears the name of a well-known segregationist. With seven other similar examples of protests over names of buildings and colleges, it clear that power issues over historical remembering and forgetting surround us. Student activists argue that when institutions use names of racist or sexist figures from the past, the university appears to be endorsing those harmful historical acts of that figure (why, in fact, would you memorialize a building or statue after someone and what they have done or what they represent to society?). They also explain that memorializing racist historical figures will painfully remind campus members of color of the historical past. University officials counter that institutions should use those figures and the naming of them as historical lessons and debates around morality of certain historical periods. Alumni of those universities highlight the absurdity of the protests and the need to rename their colleges. Instead, they argue that those names do not mean anything and that those represent time-honored traditions that are linked to their positive and nostalgic memories in college.

In 2017 in Palo Alto, California, a middle school student conducted research on the namesake (David Starr Jordan) of his school for a history report (Lee, 2017). This

College campuses are embroiled in controversy over the naming of buildings and statues in memory of racist or sexist figures from the past. This raises the question of what and who should be memorialized and if painful historical legacies should be preserved.

student examined the background of David Starr Jordan and discovered some horrible things, namely that the namesake was a fierce proponent of the eugenics movement (a larger group that argued that some races—Whites—were superior over other groups—African Americans). This student's report created an uproar that led to a district-wide committee that began a process of renaming the school (and one other in the district) (Lee, 2017). The process revealed differing opinions of community members about renaming the schools, the power of historical memories and the memorialization of memories through names. Some argued that the names represented important, and nostalgic souvenirs of their childhoods (and argued that the protestors are "whiners" in a PC-dominated era). Others argued that names are symbolic of the values of an institution and the value placed on cultures, communities, and their experiences. What has taken place is a larger and meaningful conversation about the role of names in relation to historical memories. It also raises the question of how we remember the lessons of the historical past without celebrating those memories of oppression. Can these two notions—lessons about the past and the past itself—ever be separated?

Even more questions arise here, in terms of the power interests at play: What constitutes the process of naming buildings and statues? Was history not considered a factor in the naming process? To what extent does a nod to historical tradition (or recognition of a person from the region of this university) supersede the historical memories of oppression and/or the racist ideology promoted by those individuals? Did these institutions just forget about these historical memories of oppression and racist ideologies, or to what extent did the influence of that historical figure (and any donated money to do such naming) outweigh (and defuse) any negative historical memories brought about by that figure? Is there a moratorium on when historical memories stop being painful? How do we learn about historical memories of cultural oppression without celebrating those memories (via the memorialization of figures) and under what conditions?

What is *not* remembered about the past reveals the power-slanted version of what we know about important achievements in a country and the tremendous power it is to widely circulate a narrative about what happened long ago. Such selective historical memory was highlighted in the popular film *Hidden Figures*. In 2016, the film was released and received rave reviews. The film showcases three African Americans who worked at NASA in the 1960s and how these African American women were essential to getting the astronaut John Glenn into orbit. The movie highlights how these women possessed important skills (mathematics, engineering, computer programming, leadership and management) for NASA operations and yet were discounted given their race and gender. These women—Katherine Johnson, Mary Jackson, and Dorothy Vaughn—had to complete their difficult jobs, all while still having to endure separate bathrooms and separate treatment from their White peers. Audience members praised the show while admitting to not knowing about the important role these women played in the United States' space race. This historical memory was not publicly or visibly shared, which reveals how knowledge about cultural groups in the past, and the kind of contributions they make in the face of unfair social and working conditions, is left out and absent from our historical telling.

This middle school in Palo Alto, California, has been renamed because its namesake was identified as a strong proponent of the eugenics movement (a larger group that argued that some races—Whites—were superior over other groups —African Americans). Community members debated over the need to rename a school in light of negative historical memories.

We also must ask the following questions: Whom do we memorialize? Why? Who has the power to do this? Why are most buildings in the United States named after White/European American men? Who decides this? Why do we not know about other cultural groups and genders and their different contributions to society? What about the 4,000 female code breakers who broke and deciphered codes by Japanese and Nazi military during World War II? Why don't we know we know more about these women?

Historical Amnesia

Another key aspect of historical memory and remembering is also what is forgotten about the past or historical amnesia. Several scholars, such as Hutton (1993) and Hobsbawm and Ranger (1983) explain that certain events, traditions, and elements of the past are repressed and forgotten in historical memory and History narratives because of the power interests involved and the large stakes at hand in projecting a specific version of the past. Thus, what is forgotten and elided is just as important as what is remembered. As emphasized in cinema and film studies, we need to look at both the symbolic presences (what is told and what this reveals) and **symbolic absences** (what is not told or ignored and what this reveals) of depictions of the past.

As another example, Japan has become a recent target of attacks for its historical construction as a solemn, proud, and untainted nation. In her hailed book, *The Rape of Nanking: The Forgotten Holocast of World War II*, historian Iris Chang (2012) painstakingly traces how Japan (via the Imperial Japanese Army) committed major human atrocities and war crimes against China in the 1937–1938 Nanking massacre when it captured Nanjing, then capital of China, during the Second Sino-Japanese War. Her book details the cruel torture and raping of the Chinese people (women and children) during this massacre and how Japan, to this day, selectively forgets and elides this event in their national history. Chang also points out how the Japanese government has failed to formally redress and apologize for the atrocities. What is forgotten is just as revealing as what is remembered. When examining the national museum displays and history texts in Japan, one can see how the steady

The movie, *Hidden Figures*, showcased three African Americans who worked at NASA in the 1960s and how these African American women were essential to getting the astronaut John Glenn into orbit. The movie highlights how these women possessed important skills (mathematics, engineering, computer programming, leadership, and management) for NASA operations and yet were historically omitted given their race and gender.

and streamlined focus on how Japan is the martyr and savior of Asia, while forgetting "the Japanese-led massacres, Korean comfort women, Chinese sex slaves, or tortured POWs in this history" (Chang, 2012, p. 5).

The wounds of the Nanking massacre by Japan against Korea went deep. In a PBS newscast that highlighted her book, Chang demanded that a Japanese ambassador apologize to the Chinese people for what happened in the past. After that ambassador expressed regret for "unfortunate" happenings and the acts of violence committed by Japanese soldiers, Chang expressed dissatisfaction with his statements and in subsequent years joined a larger movement to press Japan for compensation to the Chinese.

Cultural groups (and even nations) worry about the possibility of historical amnesia, especially when significant historical events risk being forgotten. For example, the Taiwanese people worry about people forgetting the importance of the 228 massacre (Fleischauer, 2007; Hwang, 2016). The 228 massacre refers to the violent killing by a Chinese government unit of 10,000 Taiwanese civilians in an anti-government uprising in 1947. This historical event served as a catalyst for the Taiwan independence movement. But, many survivors of the 228 massacre have since died and the Taiwanese community worries that the memory of the massacre and what it meant for the formation of the movement to gain independence of Taiwan from China will also be lost. As a result, community members are trying to capture the oral histories and narratives of the survivors in order to preserve this historical memory so that the Taiwanese community never forgets the beginning of the independence movement.

When the past is forgotten and or not actively remembered, some worry that the harsh oppressions of the past will re-emerge and continue. According to economist Diego Rubio (2017), historical amnesia is risky for European countries as the younger generations seem to support authoritarian-like government forms over democratic types of leadership. This, he argues, is due to the lack of historical knowledge and the preservation of memories through historical education in schools. Rubio (2017) states that

> [a] recent study by the University of Leipzig found that one in every ten Germans (10.6 per cent) want their country to be led by a 'Führer to rule with an iron fist for common prosperity.' Likewise, 61 per cent of Austrians favour supporting a 'strong leader who does not have to worry about a parliament or elections' and 40 per cent of the French state that their country should be put in the hands of 'an authoritarian government' free from democratic constraints (p. 1).

He details the loss of historical memory further: "According to a study by the Berlin Free University, half of German teenagers 'don't know Hitler was a dictator', and a third believe he protected human rights. A quarter of British schoolchildren could not say what Auschwitz was" (Rubio, 2017). Without knowledge of the past, European youth are not remembering the past with regard to dominant regimes and historical oppressions. Historical amnesia is therefore looming as historical education is not being fully maintained and instituted.

What is collectively forgotten could be an act of oppression onto another group or an example of a structural barrier for some groups over others. In the end, collective historical memory from a dominant position remembers only what advances its interests and forgets or strips away what jeopardizes such interests.

Remaking Collective and Historical Memories
We are not forever doomed to History as our only source of memory. Instead, the Popular Memory Group (1982), led by Richard Johnson, argue that communities re-create dominant historical memories, or the formal constructions of cultural histories and subjectivities found in state forms (e.g., museums, History textbooks, national commemorative discourse, administrative and legal documents). In social life, community members make different sense of the formal past by selectively remembering, forgetting, and re-articulating images, histories, and narratives of who they are, thereby constructing private memories. We rely instead on what is already within our reach: a generative materials memory of life moments, pains, joys, displacements, and structural pressures experienced by a racialized, gendered, and overwritten cultural group. The Popular Memory Group refers to these re-makings of dominant historical memories as private

memories: "Private memories cannot in concrete studies be readily unscrambled from the effects of dominant historical discourses. It is often these that supply the very terms by which a private history is thought through" (p. 211). Such a notion resonates with Marx's popular explanation of social life: "that people make history but in conditions not of their own making" (Grossberg, 1996b, p. 151). Private memories, therefore, are framed by dominant conditions but not determined by them.

Communities create private memories through which people come to imagine a shared experience of identification with those to whom they are in some way historically, politically, and culturally connected. For example, feminist ethnographer Soyini Madison (1993) and intercultural scholar Tamar Katriel (2013) highlight personal narratives as spaces where identities are performed, addressed and in dialogue with "the cultural, geopolitical, and economic circumstances" touching their lives (Madison, 1993, p. 213). By narrating their lives, (mis)recognized social members can re-tell the identity constructions through which they have been narrated. These individual stories spill over with rich theoretical insight. Community members' remembrances, though captured through individuated interviews, reveal the presence of pluralized subjects who achieve their identities as extensions of a historical- and locational-bound collective. No longer a single subject, the pluralized community subject, according to McClintock (2013), "cannot be heard outside its relation to communities" (p. 11). For instance, there are many "her stories" of women in different cultures and countries articulating their experiences as females in male-dominated regions and how they contributed to social life in major ways. Private memories and re-tellings of minority groups and their experiences in multicultural countries such as Canada, Brazil, and the United States, are emerging in varied forms (documentaries, blogs, oral histories, theatrical performances, written documents). Communities can and do recreate private memories that represent and articulate their individuated and shared experiences of the past as a version of what actually happened.

Alliance Building Around Historical Memories and Experiences

But, historical memory can also stand as a meaningful bridge and not just a divide. Cultural groups have also bonded over their shared historical experiences, and over contemporary ones, as well formed alliances (or an association or partnership with a shared goal, experience, or viewpoint). Japanese-American communities (who have endured a history of internment in the United States) have spoken out against the threatened removal of rights from Muslims in the United States. In the wake of 2017 travel ban against Muslim persons into the United States, Japanese Americans have used their past experiences with the US government as a means to speak out against any discrimination against Muslims in the United States. For instance, the Graceful Crane theater troupe performed its internment experiences at the Arab American National Museum and for Muslim-American communities (Wang, 2017). The performance was followed by a panel in which Japanese-American representatives dialogued with Muslim Americans about how to combat any threats to their rights (and of a rumored national registry for Muslims in the United States).

Also, Karen Korematsu (the daughter of Fred Korematsu who sued the US government for then-president Roosevelt's internment executive order) spoke to the media about the legal rights of Muslims and past legal decisions (Wolf, 2017). She and other Japanese American leaders addressed the historical wrongs done to Japanese Americans and the need to not let it happen to any other group in the country, namely Muslims in the United States. Historical memory can indeed meaningfully connect cultural groups into specific alliances.

Historical Memories and Intercultural Communication

Historical memory and depictions of the past (as History), as embedded in power, are not just relegated to yesterday; these articulations continue to touch our lives in the present day and for the future. Oftentimes, dominant historical memories (to which we are exposed to more than other forms) become our first encounters with a group and seal our first impression. Cultural groups are often identified and understood by expressions, images, and myths of the past. Indigenous groups in particular are remembered through constructions of the past, such as the first mystical meeting between natives and Western explorers, and images of naked, exotic savages, tribal dance spectacles, and native kings and queens. Enunciations of the past powerfully constitute and frame the nature of a specific group, its origins and collective experiences. These enunciations, whether in a museum display, a historical portrait, or popularized cultural legends, derive from the historical imagination, a force too seductive and powerful to reside as merely a physical structure or a matter of interpretation. It stands as a visual and narrative dialectic of selectively shaping, remembering, and forgetting the past and, in this specific context, historically identifying a culture. The historical imaginary is a multi-vocal, multi-vested collection of memories that call forth and activate particular myths, fantasies, and hegemonic beliefs over others. Such a force is just as much spoken as it is ideologically engrained into popular thought and is made up of several colliding forms: dominant memory (official histories by the colonial, nation-state, and local governments), popular memory (public representations of history in museum displays, tourist discourses and souvenirs, consumer products, widely reproduced legends and social histories), private memory (the practices and performances of the past—historical re-tellings, dances, celebrations and traditions—within a lived indigenous community), and counter or oppositional memory (politically resistive narratives and rhetoric by activist movement groups and everyday social actors). Our first intercultural contact with a group could be in the very moment we learn a dominant historical memory of another group in school or we read a commemorative statue in our country that depicts a historical event. Even hearing a national story told to us by family members at the dinner table is a sediment of a historical memory and an impression of another culture. Hence, historical memories shape how we view others, which can inevitably frame and guide our behaviors toward these group members. Remember, we act on perceptions and sense-makings that we have inherited from others around us and power structures in our lives.

Historical memories shape our specific intercultural relations in ways that we may not fully understand. Rhetorical scholar Marouf Hasian (1998) shares how several historical and political events (such as the Balfour Declaration) shape interactions between Israelis and Palestinians. He discusses how different memories of cultural entitlement to a territory, land, and people constitute the major struggle between the group. Who is entitled to a cultural land and by what criteria? Who first physically settled a land? Who is deemed by biblical right that they are the chosen people of the land? Who decides? These complex memories and entanglements limit intercultural relations in the Middle East to a narrow set of perspectives, behaviors, and viewpoints.

Intercultural scholar Thomas Nakayama (1993) also highlights how historical memories explain why some groups interact with one another and why others do not. He shares stories and experiences of growing up Asian American in the United States and in areas where all Asians were deemed immigrants and foreigners and rendered invisible in a dominant Black-White framework of the South. Nakayama also contends that history explains why some Vietnamese American youth do not want to learn to speak French because of the colonialist history of the French in Vietnam and Indochina and the perception by many Vietnamese that French is the language of the colonizers. This scholar emphasizes the following about historical memory:

> History is a process that has constructed where and how we enter into dialogue, conversation, and communication. It has strongly influenced what languages we speak, how we are perceived and how we perceive ourselves, and what domestic and international conflicts affect us (Nakayama, 1993, p. 15).

While historical memories can position us in specific intercultural relations and with specific predispositions, history can also connect us in ways that enable us to build intercultural alliances and partnerships through shared or similar historical experiences and oppressions. As a case in point, Muslim and Japanese American residents in the United States and worked together after the September 11th attacks to share information to help each other out. Japanese-American citizens, many of whom were interned in the World War II internment of Japanese Americans by the US government or whose family members were, educated Muslim residents on their rights as citizens given the heightened hysteria over Muslim people as terrorists after the attacks at the World Trade Center and the Pentagon. These groups educated each other and worked together (and continue to do so to this day) on community and legal fronts to form an alliance to prevent what happened to Japanese Americans to others in this country. Such an alliance reveals how historical memories—those filled with pain and injustice—can bridge groups together and create constructive intercultural relations in a hierarchy of power. We must remember that historical memories can bridge us and create constructive pathways for a better tomorrow.

Summary

History is a power-laden collection of events, images, experiences, sentiments, relations, and perceptions (memories) for a specific nation, culture, or group. History and historical memory (in terms of what we remember and what we forget) shape and constitute our intercultural encounters, relationships, and surrounding contexts.

Keywords

Alliances

Historical amnesia

Historical memory

History as a field of power

Private memories

Symbolic absence

Symbolic presence

REFLECTION activity: What historical memories were you exposed to in your culture?

Think about the ways in which your country, culture, and family have narrated the historical past to you and write down your response to the following questions:

- What historical memories or narratives were you exposed to as a child? From which sources (family member, religious institution, school, book, or other forms)?

- How did these narratives depict your country and culture? What did you make of this? How did these narratives shape how you felt about your country and culture?

- Were the memories a seamless narrative of unity among all citizens? Does a tale of struggle over foreign influences prevail? Is there one deemed hero or glory period to be hailed by your culture?

- How did these narratives depict other countries and culture? How did these narratives shape how you felt about other countries and cultures?

- Did your own historical memories of your country and culture change over time? If so, how? If not, why?

REFLECTION activity: To remember, forget, or repay?

Reparations refers to the ways in which an individual or party makes amends for a wrong whether it is through payment or some other act.

- In the United States, there have been movements to pay reparations to African Americans for slavery.

- Japanese Americans who were interned in this country during World War II received modest financial reparations from the US government.

- The Polish government has argued for the need for Germany to pay reparations for the violence and damage done to their country during World War II. War victims are demanding reparations from Bosnia for the violence and oppression experienced during the early 1990s Bosnia war.

So, given these examples, answer the following questions:

- To what extent, should cultural groups who have experienced gross unjust enslavement, imprisonment, and degradation be given reparations?

- Why or why not?

- Can we ever make up for a historical injustice?

- What could possibly be repaid?

- What are your thoughts?

Consider the symbolic power of a nation making reparations (in the most meaningful form to a Western nation—financial currency) and what it communicates to a cultural group in terms of apologizing for a historical injustice. Wouldn't that stand as a powerful form of historical recognition, which could open the way for a cultural group's healing?

DISCUSSION activity: The nature of historical memories that were passed down
Think about any of the historical memories that your family brings up (or did when you were a child or growing up) or talks about in relation to your cultural group and answer the following questions:

- What is the nature of these memories? Are these memories of the ways in which they practiced cultural traditions or prepared food? Are these memories of what grandparents or elders told them about life in their homeland? Are these memories about the government in their homeland and of any significant past events in that country? What do you notice about those memories?

- If there were no historical memories brought up by your family, why do you think that is the case? Was it in response to how they were raised or even in response to a historical event?

- Share your thoughts and reflections on historical memories.

Chapter 8

Racialization and Intercultural Communication

Learning Objectives:

▶ To understand race as a taken-for-granted structural formation that is *personally lived and experienced* by everyday persons in in both macro contexts and micro instances (interactions)

▶ To explore race as a structure of power that has been historically sedimented and naturalized into the way our society is governed

▶ To examine the ways in which race classifies us as individuals and as groups

Introduction: Lee and Race

Lee anxiously checked his inbox, thinking an e-mail notification would come. He was tired of checking the mailbox outside. The package had yet to arrive. This package would definitely tell Lee what his true identity was once and for all. Three months earlier, Lee had submitted a registration for his ancestry through 23andme.com. As a part Chinese and part African American male who resides on the West coast, Lee, a 22-year-old gaming tester and part-time college student, had been through a lot with his multiethnic identity. He felt as if he was not truly accepted by either side of the family. Family members on his Chinese side (his father's side) also told him he was "too dark" or looked "too Black." Lee's Chinese family members told

him to focus more on school, which made him wonder why they thought he wasn't already focused on school. His African American family members (on his mother's side) encouraged him to be more of a part of the Black community and to make sure he kept it "real" and to not sell out.

All his life, Lee feels that he has experienced "race" in so many ways. He has encountered societal and media messages that highlight how his African Americanness is associated with criminality and poverty and his Asian-ness (Chinese-ness) as always reflecting a foreignness or natural inclination to succeed academically (as a model minority). Lee has faced criticism of his skin color, hair texture, and eye shape by society, and these physical markers have also been taken up as automatic indications of his identity, intelligence, and authenticity. According to Lee, the 23andme.com DNA test would help to sediment his racial identity and prove that he truly belongs (via scientific evidence) to his cultural groups. Race, for him, revolved around self-acceptance and the acceptance of others around him.

The notion of race—often thought of as skin color, physical appearance, biological content, and blood amount—has become a major frame for United States' society. It stands as a concept that seems immediately divisive, exclusionary, politicized, and to many, as completely irrelevant (and counterproductive to positive intercultural relations). You may recall many around you and even yourself saying, "Why does it always have to be about race? Can't we just get over it?" It would seem that intercultural divisions and problems could be solved by merely erasing the concept and use of race.

However, it should be noted that the notion of race is not something we can merely choose to forget, discard, or ignore; it is a very present and persistent structural formation that constitutes society and has done so historically whether we like it or not. Race has shaped, constituted, and outlined our experiences, behaviors, and social responses to others.

In the introductory narrative, Lee represents the concept of race on a personal level. Indeed, Lee's racial marking as both African American and Chinese American (and how society sees him as either Black or Asian) reveals how race involuntarily punctuates and seeps into our everyday experiences and sense-makings of the world in both affirming and disconfirming ways. Lee experiences "race" in terms of biology and social perceptions. He is constantly judged in terms of the biological markers attached to race (skin color, hair texture, eye shape) and the societal perceptions that categorize racial or ethnic groups (via stereotypes such as "African Americans engage in criminal behavior" and "Asian Americans are excellent at math and in academics"). Biology and social perceptions around race therefore represent different types of social constructions of race or meanings around race that are created and circulated by society and put into motion through structures of power. The narrative example of Lee demonstrates how race stands as more than an individual behavior or attitude; instead, it stands as a structure and dynamic of power that is out of one's control.

This chapter highlights how race is much more than an intentional, individuated behavior or attitude. Rather, race is a taken-for-granted structural formation that is *personally lived and experienced* by everyday persons in complex ways (ways that make us deny race's existence in some contexts and then pronounce its presence in others). This is to say we personally engage in and live out race in real, concrete, and deeply felt ways—in both macro contexts and micro instances (interactions). Race is a structure of power that has been historically established and stitched into the way our society is structured and governed, as well as the way in which we think about ourselves and others around us. At the same time, we, as individuals and groups, also can reassemble and remake the structural and ideological encodings of race into productive points of dialogue, connection, and analysis for a more just intercultural world.

What Is Race?

One of the most frequent questions people ask in university and training contexts is "What is race?" Youth and students are often intrigued and fearful by the concept as they have typically heard this to be a negative concept that brings harm on others. Some students have raised excellent questions such as, "Race seems bad, and if it is, why do we keep talking about it? Why do we need to learn something that we should 'un-learn'?" Adults often bypass questions around the topic of race altogether because it brings up uncomfortable concepts, issues, and hard-to-resolve answers, let alone intimidating divisions among groups. These questions and concerns are valid in the sense that building intercultural relations would be most productive if done so through a positive, constructive sense of understanding, and oftentimes that would seem more possible without the concept of race.

However, it is also important to re-examine race not just in terms of how societies have defined it but in terms of its larger historical formation and framework and its connection to power. You most likely have not been exposed to such a re-examination as presented in this chapter, and it may be overwhelming at first. But it is crucial that we re-engage race according to larger logics of power, history, and context so that we may pose new questions about race to allow for more reflexivity, dialogue, and insight about how race permeates our lives. Race relations have long been a major source of contention in the United States (especially with its legacy of slavery), as well as the in United Kingdom, Europe, and Asia, and continues to be so. As a critical scholar, the best pathway toward reimagining race relations and constructive relations among cultural groups (that are framed as separate races) is to first re-conceptualize race and then analyze, question, discuss, and brainstorm around this concept.

What is Race?

We often ponder the question — "What is Race?" What do we mean by "race" and how does that shape how we see society?

Defining Race

To begin, as discussed in Goldberg (1993) and Omi & Winant (2014), race can be defined as a social category or classification created for specific cultural groups in terms of how and what a group is, who is a member, on what criteria constitute belonging, and what it means to be in the group. Such classifications of race have often deemed some groups more superior over others based on their skin color, cranial capacity, IQ scores, educational status, and blood lineage; the intelligence level, potential mobility, morality, and productivity of cultural groups have also been determined based on specific classifications (Goldberg, 1993). These classifications fix and define a cultural group's existence, way of being, and nature, all in one fell swoop through the marker of race. Race therefore differentiates, categorizes, and classifies who we are based on a hierarchy of differences (with some being deemed superior over others). Race also has taken on such a hardened and concrete physicality as a truth that it imbues great power over how we think about and act toward these cultural groups. In order to unpack race, we must first explore several key attributes of this concept.

Attributes of Race

Race Is a Social Construct

Many scholars and experts about race and race relations typically frame race as a social construct. The notion that race is a social construct means that race is a concept that has been variably defined, shaped, and reproduced by structures of power and groups in specific historical periods. So, in this sense, race is not one thing that is fixed, permanent and out there; it's not just our skin color, biological material, or blood as we may have come to believe from the Western media. Instead, race has been defined in these ways and in different historical moments by governments, scientists, political figures, and structures. As race scholar David Theo Goldberg (1993) explains, race has been defined in various ways over time. He explains that race has historically been conceptualized as "a group of persons linked by common origin or descent" and "as a group having some feature(s) in common" (p. 63). While these general frames of race have remained constant, the substance or

Classifications of race have characterized some groups as being more superior over others based on their skin color, cranial capacity, IQ scores, educational status, and blood lineage.

content of what defines a group internally, and in comparison against other groups, has changed throughout time. Goldberg (1993) traces the framing of racial classification of groups based on physical or biological markers such as lineage, gene pools, skin color, cranial capacity, hair texture, physical size and body characteristics, and DNA (genetics), among others. This is why race is most often associated as biology across the globe and why so many think negatively of race in this way, because it seems so obviously discriminating based on the way we were born. But, Goldberg also discusses how social markers such as morality, religion, national belonging, linguistic and speech style, residential origin in city spaces, and educational status and intelligence scores (IQ, standardized testing) also stand as classifications of race in separating out cultural groups from one another. Thus, race as a social construct demonstrates that the content and substance of the classification is what changes over time, while the effect takes on a more natural and permanent status (in terms of pinning down how groups "just are"). The variability in classifications of race highlights how societies and groups or structures in power are responsible for creating, crafting, and reproducing race—in both biological and social or non-biological forms. This is an important point: The fact that race is socially created provides some hope that it can be reconfigured in ways to speak to issues of social justice, intercultural understanding, and against historical inequalities. At the same time, though, this very notion—that race is a social construct—also attests to the sheer power and persistence of social forces and structures of power in sedimenting race in such a way that it seems so real, natural, fixed, and permanent.

Race Is Created in Context of Power

As discussed earlier, race can never be separated from social and structural relations of power. Intercultural communication scholars have mostly conceptualized race as an identity marker and group category as opposed to a socio-political construct. Such a tendency has therefore glossed over the construction of race as a power-vested formation. In response, critical intercultural communication scholars such as Judith N. Martin and Thomas K. Nakayama (2006) have highlighted race as a power-vested construction that invisibly and visibly positions certain cultural groups over others. Designations and classifications of race carry the powerful effect of hierarchically positioning cultural groups in relation to one another. For example, in some national contexts, Whites, Europeans, and deemed Westerners have been positioned superiorly over other groups—Blacks, native/indigenous, and non-Whites (Asians, Latinos, among others), albeit through various constructions of race. These classifications, while applied to all cultural groups, carry very different effects and consequences for these groups, with some gaining prestige, privilege, and social distinction and mobility over others who suffer from castigation, discipline and punishment, marginalization, and even death (as in the case of Nazi Germany with Jews, mixed races, and homosexuals).

Cultural studies and critical studies scholars such as Stuart Hall (1979), David Theo Goldberg (1993, 2002), Michael Omi and Howard Winant (2014) have primarily theorized race as a structural formation. They articulate that race stands as much more than some contrived or socially agreed on category—it is a structural apparatus known as the "racial state," which is composed of local, state and federal governmental structures and backed by the courts of law, military power, public policy, public educational institutions, and local and national media. Through administrative policies, race as a structural formation lays down official procedures and conditions for identification, which permeate the private, everyday experiences of social subjects. As discussed in the next section, race constitutes structures of power that divide groups based on socially designated classifications and markers of difference.

Today there is also a push to scientifically verify one's race. There are several companies that feature the scientific verification of individuals' ancestry and identity make-up. For example, 23andme.com invites us to "go beyond" our family tree and "find people who share DNA" with us. Ancestry DNA encourages us to "experience [our] ancestry in a new way." These companies offer the promise of proving ones' racial or cultural identity. Such proof comes in a detailed report with the breakdown of your DNA make-up and ethnic mix. This information emanates from an individual's DNA (via the swabbing of one's saliva) and therefore represents indisputable (irrefutable) scientific evidence. Here, race (and proof of such race) is legitimated through scientific matching and verification and percentage breakdowns through

Many individuals in society misinterpret the work of companies like 23 and Me and take ancestry information as indisputable proof of the their racial/cultural identity.

a larger discourse focused on uncovering one's ancestry. Questions arise with these types of sites: To what extent do the received DNA results make individuals feel more attached to the proven identities? To what extent will an individual experience trauma over a DNA report that challenges or denies her or his current identity membership? How will the verification of small percentages of non-White racial composition for a White person exploit and dilute the identity claims of communities of color? How will the scientific framing of race through these DNA verification companies become privileged and the only accepted form of racial identity proof?

Race as Identity Marker

Race serves as an identity marker for dominant and marginalized groups. Certainly, race has marked all groups, but in different ways. For dominant or privileged groups in society, race has created the basis for their ascendance in social rank and status but in invisible form so that these social and material gains seem natural, without bias, and by virtue of hard work and achievement. On the other hand, race, as a marker, has constituted the lives, experiences, and identities of marginalized groups in significant ways. African American and Black British communities have underscored how race and its effects lingers over their everyday experiences and is something that is unavoidable. Race goes with them every day of their lives. In turn, race has been reconfigured to represent a significant factor in the forming of marginalized group members' histories and outlooks on the world. Communities often highlight racial pride or race as a source of communal belonging and unity among their members; this illustrates how race for marginalized groups has shaped their contextualized subjective sense-makings, identities, and cultural pride. Race can carry this double-sided effect; it can have different effects, implications, and functions for different groups based on where in the hierarchy they are positioned. For historically disadvantaged groups, race and the experiences attached with it, as a marker of inferiority and difference, has served as a common source of understanding, solace, coping, and survival for group members in a race-conscious world.

Race Is Naturalized Over Time

Race has become naturalized and historicized over time through its reproduction. While race is socially created and not necessarily permanent and fixed in and of itself, it is the nature of how racial designations and classifications get continually reproduced over time (through historical power structures, world views, persistent historical relations, media representations, and structural procedures and policies that are still in effect for centuries when biological markers of race reigned supreme) that allows constructions of race to become naturalized and historicized over time. History is a powerful force that manages to perpetuate racial classifications (_____ group is this way; _____ group is that way) in macro (structural) forms and micro interactions (conversations, personal, familial beliefs, traditions, and views). Thus, race can take on a concrete, impenetrable feel precisely because it so often gets reproduced in various forms and by different structures and interests of power. In our postmodern world, we must still face the reality that race and its constructions will continue to be reproduced and intensely naturalized and historicized, which makes it a challenging and daunting problem to interrupt and reconfigure.

Racialization in Society

If race is a social construct, then racialization captures the active use and assigning of race across contexts with major consequences, or putting race into action and for effect. Racialization is the deployment and assignment of race by various structures and interests of power as a construct or marker to differentiate groups and place them in a hierarchy of value (Goldberg, 1993, Omi & Winant, 2014). A hierarchy of value refers to the unequal or asymmetrical positioning of groups for a society through which those at the top of the hierarchy are positively and distinctively valued over those lower in the scale (and deemed as inferior, weak, less than, and underdeveloped). Through racialization, race places groups in unequal relation to one another and with dire consequences.

In intercultural communication studies and social and cross-cultural psychology, researchers have discussed ways in which the use of race has caused the prejudicial and discriminatory treatment of many groups members throughout time (Allport, 1954; Hecht, Collier, & Ribeau, 1993; Orbe & Harris, 2013). However, this research has often framed such treatment as based on rational and intentional acts of hostile and direct discrimination and prejudgment by individuals or cultural group members against other individuals or cultural group members. While this happens, racialization frames the deployment of race as more than just rational and individualistic intent toward other individuals and instead as a structural and ideological formation of racism, inequality, and power interests. The next two sections highlight two such structural and ideological formations based on racialization: the racial state and the racially biased legal system.

Structural Formations of Race

The Racial State

According to David Theo Goldberg (2002), the racial state is a structural apparatus made up of local, state, and federal governmental structures and backed by the courts of law, military power, public policy, public educational institutions, and local, regional, and national media. Indeed, society has come to view the state as not subjective or racial in the first place. Instead, we tend to see the state a merely an impartial and disinterested body that oversees and delimits social order according to a set of neutral rules, conditions, and procedures. Such a guise illustrates the ideological power of the state and the central role it plays in our lives. For instance, the modern racial state creates, modifies, and reifies racial expressions, inclusions, and exclusions and how groups are situated in relation to one another. Moreover, the racial state legally and administratively defines non-racial admissions and employment criteria for public institutions of learning and business and class-based criteria for residential districting, thus shaping which groups—by race and class—will occupy specific contexts. Through these guised racially learning acts, the state "manages and oversees what individuals can do, where they can go, what educational institution they can access, with whom they can interact, and where they can reside" (Goldberg, 2002, p. 108). The racial state primarily exerts its power through dominant forms such as state policy and definitions; legal rulings, such as the ban on affirmative action in university admissions; and on race-based admissions in school districts and mainstream media discourses.

More specifically, the racial state establishes its predominance by reproducing racial power and racial order (Kim, 1999, 2003, 2004). Racial power is defined as "the cumulative and interactive political, economic, social, and cultural processes that jointly reproduce racial categories and distribution and perpetuate a system of White dominance" (Kim, 2003, p. 9). The states come into existence by the systemic nature of racial power, or the continuous reproduction of racial categories, meanings, and distributions that maintain the racial status quo. But, the racial state also remains dominant in that it racially orders cultural groups. The racial categories and meanings are reproduced in a distinct order as groups are positioned relative to one another. In her analysis of Black-Korean relations in New York City, Kim (2003) explains that US society is not merely a vertical hierarchy but is racially ordered as a field constructed of at least two axes (i.e., superior/inferior, insider/foreigner). She argues that this racial order "stands at the intersection of the discursive-ideational and social-structural realms; it is a discursively constructed, shared cognitive map that serves as a blueprint for who should get what in American society" (Kim, 2003, p. 10). The state, therefore, racially classifies groups in specific relations to one another, all the while maintaining its colorless authority. All in all, the racial state promotes its hidden and unspoken power interests of economic power and legal and political supremacy underneath a cloak of neutrality, fairness, and race-less-ness.

State Ideologies of Colorblindness and Multiculturalism

Aligned with the racial state are state ideologies (or dominant views endorsed by a governmental or national body) that perpetuate and reproduce their racial power (and

Military power represents one of the many layers of the racial state. The racial state is a dominant apparatus of power that is made up of local, state, and federal governmental structures and backed by the courts of law, military, public policy, public educational institutions, local, regional, and national media.

invisible authority), such as colorblindness and multiculturalism. Cultural studies and critical studies scholars Avery Gordon & Christopher Newfield (1996) and David Theo Goldberg (1994) explain that multiculturalism was hailed as the ideal goal of US society since the 1970s via the government, media, and educational system. In a historical synopsis, Gordon and Newfield (1996) trace how in the 1970s educators initially created a vision of multiculturalism that "sought to dismantle White majority control of schools and use of White backgrounds and values as yardsticks" (p. 77). Over the next 20 years, multiculturalism pervaded the political, institutional, and social realms of US society and eventually lost touch with its initial antiracist and politically edged focus of the 1970s (Gordon & Newfield, 1996). In the 1990s, the focus on multiculturalism encompassed diversity, or the embracing of cultural differences between and among groups. Diversity invoked a spirit of cultural pluralism and presumed equality across all cultures and even became corporatized as "diversity management" to productively organize cultural difference for business success.

With a seemingly innocent spirit of "let a thousand flowers bloom," the ideology of multiculturalism presumed that all cultural groups are already in equal positions relative to one another and that power was not an issue. It also reduced culture and diversity to an oversimplified encoding of demographic presence. The logic here is that a diverse environment is one which in there exists the presence of cultural groups and that such presence is inherently positive and equal. This ideological encoding limits the notion of diversity to be about nominal presence and not about relative positioning in terms of power, access, quality of life, and material gains. What is formed is a common sense that

In intercultural cities made up of more than one racial/ethnic group, the racial state reproduces racial categories in a distinct order that positions groups in specific relations to one another, all the while maintaining its "colorless" authority.

diversity is merely about the presence and existence of cultural groups on a surface level. Such an articulation is particularly dangerous in that it enables the state to publicly frame diversity in terms of its cosmetic details rather than the structural, economic, and material conditions and contexts that help to shape the dynamics and consequences of diversity. Next, if in fact cultural groups are deemed present and thus equal, an ideology of multiculturalism presumes that there is a type of signified equivalence, a type of signified sameness that connects all cultural groups: their difference. If all groups exist in the same areas and contexts, especially in a minority majority, then it follows discursively that we are all the same because we are all different from one another. Difference becomes universalized and neutralized, eliding all incongruities, contradictions, conflicts, and oppositions. In a move similar to the pluralistic rhetoric of the 1980s with its focus on societal multiculturalism (Gordon & Newfield, 1996), difference, in one fell swoop, rises as a shared characteristic on a general level that literally connects, bridges, and joins all groups.

In addition to multiculturalism, a prevailing ideology emerged in the late 1980s and continues to the present that touts the necessity of colorblindness or the erasure of color or race from consideration in any decision, topic, or social judgment. This ideology stresses that our society is race-less or colorblind. Such a societal view claims that racial difference and race, at all, do not factor into how society is lived and organized. Society is a neutral and equal playing field in which all groups can prosper depending on their effort and perseverance. According to this ideology, race is not a factor in terms of how groups differ, nor should it be a means from which to view society. The premise here is that all groups are equal to one another and afforded the same opportunities and access points to housing, education, employment, health care, and legal and individual rights. Colorblindness (or race-less-ness), however, completely ignores ways in which our society (via structures and relations of power) and world is already racialized (and has been throughout history) (Goldberg, 2002; Omi & Winant, 2014). Colorblindness therefore serves the dominant interests of government and corporate power through its continual denial of racial bias and minority oppression in power structures and its constant maintenance of a supposed neutral state, thereby safeguarding the racial status quo.

Critical race scholars Michael Omi and Howard Winant (2014) and David Theo Goldberg (2002) go further to theorize that discourses around multiculturalism, diversity, and colorblindness are always intertwined with meanings of race and racism (even the representational attempts that avoid race altogether). These scholars argue that dominant discourses that surround multiculturalism, diversity, and colorblindness are particularly important to examine because these forms advance the interests of the racial state.

Since 2008, there also has been an ideology about race that characterizes American society as post-racial. By post-racial, this refers to how race is not deemed a significant factor or obstacle in progress and achievement in society. With the presidential campaign and election of former president Barack Obama, the media and public claimed that the United States was finally a post-racial nation in which all groups—as evidenced by the leadership of Barack Obama—could succeed and prosper (Kaplan, 2011; Kiuchi, 2016).

However, the post racial ideology was challenged by the Black Lives Matter movement in 2013. In response to the killings of several African American male youth and men, Black Lives Matter argued that racial bias and racist violence were at the heart of American society. Some continued to insist that America was post racial with its "all lives matter" hashtag while others rallied around the Black Lives Matter movement.

Racially Biased Legal System and Critical Race Theory

Given that race intersects with power, the legal system stands as an important structure of power that defines and delimits race in key court decisions that impact our lives. An area of study that focuses on the relationship between race and power in the arena of law is known as critical race theory (or CRT) (Crenshaw, 1995). According to scholars Crenshaw, Gotanda, Peller, and Thomas (1995), critical race theory is a field of study that aims to critique how race constitutes and shapes American-based legal theory, doctrine, and practice in such a way that a bias toward whiteness and rigid racial or gender hierarchies is strongly upheld (Delgado & Stefancic, 2017). Here scholars analyze how law has been used to racially mark and oppress particular social groups (Crenshaw, Gotanda, Peller, & Thomas, 1995).

Think about how important critical race theory is in understanding race. When we have a dispute or feel wronged by a party or entity, we may seek out a lawyer to help defend and argue our case in a court system. That court system will have a neutral arbiter (the judge) along with evidence, potential witnesses, and a set of policies and procedures for how the case will be conducted and evaluated. We put our trust into this court system because of its promise of neutrality, fairness, and justice. Critical race theory argues that this supposed neutral court system and the framing of the law as fair, open, and just are not actually so, especially in cases and matters around race (Delgado & Stefancic, 2017).

Former President Barack Obama was deemed as evidence of a post-racial nation in which all groups could succeed and prosper.

Legal Scholarship Is Not Objective

Critical race theory challenges the idea that legal scholarship is (and should be) neutral. In fact, CRT scholars argue that there is no such thing as an objective position in the legal system and that lawyers are not neutral representatives but also persons with racial, gendered, and cultural identities and positionalities. In this way, then, the law and legal scholarship should be framed as important knowledge that acknowledges and considers race as a way to help and advocate for marginalized communities and persons. To do otherwise would be to deny that racial difference ever existed which may, in fact, disadvantage an oppressed racial group even more in the court system.

Race as More Complex

CRT pushes for more complex definitions of race and racism than in traditional civil rights discourse. In the civil rights era (1960s and 1970s) in the United States, the legal system framed racism in a specific way: as a set of intentional, irrational, and social deviant acts (Crenshaw, 1995), meaning that a person was engaging in a racist act if that person acted out of the ordinary and in an extreme way, set out to purposefully harm a racially different person. As a result, racism was codified as a behavioral practice that was irregular and non-normal and an act that was visible. So, consider this: If an allegation of racism is not visible or identifiable (meaning, that someone else witnessed it), or is not proven to be intentional or out of the ordinary, then it fails to meet the legal standardized criteria. If an individual's claims of racism then, according to popular and legal reasoning, does not fit such criteria, those claims are dismissed. Worse yet, those claims may be

However, the Black Lives Matter movement and the killings of several African American males and youth by law enforcement powerfully demonstrated that such a post-racial nation did not exist.

perceived as a racial group member's tactic for getting what he or she should be entitled to without putting in the work.

For instance, Kinna is a Latina professional who had been working for her medical device sales company for five years and is consistently exceeding her sales quota every month. On several occasions, Kinna approached her manager, Sara—an Asian American female who has been with the company for fifteen years—about a potential promotion and the steps that she needed to make to actualize such a promotion. Her manager, Sara, kept dodging her requests until one day Kinna confronted Sara in the work cafeteria: "Sara, I can't seem to get an answer about a potential promotion from you. What is going on?" Sara immediately responded by stating, "You are going to need to do a lot more to move up in this company. Just because you ask doesn't mean you will get something. Your people need to understand that you have to work for it." Kinna was surprised at Sara's response and the statement about "your people."

After this encounter and several more months of her outstanding sales performances, stellar performance reviews, as well as repeated rejections of promotion requests, Kinna ultimately filed a racial discrimination complaint and one about systemic racism in the company with human resources in being continually turned down for promotions. However, according to the legal definition of racism, there was no "out of the ordinary" or "irregular" act or intent to harm or hold back anyone. A manager was merely communicating back to her employee about work roles and expectations. Thus, Kinna's claims about a racist manager and company could never come to fruition. She was portrayed as a bitter employee who used her race (via a claim about racism) to move up in the company without paying her dues and putting in the necessary work.

Critical Race Theory (CRT) challenges the notion that the legal system (with its symbols of justice and truth) is not neutral and instead privileges whiteness over all groups.

Thus, the legal definitions of race and racism uphold and reproduce the larger American myths of equal opportunity (every person is afforded the same opportunities in life), the American Dream (you can work your way up and increase your mobility), and the social world as a meritocracy (through hard work, you will achieve your success). Legislation therefore defined racism as a deviation from the norm (or something that occurred out of the ordinary) rather than as everyday, subtle acts that were embedded in social routines and processes and reflected a systemic and historical form of oppression. Such a framing of racism was written in such a way that any challenges to such a status quo seemed useless. Moreover, legal definitions of race and racism also created an ironic stance in which anyone (and especially for persons of color and from historically underrepresented groups) who made a claim having to do with race (in terms of racism, racial discrimination, or prejudice) with the goal of racial justice and addressing a wrong, were immediately characterized as racist. Thus, the law and society would see *both* White supremacists and Black activists for racial equality—two groups situated differently in relation to power, with differential access to resources, support, and Constitutional protection—as racists, and the same type of racists. There would be no distinction between these two groups in terms of their positionalities and relationship to race and power. This has continued today in society and everyday life in which anyone who brings up race or racial difference is deemed a racist. Kinna, for example, would be characterized as someone who only sees race and uses race for personal gain and thus, must be a racist. A Latina teacher who brings up the idea of race in her high school English class in terms of how the canon of required classics literature only includes works by European/European American authors, would be labeled a racist because she is explicitly calling out and identifying race and racial difference. Critical race theory aims to dismantle the legal definitions of race and racism as being out of the ordinary and intentional acts in a presumed racially equal and neutral (and thus colorblind) world (Delgado & Stefancic, 2017).

Challenging Legal Neutrality

Critical race scholars challenge the perceived neutrality of American law. The civil rights era ushered in a narrow (letter of the law) definition of race (Crenshaw, 1995). Likewise, the procedures and criteria for determining merit, need, and qualifications were framed in the same way and were ultimately presumed to be "without race" or not be racial in the first place. From a legal standpoint, racism was delimited as the formal, overt exclusion of people of color in a world that was already presumed to be fully accessible and with culturally or racially neutral social institutions (legal, governmental, educational, housing, economic). Law was also deemed neutral and inherently beneficial for all individuals regardless of color. Here, legal policy ideologically framed race without referencing or naming race. This presumed neutrality in the legal sphere is what CRT scholars aim to expose and break down.

CRT scholars highlight the power dimensions of race in the law. CRT scholars set out to highlight race as opposed to denying its existence (as in current legal doctrine). These scholars who all hail from different racial backgrounds argue that their social experiences of being marginalized as youth and in the legal profession make them better legal practitioners in terms of understanding the communities that they serve (Crenshaw, 1995). They also see experiences of marginality and racial oppression as useful tools for social action and community service. This is a counterpoint to the civil rights era's dominant legal classification of racism as a visibly concrete, discrete act of prejudice based on skin color. Such a legal classification made all hidden and subtle social practices of racism (through language, media and popular culture, employment, education, and social relations) irrelevant to legal jurisdiction and purview (Delgado & Stefancic, 2017).

Against Legal Rationality

Legal rationality is another area that is questioned by CRT practitioners. CRT reflects on constitutional law and the case study of *Brown vs. Board of Education* as an example of how racial discrimination has been framed from specific rational logic. In *Brown vs. Board of Education*, the Supreme Court prohibited racial segregation of public schools. Such a case established the precedent that government-sanctioned racial discrimination (such as legally enforced segregation) was prohibited (Crenshaw, 1995). From the 14th Amendment, it was ruled that race was a "suspect classification," which required tight judicial scrutiny, and thus, racial classifications were defined as violating the equal protection clause unless they served a "compelling government interest" and were "no broader than necessary" to achieve such a goal. From this, several questions emerged: Is discrimination intentional? Is affirmative action subject to strict scrutiny? Does remedying past discrimination meet the standards of compelling government interest? Currently, the law operates from a legal rationality in which racial bias was deemed as not existing in the first place and or, when it did exist, it showed up as an obvious, extreme, direct, intentional, and out of the ordinary act.

Challenging the Status Quo

Critical race theory challenges the status quo approaches to racial discrimination. CRT scholar Alan David Freeman (1995) critically analyzed two dominant approaches to racial discrimination: the victim perspective and the perpetrator perspective. He traces each perspective in their respective historical contexts. The victim perspective refers to a view of racial discrimination as a set of actual, objective conditions of lower-class existence (lack of jobs, money, and housing) and the position resulting from such conditions (lack of choice and of individuality). This condition-based definition theorizes that discrimination will not be improved until the conditions are erased. But, you must first prove the condition. This victim perspective resulted in the implementation of affirmative action programs to change the conditions of racial discrimination, but this perspective would not stand the test of time and was continually challenged because it represented an explicit admission by the legal and governmental system that racial groups were being socially disadvantaged. Instead, the perpetrator perspective became more popular and dominant (Delgado & Stefancic, 2017).

The perpetrator perspective refers to a view of racial discrimination as a series of actions inflicted on a victim by a perpetrator. Thus, conditions of the victims are not considered here; rather, the focus is primarily on what the perpetrators did to the victims. The larger conditions, such as poor socioeconomic status, housing, and education, were therefore not framed as evidence of racial discrimination. These conditions were instead characterized as neutral conditions of what happens when people are not competent enough in life. The remedy to racial discrimination in this view was to stop the wrongful perpetrator behavior. But, wrongful perpetrator behavior and racially discriminatory behavior were classified in overly simple terms: visible, direct, and intentional. Anything beyond what could be proven as visible, direct, and intentional fell to the wayside.

Today, antidiscrimination law heavily relies on the perpetrator perspective. More often than not, the sociopolitical conditions that racialize a victim are thus deemed irrelevant by the law. Racial discrimination is therefore assumed to be merely the misguided actions of a few in a world in which there are colorblindness and equal opportunity for all.

Fault and cause are important components of this current antidiscrimination law. Fault stresses that proof of intent is necessary to meet the antidiscrimination principle while causation specifies the particular behaviors or mini-conditions that are discriminatory to a specific group or person. However, both these components are incredibly difficult to prove. In terms of fault, those who do not behave within the narrow scope of intentional racist behavior are not deemed racist. In turn, those who do not meet such criteria feel immediate resentment for affirmative action programs for racial groups and historically underrepresented communities: "Why should they be given a break when I have done nothing to them?" is the common attitude. With regard to causation, the victims have a large burden of proof to link particular conditions to the direct, causative principle and, oftentimes, these conditions cannot be proven with tangible evidence and are thus categorized as mere conditions beyond the scope of legal jurisdiction.

The field of CRT examines how law constructs race, not so much in the sense that a group of judges sat down and determined what race would look like. Rather, legal doctrine over time, shaped and was shaped by race. CRT scholars Richard Delgado and Jean Stefancic (2017) goes further to argue how certain racial groups dominate the legal profession, which can further shape legal thought within those group frames. This is important especially in the area of civil and minority rights legislation. Any legal research that highlights civil rights legislation is consequential for historically underrepresented groups, creating very real conditions and so-called remedies for their lives. For example, affirmative action decisions changed the nature of affirmative action programs and ultimately caused the termination of all such programs, thereby shutting out many racial groups from protection and benefits in housing, education, and employment. Immigration law cases have also influenced anti-immigration legislation, thereby shutting out thousands of both legal and illegal immigrants from basic health and social services, legal and police protection. As Delgado and Stefancic (2017) includes, "Courts do cite law review articles. Judges, even when they do not rely on an article expressly, may still read and be informed by it. What courts do clearly matters in our society" (p. 51). Policy makers, legislators, and educators read law review articles, and if they read civil rights scholarship that is not grounded in the experiences of racial group members, dominant ideologies may be maintained and held intact.

Critical race scholars also argue that resistance and social change can occur in a variety of forms (Crenshaw, Gotanda, Peller & Thomas, 1995). For example, because legal scholarship is constituted by ideologies of race and power, CRT scholars can create new, oppositional accounts of race that run counter to dominant legal narratives. They also can learn the tools, reading practices, and tactical and strategic skills for de- or re-constructing legal discourse. But, CRT scholars also remind us that for social change to really occur, there must be several simultaneous actions: changing law school curriculum and pedagogy and recruiting and supporting a diverse faculty and student body. Here, resistance exists in many forms: individual scholarship, collective activism, and community action. Resistance and social change to the legal arena require a number of different groups to engage in pointed action. Scholars can provide useful critiques of the law, which many other lawyers and judges read. Students can push for more politically useful curriculum. Communities and movements can work with legal scholars to devise strategic agendas to attain rights and reform best suited for their needs. Change is indeed possible here. While CRT scholars seem to only speak of resistance in general terms, they promise contextualized strategies for certain cases and types of law (e.g., desegregation law, property law).

The US racial state ideologies of multiculturalism and colorblindness, and a racially biased legal system, all demonstrate the operations and effects of racialization and the deployment of race in context of power. This view of our society may be overwhelming to digest, but it should propel us to continually ask questions about the seemingly neutral and colorblind structures, policies, and procedures embedded in the legal sphere and throughout society.

As discussed throughout this chapter, race involves much more than just biological attributes that we are born with. Moreover, racism constitutes much more than conscious, intentional, direct, obvious, and provable actions. From a critical intercultural communication perspective, race stands as a set of social constructs created in and through conditions, contexts, and structures of power that are used to categorize, differentiate, and hierarchically order specific groups over others (also known as racialization). Racialization occurs in everyday society and across contexts such as the governmental and legal system, educational sphere, economic marketplace, and media (television, film, social media, Web).

Summary

As a counterpoint to the dominant view of race as irrelevant or biological in nature, this chapter highlights how race is a taken-for-granted structural formation that is *personally lived and experienced* by everyday persons in both macro contexts and micro instances (interactions). A critical intercultural communication perspective reveals how race is framed by structures of power and is used to hierarchically order cultural groups over and against one another.

Keywords

Colorblindness
Critical race theory (CRT)
Legal rationality
Multiculturalism
Perpetrator perspective
Post-racial society
Race
Race as a social construct

Racial discrimination
Racial order
Racial power
Racial state
Racialization
Racist act
Victim perspective

Questions and Activities

REFLECTION activity: Race in your life

- Ponder how the concept of race plays out in your life. Is race something you think about on a daily basis? How so?
- If race is not something you think about, why do you think that is the case?
- To what extent is race relevant and meaningful to society today? How so?
- To what extent are we a post-racial society today?

REFLECTION activity: How race plays out in our neighborhoods

For this reflection activity, we will apply a critical intercultural communication approach to race in terms of our neighborhoods.

- Map or sketch out your neighborhood in terms of its racial or ethnic group residents and research the demographics of that neighborhood.
  - Sketch or map out the neighborhood in which you lived when growing up or the one in which you live now—use a paper and pencil or use shapes and/or a draw tool on one of your electronic devices (phone, tablet, computer). Demarcate which racial or ethnic groups lived in which parts of your neighborhood and/or surrounding area (the boundaries). Use shapes and arrows. Take a picture of that image and upload to this journal entry.
  - Look up the racial or ethnic demographics of your mapped neighborhood through the following web link:
    www.nytimes.com/projects/census/2010/map.html
- Place your mouse/cursor directly into the map and hold down and move it to your designated mapped neighborhood (the one you mapped).
- Scroll your mouse/cursor over the specific county of your mapped neighborhood. As you do this, examine the box that comes up with the racial or ethnic group population percentages and the noted change in that population since 2000. Do the same for the surrounding counties of your mapped neighborhood.

Based on these steps, answer *all* of the following questions:

- What did you remember about your mapped neighborhood? Was or is your mapped neighborhood a diverse one? Which racial or ethnic groups reside or resided there? Was or is there much interaction among these groups? What was or is the community like?

- How did your map or sketch compare with the information displayed on the web link?

- Is your mapped neighborhood a diverse one according to the web link?

- Are the same racial or ethnic groups in that neighborhood? Any new ones?

- How much change has happened since 2000 according to the map link data? What do you notice about the surrounding counties in terms of the racial or ethnic group data from the website?

- How would a critical intercultural communication approach view your mapped neighborhood?

- Now, discuss the extent to which your mapped neighborhood space is a racially segregated cultural space (or one in which racial or ethnic groups live in designated areas or enclaves that are separate and closed off from one another).

- How are our neighborhoods marked by racial difference and race?

DISCUSSION activity: A training intervention

Discuss the following questions in dyads and then come together as a larger group:

- If you were told that you needed to complete a racial bias training at work, what would be your initial reaction?

- What do you see as the importance of this training?

- Why do you think it was required?

- What concepts from this chapter do you think should be a part of the training and why?

- What about other concepts?

- How much impact do you think this training will have on eradicating racial bias in the workplace? Why? How so?

Chapter 9

Global Flows and Intercultural Communication

Learning Objectives

➤ To explore globalization as a structure (and context) of power that impacts our intercultural relations

➤ To better understand global culture and its circulation and fragmentation of cultural meanings and how these shape our intercultural encounters

➤ To reflect upon how global flows empower or disempower us

Introduction: Char and Globalization

Char was home at last. It had been 10 years since she reunited with her extended family in San Mateo, California—part of Northern California, north of the Silicon Valley where computers, start-ups, and promised fortunes abound. She was happy to be with her family, albeit in a two-bedroom apartment. This was not the Tonga she grew up in (in Nuku'alofa), but it still felt like home with the familiar smells of 'Ota ika, feke, and kumala. The foods, language, and family were all here in the diaspora to California and it felt so wonderful. Having family together on the weekends and at the frequent family celebrations (birthdays, weddings, voyages) made Char so happy and grateful. Char smiled whenever she was with her parents. They were getting older

and she needed to help them and her larger family in the Bay Area and in Tonga. That was her responsibility.

Char drove the Google-mapping cars all over the Bay Area to record the images and coordinates for the popular Google maps. Char was not an engineer or programmer who made the larger salaries; instead, she was part of the workforce that the Silicon Valley rarely talks about. Rather than the rich Silicon Valley elite class, Char worked an essential but lower-position and lower-paying job (like the truck drivers for Amazon, the janitors for companies, or the bus drivers for the commuter buses). She would take her earnings and make sure that her immediate family was taken care of and then she would send a portion of her money to family in Tonga and to her cousins who were in other parts of the world (Australia, Canada) trying to make a living. Char was part of the global workforce through which technology, internet and Web applications dominated the landscape for the world and yet was also a "cog" in a machine built on the extremes of income inequality, disparate access to housing, and promised fortune. Char was part of the globalization landscape, dependent on it, and yet rendered invisible by it at the same time.

Char's story reveals how our intercultural environments are constituted by global flows of goods, people, and meanings. These flows are uneven and dominated by specific forces, but they also provide new opportunities to recreate cultural identities and forms of expression. However, the West has had the most cultural influences spread throughout the world. As global shifts and local meanings combine all over the world, intercultural communication is continually being broken down and remade. Consider the following:

- American English pervades as one of the major global languages to date, with the increasing popularity of English language instruction across multiple countries.
- US-based capital reigns supreme in global markets as Western ideas, products, and meanings (Nike, Coca-Cola, NBA, Starbucks, Apple, Disney, Microsoft) have circulated to the most remote areas of the world.
- The influence of world religions and philosophies of Islam, Hinduism, and Buddhism has spread across Western countries.
- Current and past Hollywood television programs such as *Game of Thrones, Homeland, Modern Family, The Big Bang Theory, CSI: Crime Scene Investigation, Baywatch, Dallas, Melrose Place,* and *Fresh Prince of Bel-Air* have grown popular in parts of Europe, Asia, Australia, and Latin America, depicting specific versions of the West (and of the United States in particular).
- Faraway and diverse cultures that were once remote (Thai, Asian Indian, Burma, Ethiopia, Pacific Islander, Korea, among others) are now more accessible through globalized ethnic music, media forms, literature, fashion, and cuisine.
- Ethnic products, trends, and meanings (henna, yoga, feng shui, tattoos, sari) have also become global forms of culture in high demand in the Western market.
- Latin American telenovelas are increasing in popularity among immigrant groups in the United States and Europe.
- Rap and hip-hop groups have emerged in India, Samoa, Iran, Pakistan, Turkey, Russia, and Korea and follow similar musical styles (beats, rhythms) and patterns to US-based rap and hip-hop artists (namely African American artists).
- Social networking sites (Facebook, Twitter, Instagram, Snapchat), media platforms (You Tube), and communication channels (Facetime, Skype, Google Hangout) enable

These logos represent well-known global brands and companies.

individuals in different parts of the world to communicate instantaneously and frequently in convenient, accessible, inexpensive, and enjoyable ways. Individuals can more easily share their cultures with one another through these forums.

- Globalization and its effects surround us in an ever-changing world. Globalization as a structural, economic, and cultural force, though large in scope and nature, touches and shapes our private intercultural encounters, relations, and cultural identity formations.

In addition, globalization greatly influences how we see other parts of the world (nations, countries, East, West, Mideast), other peoples around the globe (cultures, civilizations, communities, citizens), and the relationship between ourselves in our localized context and others in a global society (Beynon & Dunkerley, 2014; Kraidy, 2017). This chapter will discuss globalization as a structure and force of power that dramatically transforms our intercultural relations, encounters, and contexts and in ways that we may not fully notice.

The Global Age

Each one of us is situated in a global world in the global age, meaning that we live in a larger society through which we are connected in various ways that were not possible during the childhood days of our grandparents. According to several globalization scholars such as John Beynon and David Dunkerley (2014) and Saskia Sassen (1991, 1998, 2018), these connections occur by way of travel, mobility, electronic media, the internet, business enterprises, and circuits of labor. Simply put, globalization refers to the dynamic flow of people, goods, money (capital), and cultural meanings. All these entities move in unpredictable ways across continents, vast oceans, national boundaries, and cultural communities. However, as discussed in this chapter, globalization is not a purely positive force that is free from complications around power. In fact, globalization is rife with issues of power and ideology (as discussed in chapter 4), such as uneven flows of money and cultural meanings, which often lead to inequalities among nations and communities and the imposition of cultural ways of life onto others. These issues of power undoubtedly impact and construct our intercultural encounters with individuals from around the world as well as the production of our knowledge about other cultures and the globe. In order to better understand its nature, it is important to define globalization and its key attributes.

Defining Globalization

Globalization is a much-studied concept and phenomenon. Economists examine globalization in terms of its economic impacts and the patterns of investment, capital, products, and labor between and across national markets. Differently, anthropologists view globalization as a sociopolitical force that triggers unique intercultural exchanges between and among groups and the intermingling of meanings and practices between and across cultural groups. Thus, you can view globalization in terms of different foci—whether it is in terms of its tangible products and effects (economic impacts) or fleeting social relations and consequences (newly defined relationships, encounters, and meanings between and among cultural groups). Through a critical intercultural communication perspective, this chapter views globalization as the interplay between structural and economic forces and the cultural meanings of people and groups that result from economically influenced shifts. More specifically, **globalization** is the structural shift toward greater internationalization of the capitalist economy, rooted in the multinational firm, transnational labor, the migrations of peoples, the de-emphasis of the nation state, and the dynamic production of cultural identities (see e.g., Barker, 2000; Barker & Jane, 2016; Beynon & Dunkerley, 2014; Kraidy, 2017; Sassen, 2018). Such a definition highlights some important attributes of globalization.

Key Attributes of Globalization

There are several attributes of globalization to consider in terms of issues of power and intercultural communication. These attributes include the following:

1. Globalization is first and foremost a consequential economic structure of power.
2. As a result of globalization, cultures are no longer bound to specific geographic places (e.g., East Asian cultures are not fixed to or present only in Asia).
3. There is a rapidly moving circulation of cultural images and mediated texts and forms across national boundaries.
4. There are increasing (albeit somewhat narrowly) flows of global commodities and products around the world.
5. With the creation of global cities and global culture, Western-style consumerism and capitalism are spread throughout the globe.
6. People are migrating to new sites and places across the globe.
7. The framing of what is culturally authentic is changing.
8. Globalization also gives way to the creation of hybrid identities and forms of expression.
9. Capitalism also becomes more flexible and moves across nations in the global context.

In the next section, each attribute of globalization is explained in terms of the power implications in relation to our intercultural communication encounters and relationships.

Globalization and Economic Power

Globalization is first and foremost a consequential economic structure of power. Beynon and Dunkerley (2014) are quick to point out that globalization is ultimately an economic force and a power that concretely and swiftly changes how people live, think, behave, and fare in the world. As an economic force, globalization involves the financial investment and participation of certain nations into the economies of other nations, especially when it comes to Western capitalistic practices. For example, the United States has long established an economic presence in other nations, such as China, Japan, and Mexico, among others, through its acquisition of companies in those countries and/or the investment of capital in those nations in terms of using their labor forces to assemble products (automobiles, goods). The often heavy involvement of nations in other national economies is not a new phenomenon; it began in the age of empire or colonialism (as Anne McClintock, 2013, explains) when Western/European nations invaded and seized other nations (England over India, Hong Kong; France over Vietnam, Spain and the United States over the Phillippines, Japan over Korea, France over Algeria, to name just a few in a very long list of colonialist relations) via exploration, the use of technology, religion (Western Judeo-Christian faiths), and language.

Likewise, the economic involvement of certain nations into others is not random or innocent; it is characterized by the wielding of power and influence by dominant nations over marginalized ones. This is to say that globalization does not just happen as a result or trend of the market (a notion that economic theory seems to project). These involvements or impositions are demonstrations of the accumulated strength and predominance of Western nations over non-Western ones throughout time and from as early as the 1700s (McClintock, 2013).

A prime illustration of globalization as an economic structure of power lies in how, according to Barker (2000) and Beynon & Dunkerley (2014), global media production and circulation is held by a small number of US corporations. Moreover, a small number of transnational corporations has always dominated global markets of products; transnational corporations such as Royal Dutch Shell, Ford, and General Motors have represented the world's largest economic producers of between one-third and one-half of world output (Barker, 2000). These companies have had a substantial percentage (in some cases, over 60%) of their sales and profits from outside of their home country. According to the International Labor Organization, since 1996, the US represents 31 of the 50 most profitable firms, and seven of the top ten. The most profitable, however, was Shell (the Netherlands)—with profits of $8.9 billion. Most of the largest American and European companies in terms of revenue are also the largest in terms of foreign assets. As of 2008, some of the largest American companies, by revenue, are WalMart, GM, Chevron, and Exxon Mobil (Global Policy Forum). By foreign assets, the largest American companies are Walmart, Exxon Mobil, Chevron, GM, General Electric, and Ford (Paine, 2000). According to Hearn and Parkin (2001), "Shell, which is the only European company among the ten largest by revenue, also had the largest amount foreign assets ($79.7 billion and growing) since 1995 (*p. 128*).

Another example of globalization as an economic force can be seen in the US publication, *Business Week*'s, annual ranking of the most valuable global brands or those companies with significant influence in major markets around the world. In the 2009 ranking, the United States possessed 13 of the top 20 global brands, including Coca-Cola, IBM, Microsoft, GE, McDonalds's, Google, and Disney, among others. By comparison, only two non-Western

01	02	03	04	04	06	07	08
Apple	Google	Microsoft	Coca-Cola	amazon	SAMSUNG	TOYOTA	f
+3%	+6%	+10%	-5%	+29%	+9%	-6%	+48%
184,154 $m	141,703 $m	79,999 $m	69,733 $m	64,796 $m	54,249 $m	50,291 $m	48,188 $m
09	10	11	12	13	14	15	16
Mercedes	IBM	GE	McDonald's	BMW	Disney	intel	CISCO
+10%	-11%	+3%	+5%	0%	+5%	+7%	+3%
47,829 $m	46,829 $m	44,208 $m	41,533 $m	41,521 $m	40,772 $m	39,459 $m	31,190 $m
17	18	19	20	21	22	23	24
ORACLE	Nike	LOUIS VUITTON	HONDA	SAP	pepsi	H&M	ZARA
+3%	+8%	-4%	+3%	+6%	+1%	-10%	+11%
27,466 $m	27,021 $m	22,919 $m	22,696 $m	22,635 $m	20,491 $m	20,488 $m	18,573 $m
25	26	27	28	29	30	31	32
IKEA	Gillette	AMERICAN EXPRESS	Pampers	UPS	J.P.Morgan	HERMÈS PARIS	Budweiser
+4%	-9%	-3%	+2%	+7%	+11%	+2%	+11%
18,472 $m	18,200 $m	17,787 $m	16,416 $m	16,387 $m	15,749 $m	15,375 $m	13,210 $m

This figure displays Interbrand's annual ranking of the most valuable global brands or those companies with significant influence in major markets around the world. Note that most of the countries with top-grossing global brands are in the West.

countries (Japan, South Korea) had brands in the top 20 ranking (Brown, 2015). The global market is therefore dominated by Western and mostly US corporate power and capital.

Given this, the notion that globalization yields a flat, equal, free-flowing and equal opportunity arena of goods, jobs, and products for all nations can easily be disputed (as discussed by columnist Thomas Friedman, author of the best-selling book, *The World is Flat*, 2015). Rather, today's global market actively (and continually) yields a disproportionate and uneven economy that favors and privileges specific nations over others (and namely those nations that have gained ample influence, capital, and market presence over time through colonialism) (Barker, 2000). This uneven set of economics ultimately creates an asymmetrical power relationship among nations of the world, with mostly Western and European countries as possessing the most market and financial control and gain. With such power configurations from globalization as an economic structure, money and capital also drive the capacity of some nations to sell or brand their wares and products all over the world (and with great demand), establish important business and trade arrangements with other nations in need of economic gain, and create the need for labor (via manufacturing and production outlets) in other countries (to cut costs). The capacity to do all of these enables richer countries (the drivers of globalization) to also yield great cultural influence and control over others as well, in terms of the construction of culture, identities, and social values and meanings (as discussed in the next several attributes).

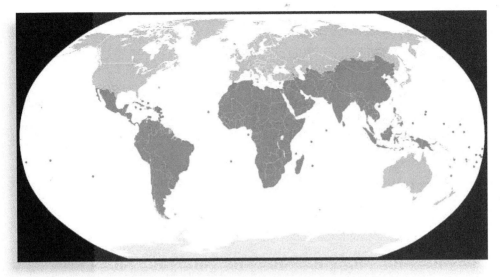

This map displays the Global North (U.S.A, Canada, Western Europe, Hong Kong, South Korea, Singapore, Taiwan, Japan, Israel, Australia, and New Zealand) which is deemed as having more wealth, resources, and development. The Global South (Africa, Latin America, developing Asia, Middle East) is also displayed and framed as poor, less developed, and more populated.

The power dynamics embedded in globalization can be seen in the terms used to identify the haves and have nots of the parties involved.

- **The West vs. The Rest:** These terms highlight the global power of Western countries (one-fourth) over the rest of the world (three-fourths), which has been colonized and disadvantaged in terms of resources, capital, and cultural circulation in terms of values, ideas, and ideologies.

- **The Global North vs. The Global South:** These terms refer to the global socioeconomic and political inequalities between two sets of nations (Parnell & Oldfield, 2014). The Global North speaks to the power of the United States, Canada, Western Europe, Hong Kong, South Korea, Singapore, Taiwan, Japan, Israel, Australia, and New Zealand. The Global North (with only one-fourth of the world's population) is characterized as having more wealth, resources, and development and thus dominates the world's income. By contrast, the Global South (Africa, Latin America, developing Asia, Middle East) is deemed as poor, less developed, and more populated (with three-fourth of the world's population) but generating less of the world's income (Parnell & Oldfield, 2014; Roberts & Parks, 2006).

Cultures Are Not Always Fixed to Place

As a result of globalization, cultures are no longer bound to specific geographic places (e.g., East Asian cultures are not fixed to or present only in Asia). When we think of cultural groups and their identities, we typically associate these with a specific geographic place or country (nation). For example, Latin American communities, their traditions, and products are thought of as being located only in Latin America; Asian identities, practices, and images can be found in Asian nations. However, globalization has changed what used to be a reliable and tight connection between culture, place, and identity. In this vein, anthropologists Smadar Lavie and Ted Swedenburg (1996) highlight how modernity and globalization, with its spread of technological and media advancements, capitalism, and new modes of mobility and travel, have opened up what used to be hardened borders, boundaries, and closed territories. There are a few ways in which globalization has loosened up cultures from their geographic place of origin.

Global conditions of intercultural context

Globalization created conditions (colonialist invasion, emigration of new labor sources, advancements in travel and mobility technology) through which cultures that never encountered one another before, met and came into (forced) intercultural contact. As discussed earlier, colonialism (the earliest form of globalization) through which Western nations invaded and seized specific territories and lands that were homes to other indigenous groups and governing structures, undoubtedly forced cultural change and exposed once closed lands to other groups (namely colonialist governments and their subjects) (Barker, 2000; Barker & Jane, 2016; Beynon & Dunkerley, 2014). Thus, cultures were pried open and their once rigid boundaries (politically, geographically, economically, and socially) were dismantled. Specific nations and their governing structures (and citizens) could enter in, travel through, reside in, and explore countries and lands that were formerly difficult to access. For example, Hong Kong, with its colonialist subjugation by the British (from mainland China), became an open, accessible space for Westerners, Europeans, and groups from all over the world. Language practices, traditions, and social life were transformed by such colonialist shifts in power. Cultural groups encountered one another in these new settings (and amid loosened political and geographic boundaries) and most often in disproportionate ways (with one group possessing more political, social, and economic power over another).

As a result of colonialism, nations were subjected to colonial rule, new forms of governance, and economic structures. Part of this entailed the emigration of labor sources (groups of workers) from other countries, often at cheaper wages and for short-term stays for colonialist governments. As one example, the Kingdom of Hawai'i was illegally overthrown and annexed by the United States; under this new authority, the United States encouraged the emigration of other cultural groups—Filipinos, Koreans, Chinese, and Portuguese—from outside Hawai'i to come to the islands and work on the sugar and pineapple plantations. Thus, colonialism not only created internal change (new governing, religious, and social structures) within subjugated nations, but also caused external change or the influx of immigrant groups into those nations (see Barker, 2000).

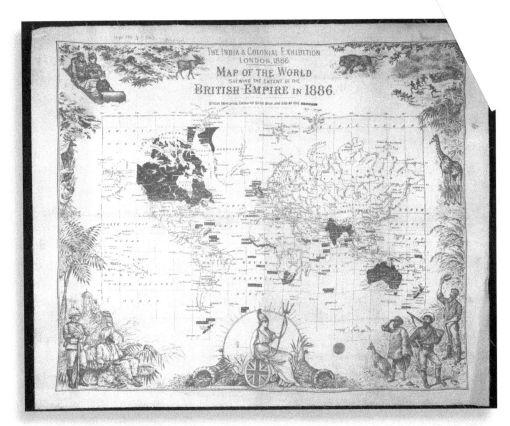

This map of the British Empire in 1886 shows the long reach of England's colonialism across multiple continents, which was made possible through early stages of globalization.

Global advancements in technology

Through modernization, industrialization, and globalization, there occurred great technological advancement in the capacity to travel across continents and vast lands, from a matter of days to mere hours. Airplane and ship travel improved and advanced in terms of machinery and affordability of cost. In the early 1900s, only the very wealthy could afford to travel by ship (which took weeks and days) to travel from the continental United States to the South Pacific; a trip that today most can afford and can reach in five hours. With such advances in modern-day travel and mobility, cultural group members could access other cultures and the potential for intercultural interaction among groups dramatically increased. As a result, not only could other cultural group members visit and traverse other cultures, but the members themselves could leave their own lands and visit others. There was an unmistakable flow in and out of cultural lands in the modern age that afforded new opportunities and challenges for intercultural contact (Beynon & Dunkerley, 2014). However, the flow was not as open as one would think; socioeconomics (cost of travel, access to leisure time, social class) factored in to who could travel to other lands and who could not. This uneven movement of who can travel (due to socioeconomic access and privilege) and who cannot, is due to the globalized conditions of power. Some cultures are always visited and thus, grow to be dependent on tourist revenue (e.g., Bali,

Mexico, Hawai'i, among others). The tourism industry therefore has shaped specific economic exchanges between cultural members and visitors as well as encounters that question and/or demand the authenticity of cultures in order to experience the real country they are visiting.

Cultural Images Move Across Boundaries

There is a rapidly moving circulation of cultural images and mediated texts and forms across national boundaries. In relation to the global unbinding of cultures from their geographic boundaries, the circulation of cultural ideas and images in media and popular culture have also created new intercultural encounters and cultural impressions, versions, and forms. With the onset of dominant media (films, televisions, music videos) that accelerated from the 1980s through the 1990s, cultural images from outlets such as MTV, network television, and Hollywood films, grew in number. We were able to see music videos with African, African American, Asian, and Latino/a influences. Hollywood featured some stand-alone films set in other cultural settings (*Hidden Figures, Fences, Ghandi, Mississippi Masala, Gran Torino, Black Panther, Selma, My Big Fat Greek Wedding, Smoke Signals, The Joy Luck Club,* among others). Recent television shows such as *Empire, How to Get Away With Murder, Black-ish,, Brooklyn Nine-Nine, Orange is the New Black, The Fosters, Jane the Virgin, Shades of Blue, Quantico,* and *Fresh Off the Boat*

Bollywood films represent an influential form of global media that has circulated specific images of Hindi cinema to many countries and corners of the world. With video sharing websites like Youtube and Vimeo, Bollywood images are accessible across many cultures and countries.

have all showcased cultural groups and their experiences. However, it is in important to note that these media texts were, at one point, predominantly made in the United States and dispersed and exported to many other countries. Thus, American media images have had a greater global dispersion and reach to other countries than can be said for other countries' media products (music videos, television shows, and films) being made available to consumers in the United States. This means that historically individuals across the world have had more access to American media forms and images than to other countries or cultures' media images. For this reason, countries have resisted such access to and circulation of Western media forms. The French government in particular has created sanctions against American television imports, while satellite dishes have been deemed illegal in Saudi Arabia, Egypt, Bahrain, and Iran. Moreover, consumers in the United States have had less access to foreign images and texts; consider how many foreign films are played in local and regional theaters. You, for example, can probably only identify one theater (and no more than that) in your city that plays foreign films.

However, the circulation and distribution of popular media forms has changed dramatically in today's day and age with the creation of YouTube and Vimeo (video-sharing websites), and streaming media and video on-demand sites such as Netflix, iTunes, Hulu, Amazon Prime Instant Video, and Google Play. Now we have more access to music videos, television shows, and films from other countries and cultures beyond the United States. For instance, one can view Korean dramas, Swedish rap music videos, Bollywood movies, and telenovelas through YouTube, Vimeo, Netflix, and Hulu. Such access, albeit paid on some outlets, provides a never-before experienced window into the music and stories of other cultures. People in the United States have enjoyed this access especially since such availability has been so limited before the beginning of the democratization of media outlets and video-sharing sites in this global digital age. Consider the possibilities for intercultural communication:

- Individuals can become exposed to different cultures than ever before (Muslims, Pacific Islanders, Cambodians, Black British, Jamaicans, among many more).

- Individuals in the United States can have more access to information and narratives from or about other cultures beyond the United States. They no longer have to rely on that one foreign film playing in that one theater or wait for the more popularized or mainstream foreign films (often backed by the larger Hollywood studios) to come to mainstream networks or video-on-demand sites. This will help provide initial doorways for meeting other cultures and create the catalyst for interest into other cultures, which could set the tone for positive intercultural contact. On the other side of that, the images or videos may also negatively depict other cultures. Although, with more video-sharing sites and social media channels, cultural members can provide more narratives and content, thereby providing a range of cultural experiences. There also stands an unequal proportion of popularized media texts from the United States to other parts of the world (which is plentiful) in comparison to the opposite direction.

- Individuals of cultures from all over the world can create their own video stories about their identities and share these on YouTube or through social media outlets such as Facebook, Instagram, Snapchat, or Twitter. Thus, cultural members exercise more creative control over their own cultural stories and the enactment of their cultural identities. This helps to create a larger global community of intercultural creators of media content and popular culture than just the dominant media industries (studios, networks, mainstream music labels).

The Flows of Global Commodities

There are increasing (albeit somewhat narrowly) flows of global commodities and products around the world. Similar to the circulation of cultural images through media texts and forms, another key aspect of globalization is the flow of commodities and cultural products throughout the world. According to the rankings of global brands from Forbes and Brandirectory, Apple, Google, Microsoft, Facebook, Coca-Cola, Amazon, Disney, Toyota, McDonald's, and Samsung stand as the top grossing global companies in the world. More specifically, the United States possesses the highest number (56) of global brands, followed by Germany (11), France (7), Japan (6), Switzerland (4), Spain (3), Belgium, Korea, the Netherlands and Sweden (2 each), and Austria, China, Denmark, Ireland, U.K. (all with 1). Thus, even though globalization is often framed, theorized, and discussed as opening the sharing and exposure of global ideas and images, it is important to note that only a small number of global brands and companies dominate the ownership, control, and circulation of specific cultural products and commodities for the world. As the critical intercultural perspective illustrates, only a handful of companies dominate the power reins of the global flow of products. So, many countries and their people will know what an iPhone is or spend a great deal of time "Googling" information (or listening to "Alexa"), playing games on their Microsoft tablets, sharing photos on Facebook while ordering their favorite items through Amazon Prime, and/or watching Disney movies and ordering McDonald's big macs. The circulation of specific global products from these companies is widespread in terms of its popular visibility, while many cannot partake in consuming these items due to the costs that are required (high product prices, subscription fees). But, these global products are indeed known and often coveted. The circulation of global goods and the specific meanings associated with these products are also not free-flowing in terms of having all nations having equal access to these goods. But, there is more distribution and visibility of these goods as compared to local, regional, or national products such as specialty foods, attire, and artifacts. Thus, some argue that the global flow of commodities tends to create more homogenous cultural forms with specific cultural meanings from Western countries (the Global North) or parts of East Asia (Japan, China, Korea) and thus, creates a particular type of global culture. The domination of global brands by a smaller set of companies has indeed created a global culture, or a larger arena through which a certain set of goods and cultural meanings are produced, sold, consumed, and experienced by multiple nations and through which specific ideologies (or world views) are circulated and embedded. For instance, a global culture (which features goods and values from the United States, England, Australia, New Zealand, and some Asian countries, such as Japan, China, Korea) push a view that promotes materialism, status and wealth (via consumption and possession), the heralding of technology and science, the immediacy of information, masculine-driven values, and the valorization of the English language and Western ideals (individualism, low context styles).

The Spread of Western Consumerism and Capitalism

With the creation of global cities and global culture, Western-style consumerism and capitalism are spread throughout the globe. Global culture can appear to circulate more Western ideologies (meritocracy, consumerism, the goodness and necessity of technology and science, democratic voice and choice) and privilege capitalism (and its associated values). Some scholars, such as George Ritzer (2009) and Zygmunt Bauman (1998), argue that global culture ultimately homogenizes other cultures and transforms them into Westernized or more uniform cultures with Western embedded values and ideologies. Others, such as John Tomlinson (1999), Chris Barker (2000), and Saskia Sassen (1998), see the global culture as indeed providing exposure to a common set of products and ideas but that individuals represent complex beings who do not necessarily read or understand these cultural forms in the same way or even in line with dominant framings (for example, to see the United States, the West, or the Global North as superior and desirable). These two differing perspectives represent an ongoing debate in globalization and cultural studies today. We will engage this debate later in this chapter.

Global culture, however, adapts to its surrounding local, regional, and national contexts in a process known as glocalization. Glocalization refers to the adaptation of global brands to the local and ethnic identities, tastes, and preferences of its market. For instance, McDonald's changes its menu offerings and advertising depending on the local or national culture at hand. In Japan, McDonald's features the EBI filet-o-shrimp burger or one made of panko-coated shrimp with tempura sauce, lettuce, and a bun. In Middle Eastern countries, there is the McArabia, a pita bread sandwich filled with

What kind of global culture is being created through these global brands and their goods and embedded cultural meanings?

grilled chicken. McDonald's will not advertise its food or drinks in Muslim countries given the observance of Ramadan and fasting rituals. Starbucks also glocalizes its products with its Asian décor and green matcha tea drinks in Japan and rice and Cantonese style pancakes in China. In Bejing, Kentucky Fried Chicken serves porridge for breakfast. These glocalized changes made by global brands serve as a way to adapt to different localized needs while also maintaining the dominant global brand culture (and its corporate profit share across regions) (Barker, 2000; Barker & Jane, 2016; Beynon & Dunkerley, 2014).

Global Migration

People are migrating to new sites and places across the globe. Given the political changes (leadership shifts, civil wars), economic shifts (crises, loss of jobs, scarce housing and increased costs of living), and cultural uncertainties (changes in cultural communities and the decreased feelings of home and belonging) brought forth by globalization, cultural groups often migrate from their home to another site of settlement. The migration or movement of one cultural group to at least one to two sites of settlement refers to a diaspora (Clifford, 1994; Safran, 1991; Swedenburg, 1996). There have been countless diasporas throughout history: the migration of Jewish, Armenian, Afro-Caribbeans, Irish, and Germans throughout the world; Chinese communities to Cuba and Mexico; Japanese migrants to Brazil, Peru, Mexico, and Chile; Cubans to the United States; Koreans to El Salvador; Asian Indians throughout the world; Chinese to Vancouver, Canada; and many more. These diasporas occur largely because of difficult economic conditions at home and/or for political reasons through which they must leave to flee persecution. Diasporic movement can be voluntary (by choice) or involuntary (through force or limited choice in terms of survival).

When a cultural group becomes a diaspora to another site, it engages in a process of "re-homing." Re-homing refers to the ways in which cultural groups remake their new

Global chains like McDonald's and Kentucky Fried Chicken have localized their products to fit the ethnic customers of each particular country that they are in.

site of settlement into a home by creating enclaves or demarcated areas for their cultural members and shaping a community for their members. Such community building involves building neighborhoods and businesses catered to and opened by their members for economic survival.

These diasporas have become so strong and continuous over time that they are known to their cultural counterparts at home or in the primary cultural site. Communities in Mexico who want to migrate, for example, set their sights on known diasporic sites such as Redwood City, California; Riverside or San Bernardino, California; Phoenix, Arizona; and Houston, Texas, among others. Thus, diasporas develop their own interregional, cross-national circuits of identity and belonging. Because diasporas originate from political and economic shifts created by the forces of globalization, diasporic communities around the world, provide new forms of cultural exposure and intercultural interaction in regions and nations where they have not had a historical presence. Thus, the flows and circuits of cultural groups provide greater intercultural interaction potential, but these migrations also can ignite xenophobia, fear, and exclusionary measures to maintain the original citizenry of the area (giving in to nativist sentiment).

Cultural Authenticity

The framing of what is culturally authentic is changing. With diasporic migrations now occurring and sedimenting across multiple (often to eight or nine) sites of settlement, the definitions of cultural authenticity have also shifted. The questions now are, "Which is more culturally authentic?: a Russian cuisine restaurant in Moscow or a Russian cuisine restaurant in Chicago? Is the restaurant in the original homeland site always the truer, more authentic one? What constitutes the difference between the homeland site and the diasporic sites? Is there a difference at all? Is the homeland always closer to tradition and the real culture while the diasporic sites are always the lesser than, less authentic, and more modern versions of what was at home? Globalization does not provide easy answers to these questions. While there is a dichotomy between the cultural homeland and the mainstreamed (acultural) diasporic site, there is no guarantee that such a dichotomy always prevails in global contexts. There could, in fact, be the presentation of more cultural traditions in the diaspora as a way to maintain the cultural connection to the homeland. The Russian restaurant in Chicago could feature a menu and décor that is no longer in existence in the homeland, thereby flip-flopping what is deemed as the culturally true or original version of Russian culture. Globalization, therefore, stands as a vibrant context in which diasporic groups move and reconfigure their homes and what their cultures mean in that specific context. We all, therefore, interact with different and yet intermingled versions of culture, which complicates and also enriches our intercultural interactions.

At the same time, however, globalization produces some effects that defy stability, predictability, and complete domination by a power force. One of these effects is the formation of cultural hybridity (Barker, 2000; Barker & Jane, 2016; Beynon & Dunkerley, 2014). Through global flows of goods, meanings, and people, culture can become more

This image displays a Japanese family who migrated to Brazil. This family was part of the larger diaspora of Japanese to different Latin American countries such as Brazil, Argentina, Chile, and Venezuela, among others

than its original shape or form. Younger generations can take new forms of expression (rap, hip hop, video stories, blogging, photography, art, tattoos) and use these to remake their cultural voices and narratives with the recombination of multiple languages, dialects, and art forms. Samoan rap, Latin hip hop, Hinglish films, and Bollywood television shows and movies all represent examples of culturally hybrid forms of expression and creation brought forth by globalization. With the interplay of multiple cultural influences, new intercultural exposures and meetings, and the presence of more diasporas across the world, cultures are reconfiguring and redesigning themselves in unexpected and exciting ways. Scholars such as Stuart Hall (1997a) and Paul Gilroy (1993) frame cultural hybridity as an exciting resource for cultures to stay alive and connect with new generations in new cultural homes. By creating more fluid and recombined cultural expressions, perhaps cultural groups will open and expand their boundaries of membership and identity so as to connect with other cultures more in this global age.

Capitalism Moves

Capitalism also becomes more flexible and moves across nations in the global context. A marker of globalization is that Western-based capitalism (market economy) spreads across nations and cultures. This demonstrates the notion of **transnationalism**. Transnationalism refers to the uneven movement of global capitalism beyond and between single nation-states. David Harvey (2006) emphasizes the importance of flexible capitalism, which is one specific movement of transnationalism. This notion of flexible capitalism explains that with shifting

Which is the more authentic Chinese restaurant: the one on the left or the right? The one on the left displays more of a "traditional" Chinese exterior even though it is in Washington D.C. in the United States (a diasporic site). The one on the right looks more modern and contemporary and is located in China (a homeland site). Globalization has reconfigured what we mean by "cultural authenticity."

modes of labor, development, markets, and consumption, capitalism as an economic structure and ideology can move across multiple boundaries rapidly. With capitalism, national cultures and political structures also shift and change in terms of materialism, individualism, and structured economic inequalities. Transnationalism (as the structural push of capital and citizenship between and among several nation-states) has changed how groups understand their identities and belonging and their encounters with other groups. For example, Hong Kong-based Chinese have negotiated a transnational sense of who they are in relation to Hong Kong's past British rule and its tense political and ethnic connections to mainland China (Ong, 1999). Before 1997, the year when China reclaimed Hong Kong as part of its national territory, Chinese individuals in Hong Kong would carry a both a British passport and a Chinese passport, given the contention fight over the sovereignty of Hong Kong between Great Britain and China.

Taken together, these aforementioned nine characteristics highlight how globalization has undoubtedly impacted our intercultural world. There are different ways to view such globalization. One view—globalization as cultural homogenization—sees globalization as a massive reproduction of Western institutions and cultural formations over the rest of the world and thus, homogenizes places in terms of Western values and capitalism. Another view—globalization as cultural hybridization—understands globalization as the creator of a dynamic set of unpredictable, chaotic, disjointed, and multidirectional cultural flows that bring about new forms of cultural expression and cultural identities. These views point to different interpretations of the power implications of globalization and how this positions us in terms of intercultural communication.

We should remember that globalization and its aspects are not something that are "out there" or removed from our own daily existence. Globalization has that local touch on our own lives and connects our experience with the global dynamics and dimensions featured in this chapter. Consider, for example, the power aspects of globalization that emerge in the experience of this book's author living in Silicon Valley, California. The author—Rona Tamiko Halualani—has lived in East Palo Alto, California for the last 18 years, albeit in one of the first gentrified neighborhoods in the city. This is a city that exists on the Silicon Valley border, with Facebook, Amazon, and Google right around the corner. However, East Palo Alto, a city that

This image represents the British Hong Kong flag from 1959 to 1997 which marked a period when Hong Kong-based Chinese had to negotiate a transnational sense of who they were in relation to Hong Kong's past British rule and its tense political/ethnic connections to mainland China.

has long been a home for African Americans, Latinos, and Pacific Islanders in an area framed as an economically depressed and crime-fueled space is experiencing dramatic change to globalization. What was once deemed the "murder capital of the country" is now characterized by gentrification (the creation of new, higher-priced homes and the displacement of local residents of color) and by the influx of large businesses and technology companies to occupy more affordable leases. Globalization has therefore exerted its presence through the influx of technology companies (and their demand), higher-priced homes in an area with scarce housing, and a distinct separation between white collar professionals (entrepreneurs, engineers, programmers/coders, doctors, lawyers) and service workers (delivery drivers, customer service agents, retail clerks, janitors, inventory stockers). The author works as a university professor in the area, and it is interesting that most of her students will seek employment in this globalized economy of Silicon Valley and in terms of the economic classes. Globalization has also put the emphasis on professions and jobs that advance technology, science, and business over those in education, social work, nonprofits, social justice, and/or community building. East Palo Alto now houses Amazon (which has dominated the delivery of consumer goods) and is located near Facebook, Google, and YouTube. This city also still houses longtime residents of color who have been displaced and still face economic challenges as opposed to the ample startup wealth and capital in Silicon Valley (which mostly benefit Asian, Asian Indian, and White/European American professionals). There is now a disproportionately uneven hierarchy of the haves and have nots and a separating out of the wealthy from the middle class and the working class in the area. Globalization has changed the capital coming into the city of East Palo Alto and its composition and yet at the same time has exacerbated the disparity between the affluent homeowners and technology workers who have moved into the area and the longtime residents of color (namely Blacks/African Americans, Latino/as, and Pacific Islanders) who have settled in the area. What was once considered the worst area to be in and the city you want to avoid (especially at night) is now fast becoming a gentrified locale where global technology sectors, big-box retail outfits, and upper middle class suburban life (with the influx of Asian/Asian American and White/European American families) have arrived.

Power Dynamics and Implications of Globalization

It is important to consider the power dynamics and implications of globalization. Key questions that arise include the following:

- Are we growing together or further apart in this increasingly global society?

- Is cultural identity something to be kept pure or something to be enriched through mixing and matching?

- To what extent does a global capitalist economy lead to more intense Western domination or a more vibrant world filled with possibilities for resistance?

- How does globalization impact and shape cultural group authenticity and intercultural relations between groups?

- To what extent does globalization impose Americanized culture (in the form of television, videos, pop music, films and other Western goods) on vulnerable communities unable to protect themselves?"

- To what extent does globalization lead to more homogenization or hybridization of meanings and culture?

- Critical scholar Chris Barker (2000) asks: "If Africans listen to some forms of Western music, watch some forms of Western television and buy Western-produced consumer goods, cannot this be read as domination or false consciousness? Does the consumption of Western goods have the same meanings and outcomes in Africa as it may in the West?" (p. 44)

What is clear is that globalization has historically and continually ushered in a set of power shifts, economic and political changes, and an uneven flow of cultural forms and influences. How we understand and experience our own cultures and that of others has inevitably changed due to globalization—whether that change occurs within that culture and/or that culture enacts more rigid boundaries to ward off any external cultural influences. What do you think of globalization and how it impacts intercultural communication? Which view of globalization—globalization as cultural homogenization or cultural hybridization—resonates the most with you and why? We ought to pay serious attention to the global environment as it continues to change every day, for our lives and for those of our cultural communities, and for how we relate to one another.

Summary

Globalization stands as a major structure and force of power that has forever changed our intercultural relations, encounters, and contexts. The characteristics of globalization and global culture all highlight how rapid and continuous shifts in meaning, access, and cultural influence occur across the world. Two primary views—globalization as cultural homogenization vs. globalization as cultural hybridization—dominate the global landscape as new economic, political, and cultural shifts emerge on a daily basis, thereby impacting our cultural identities and contexts and our intercultural communication exchanges and relations.

Keywords

Cultural homogenization

Cultural hybridity

Diaspora

Global flows

Global North

Global South

Globalization

Glocalization

Transnationalism

Questions and Activities

REFLECTION activity: Global brands activity with accompanying journal entry: Please closely go through each of the following links. Each of these links identifies the top grossing global brands and companies. These links also indicate the countries of origin for each of the brands/companies.

- https://www.forbes.com/powerful-brands/list/#tab:rank
- https://www.forbes.com/sites/kurtbadenhausen/2017/05/23/the-worlds-most-valuable-brands-2017-by-the-numbers/#4c6d800a303d
- http://brandirectory.com/league_tables/table/global-500-2017

As you go through each of the links, see if you can trace one or two of the global brands or companies by looking up its products (you may need to do a Google search on the brands or companies). What do you notice about the products?

Write in response to the following questions:

- What conclusions can you draw regarding the top global brands and companies?
- Which countries seem to hold the top spots?
- What kinds of brands or companies dominate the rankings?
- To what extent were you surprised by the rankings and information?

Write in response to the following questions:

- What conclusions can you draw regarding the top global brands and companies?
- Which countries seem to hold the top spots?
- What kinds of brands or companies dominate the rankings?
- To what extent were you surprised by the rankings and information?
- In terms of this chapter's focus on globalization and the global flow of goods, people, and meanings, what kind of impact do you think these global brands and companies have on different parts of the world? Do you think these rankings indicate that there is cultural domination (and therefore cultural homogenization) by certain brands? Or, might it be more complex than this? How so? Discuss.

REFLECTION activity: Globalization-focused video and accompanying journal entry:

- Select one of the two following globalization video options to view.
- Become familiar with your selected video.
- Then, identify and discuss two major takeaways or key insights that you gained and found fascinating

- Option #1:
  o *Freightened—The Real Price of Shipping*
  o Ninety percent of the goods we consume in the West are manufactured in far-off lands and brought to us by ship. The cargo shipping industry is a key player in world economy and forms the basis of our very model of modern civilization; without it, it would be impossible to fulfill the ever-increasing demands of our societies. Yet the functioning and regulations of this business remain largely obscure to many, and its hidden costs affect us all. Due to their size, freight ships no longer fit in traditional city harbors; they have moved out of the public's eye, behind barriers and check points. The film answers questions such as "Who pulls the strings in this multi-billion dollar business? To what extent does the industry control our policy makers? How does it affect the environment above and below the water line? What's life like for modern seafarers?" Taking us on a journey overseas and oceans, *Freightened* reveals, in an audacious investigation, the many faces of world-wide freight shipping and sheds light on the consequences of an all-but-visible industry.
  o Running Time: 53 mins
  o Year: 2016

- Option #2:
  - *Sweatshop: Deadly Fashion Bloggers Spend Time as Garment Workers in Cambodia*
  - It started off as a web-series, charting the experiences of three young fashion bloggers who spent a month living the life of Cambodian garment workers in Phnom Penh. But following headlines and articles all over the world, more than a million hits and lots of inquiries, the Web series has been re-versioned into an hour-long documentary.
  - Frida, Anniken, and Ludwig live, breathe and dream fashion. They spend hundreds of euros every month on clothes and make a living promoting the latest catwalk trends. Except for speculation that factory workers must be used to their hard lives, they have never given much thought to the people who make their clothes. Now, they're trading their comfortable lives for those of Cambodian garment workers. As well as working in the factories, they have to survive on $3 a day. But this is no exploitative documentary, relying on shock value. It poignantly shows the consequences of cheap fashion.
  - Running Time: 54 mins
  - Year: 2015

REFLECTION activity: Globalization in your life:
Think about globalization and its key characteristics as discussed in this chapter.

- What are some examples of how globalization touches your life and everyday experience? In terms of where you live and work and socialize? Your roles and job? What you like to eat and consume? In terms of who you interact with?
- How is globalization localized in our experience? How does our local experience impact global flows of power?

DISCUSSION activity:
Discuss the following in small groups and then with the entire class.

- Reflect on this chapter's material. What do you think of globalization and how it impacts intercultural communication?
- Which view of globalization—globalization as cultural homogenization or cultural hybridization—resonates the most with you and why?
- What are the limits *and* possibilities afforded by globalization today?

DISCUSSION activity: Predicting Globalization:

Discuss the following in small groups and then with the entire class.

- Create a prediction about what the role and impact of globalization will be like in 10 years.
- Will globalization still be a major factor or will national boundaries and powers be more prevalent?
- To what extent will globalization still be a dominant force? How so?
- What will this mean culturally, economically, and politically? What will this mean for individuals and groups and how they can resist forces of power?

Chapter 10

Intercultural Relationships and Power

Learning Objectives

▸ To understand the role power plays in private, one-on-one intercultural friendships and romantic relationships

▸ To identify the unexpected ways in which power operates and manifests in our intercultural relationships

▸ To understand how intercultural desire for specific cultural group members, is shaped by power

Introduction: Meg and John in an Intercultural Romantic Relationship

Because this chapter focuses on intercultural relationships and how people connect with one another, five narratives that highlight different aspects of intercultural relationships will be featured throughout this chapter.

In the first narrative, John is a second-generation Korean American male who lives in the San Francisco Bay Area. He attends a four-year university and has been busy with his classes, a part-time job at an electronics store, and a new significant other. His new girlfriend is Meg, who hails from Los Angeles and attends the same school as John. They met in a communication class a year ago and have been inseparable ever since. John and Meg spend as much time as possible with one another. They have met each other's friends and Meg even introduced John to her parents. But, John has yet to do the same. He is anxious about introducing Meg to his traditional first-generation Korean parents because Meg is part Black and fourth-generation Chinese. It is the fact that Meg is part Black that worries John. Meg is worried about John's reservations in terms of what his family will think of her. She does not think that it should matter and, after all, she is part Asian as well. John has not even told his parents that he has a new girlfriend. They still think he is dating his former girlfriend who was Korean American. Meg and John have been fighting over his reservation to introduce her to his family. To Meg, it's not the 1950s anymore; it's 2018! She believes that their intercultural difference should be embraced and not looked down on.

John and Meg's relationship represents an intercultural romantic relationship. Both come from different racial and ethnic cultures and backgrounds in terms of nationality from birth and generational identity. However, the larger pressures from family and society enter their private relationship. But, how can macro layers and power issues play a role in our interpersonal relationships and friendships across cultures? This chapter seeks to explore how power relations and ideologies impact our micro episodes and intercultural relationships. Power is indeed present and embedded in our one-on-one intercultural relationships and to examine such power is to acknowledge the complexities and dynamic nature of our intercultural relationships.

Intercultural relationships surround us—friendships, work-relationships, or romantic relationships. Intercultural relationships represent ongoing exchanges between two individuals that are from culturally different backgrounds (via gender, race/ethnicity, nationality, religion, socioeconomic class, sexual orientation, among other identity aspects)

Types of Intercultural Relationships

Reflect on the relationships in your life. You may have a few that can be defined as intercultural relationships. An **intercultural relationship** refers to an ongoing exchange between two individuals who are from culturally different backgrounds (gender, race/ethnicity, nationality, religion, socioeconomic class, sexual orientation, among other identity aspects). What makes a relationship intercultural depends on the degree of difference in terms of the identity and background of the people involved. There are several types of intercultural relationships:

- **Intercultural friendship:** A relationship that represents an ongoing exchange between two individuals who have a positive affinity for one another (common interests, shared settings)

- **Intercultural romantic relationship:** Relationship of a romantic nature (dating, long-term) between two culturally different members (whether international, interracial, or interethnic)

- **Intercultural work-relationship:** A connection to culturally different others whom one works with in a professional/organizational setting; these people may occupy the same work team or division for a larger organizational goal. Individuals in work situations may not consider themselves to be friends but just professional colleagues or co-workers

- **Intercultural marriage:** A formally recognized union between two individuals of different cultural backgrounds (nationality, race, ethnicity, language, sexual orientation, religion, disability, among other aspects)

As the second featured narrative in this chapter, Mike and Rich have been friends since elementary school. Mike is a White/European American high school student in Boulder, Colorado, while Rich is a Mexican American originally from California and now living in Boulder, Colorado. They met one another in first grade and were inseparable. Mike and Rich gravitated toward each other because they liked the same things: basketball, cars, and robots.

Each year, they would enter a new grade together and would continue to be recess buddies, sports partners, and all around best friends. They would occasionally see each other outside of school, but they lived in different areas.

Mike lived in the suburbs around their school, while Rich lived across town near an industrial area and was able to attend the same school as Mike through a special equal access program. Their families did not really socialize as there were cultural and language barriers: Rich's parents did not speak much English and worked most of the time, while Mike's mom stayed at home and his father traveled a lot for his business.

But, Mike and Rich remained best friends in school all the way through seventh grade. Then, things started to change. Mike started to hang around with more of the popular crowd who were mostly White. Rich, on the other hand, socialized more with the athletes of his school, playing on the sports teams (which were made up of some Blacks/African Americans and Whites/European Americans). Rich was always one of the few Latinos at the schools that he attended.

It appeared, then, that racial dynamics and racial difference affected Mike and Rich's intercultural friendship as they got older. Although race and racialization (as discussed in chapter 8) were always present in terms of how they met (via the equal access program for Rich and the cultural differences between the families), these factors would not become as apparent until Mike and Rich grew older.

Macro influences, such as zones of contact and access, cultural and socioeconomic class differences, and differential positions in terms of race, all impact intercultural friendships. But these influences play out in a more calibrated way than intercultural romantic relationships. In the case of intercultural friendships, there are lower stakes in terms of the mixing of culturally different families. Still, intercultural friendships are indeed impacted by power.

How Power Touches Our Intercultural Relationships

It is hard to think about how power inequalities from a macro level impact our personal relationships. After all, we exert control and our own wishes in our intercultural friendships and relationships. If power was a part of our relationships, we would know about it, right? This is indeed the potency of structural and historical layers of power—on the macro level, it is invisible and under the surface yet still very present. Typically, when we discuss interpersonal and intercultural relationships, we focus on the micro aspects, such as individual perceptions and the behaviors of the people involved. But, a critical intercultural perspective seeks to uncover how macro layers of power constitute and seep into our private, one-to-one interpersonal and intercultural relationships.

There are a few macro layers of power that impact our intercultural relationships. These are as follows: a) zones of contact, b) historical memories (via myths and narratives), c) structural influences of power, d) cultural capital, and e) intercultural desire.

Zones of Contact

Our intercultural relationships do not exist in a vacuum. Instead, these relationships are shaped by the surrounding zones of contact that each person brings with them. A zone of contact refers to the set of surrounding settings or contexts of possible interactions with other cultural groups that are made available or accessible to an individual. In the 1950s, social psychologist Gordon Allport (1954) identified several ideal conditions through which culturally different groups could positively interact with one another, or what he framed as "contact" (as the meeting or interchange between culturally different persons) (Pettigrew & Tropp, 2005). Such work became known as the "contact hypothesis," which shaped intercultural and interception contact research (Allport, 1954; Pettigrew & Tropp, 2005). What was not fully theorized in this work was how each person brings to bear a record of intercultural contact from his or her own childhood through adulthood.

These records of contact include the following:

- Which racial/ethnic groups lived in the person's neighborhood as a child

- The nature of these interactions (if any): cooperative, separate but equal, hostile and negative, avoidance related

- The interaction exposure and potential with culturally different groups in that person's neighborhood

- The type of community the person lived in (enclave, pluralistic city space, impoverished area constituted by multiple groups)

From the introductory (first) narrative in this chapter, John came from a childhood in which there were other Korean families in South Korea and then in the Oakland area in California. His family (and he, himself) was accustomed to being around other Koreans, and this shaped an expectation of such intracultural contact with other Koreans for friends

We enter into a specific intercultural contact zone when we enter a college or university setting. But, keep in mind that not everyone attends college or university and certain institutions speak to specific socioeconomic statused persons and groups. So, contact in college is inherently segmented based on racialized and class aspects of society.

and romantic partners. Meg, on the other hand, grew up in a largely diverse neighborhood in Southern California. She went to school with Latinos, Asian Americans, and African Americans and had friends of all backgrounds. Meg also dated across multiple racial or ethnic groups. Thus, these zones of contact shaped the preference and expectations for contact with certain groups in different ways for John and Meg.

The demographic makeup of our settings can indeed provide specific zones of contact, but these are not randomly provided. For example, at a college or university setting, we may become friends and/or romantically involved with individuals who attend the same school and/or are in the same major or clubs. But, not everyone attends college or university, and certain institutions speak to specific socioeconomic persons and groups with status: Ivy League schools, state universities, private schools, and public community colleges. Thus, contact is inherently segmented based on the racialized and class aspects of society, which also includes the historical placement of said groups in those institutions. So, later in life, we may hang out with friends that we made in college (if we attended school) or date individuals (perhaps even marry them) we met in college. A more frequent intercultural pairing in the Silicon Valley and the East Coast are Asian Indian and East Asian couples. Many of these individuals attended the same schools, colleges, or graduate and professional schools together and thus comprise the same zones of contact and thus meet, date, and marry. (College majors also reflect specific racial or ethnic and gender

We are also racially and socioeconomically segmented into our workplace zones of contact as well. Depending on the nature of the job, profession, and industry and the specific regional/national setting, individuals are exposed to specific genders and cultural groups members.

demographics in terms of who occupies specific fields of study—business, engineering, social sciences, health sciences, pre-med, pre-law, among others.)

The same could be said for who we work with. You may work at a job and in a setting that possesses a specific racial or ethnic and gender demographic in terms of the location of the workplace or the type of industry/profession. Who you work with and that specific zone of contact presents you with specific interactional partners and relationship opportunities in terms of the cultural background. These zones of contact, then, are shaped by the racial or ethnic and gender segmentation, placement, and structured inequalities of our society, which play into who we come into contact with and form intercultural relationships with.

But, history also plays into these zones of contact in that groups don't just freely move to where they want to go. Instead, cultural groups are differentially placed in specific areas based on socioeconomic status and racial designation. Over time, some groups were afforded the privilege to be homeowners and live in prime areas, while others were relegated to economically depressed spaces (also termed as slums or ghettoes). Thus, historical memories play into our zones of contact and, in turn, our intercultural relationships.

Histories, Myths, and Narratives

Chapter 6 emphasized the power of historical memories and how we carry certain remembrances of culture, nations, and the world that are circulated in the media, news, history textbooks, and public memorials. A key aspect of historical memories is that these shape our impressions, interpretations, and even possibly our own desires for intercultural relationships. These historical memories shape who we may approach or have around us for friendships and who we may seek out for romantic intercultural relationships. These historical memories are constituted by lingering memories and myths of the past and shared narratives about other cultural groups.

Memories, Shared Narratives, and Myths About Cultural Groups

The third narrative featured in this chapter hones in on a serious romantic intercultural relationship between two women—Erin and Kala—of different backgrounds. Erin, a Latina from New York, has been in a year-long relationship with Kala, a Chinese Filipina woman she met at a concert. Erin and Kala have fallen in love and want to move in together. They are wanting to introduce each other to their families. However, Erin's family does not accept her identity as a lesbian as it conflicts with their cultural and religious beliefs. In Erin's culture, same-sex relationships are still taboo.

Erin still thinks that she has to push the issue with her family because Kala wants to meet them. On her end, Kala told her parents (who are divorced) about Erin and they are thrilled to meet her. They have embraced Kala and her sexual orientation since she was a teen. Kala's parents also feel that although their respective cultures (Chinese on the mother's side and Filipino on the father's side) often negatively view gay, lesbian, bisexual, and transgender identities, they will be different for their family and Kala.

A week later, Erin approached her mother and father and told them about Kala. "I've met someone and it is serious. We are moving in together. I want you to meet her. Her name is Kala."

Her mother says, "Her? What? It's a she?"

Erin responds, "You know who I am. I told you years ago, and I think you just thought that was a phase. But I found someone and she is amazing."

Her parents were silent.

Her father calmly says, "Let's meet this person."

Erin says, "Her name is Kala and ... ."

Erin's mother interrupts her. "We don't need to meet her. This is not right. Our faith is about marriage and family."

Erin chimes in, "I can get married to her. It is legal now. I can have a family."

Her mother raises her voice, "It is not natural. It's not. It should be a man. You know this."

Erin states back, "No matter what you say, it won't change who I am or who I love. If you want me in your life, you will need to fully embrace me and the person in my life."

Since Erin left her parent's house, she has not spoken to them in a year. She did meet Kala's parents and they were friendly and warm toward her. Erin and Kala are planning their wedding.

In the case of Erin and Kala, this intercultural relationship collided against two larger ideologies—one based on gender ideology and another based on a heteronormative ideology.

Gender ideology refers to a specific dominant view of what women and men should do and be like in society (Gill, 2015; Kroska, 2007). So, the notion that women should be married, have a family, and tend to the home represents a specific gender ideology. This ideology frames the conversation that Erin has with her parents about her romantic relationship with Kala. For a woman to be with a woman is to not fulfill the dominant gender ideology that circulates in some societies in which women are to be married to men and have children. Added to this gender ideology are the religious and cultural ideologies that also proscribe and frame Erin's behavior and role as a woman. Marriage and procreation are often deemed as important hallmarks of life according to some religions. Cultures also create spoken and unspoken expectations and rules that women should act and be a certain way. Thus, Erin's parents see her identity and relationship through the gender ideology of what it means to be a woman as well as the ideological influences of religion and Latino/a culture. These represent larger social and structural pressures of power that seep into and impact a private intercultural relationship.

Intensifying the pressure even more is another ideology—the heteronormative romance ideology—that presumes that the natural or normal type of romantic relationship that every individual will have will be with the opposite gender (for a woman to be with a man or for a man to be with a woman). (Keep in mind that this ideology, as well as dominant gender ideology, only recognizes and presumes two distinct genders—woman or man.) According to Ingraham (2009) and Warner (1993), heteronormativity represents a powerful social institution shaping our expectation that everyone around us is heterosexual and straight (Yep, 2003). This heteronormative romance ideology also frames Erin's parents' reaction and level of acceptance to her relationship with Kala. These ideologies constitute and shape the social values and understandings around gender roles, cultural and religious identity, and even romance, and thus represent powerful frames through which to view, evaluate, and behave in the world. Erin's parents are heavily influenced by these ideologies (as many people are), and it impacts their relationship and closeness with Erin, their only child. Ideologies of power, therefore, powerfully shape and mark our one-on-one intercultural relationships.

These ideologies of power inform our family members' perspectives and framings of cultural groups. In turn, our family members' memories about other cultural groups— from their childhoods to the present—can influence our own. So if, for example, Erin's parents have positive and warm memories of and expectations for straight (heterosexual) intracultural relationships with other Latinos, then these will be passed down to Erin and her siblings. This actually stems farther back than her parents, perhaps to her grandparents and before, and quite possibly in terms of a larger group memory (and of society). Similarly, with the first narrative, John's Korean family may widely circulate historical memories, stories, and cultural expectations around how Koreans marry other

Koreans and marry within their own kind. Our family's memories therefore shape how we see other cultures (and genders) and envision them as friends or romantic partners.

We may not even be able to pinpoint where and how we first came to the impressions we have of other cultures. These may be subtle messages or stories that we have heard from our families about their encounters with cultural groups. For example, a family member could relay a story about a cousin who married outside of his or her religion and then point out how that cousin was never heard from again. Or, a family member could describe how a relative married an Asian Indian man and he was so controlling that she was so unhappy. These narratives embed themselves in our understanding of intercultural relationships and interactions with culturally different others.

Such narratives may pull gender, racial, and religious stereotypes and myths about other cultures. Stereotypes about how some cultural members are sexually aggressive, opportunists, prone to being alcoholics, lazy, and unintelligent can feed into family stories about other cultures. In this chapter's introduction, John's parents told his siblings that African-Americans made up a lower uneducated class and were inferior to them. Over time, these messages shaped how he perceived and ultimately avoided most African Americans that he met. As he got older, John realized that his parents' views were not accurate and were narrow, thereby opening him up to meeting Meg.

Historical memories and myths can constitute family narratives and stories about other cultural groups. These may not be based on actual experiences. In fact, family memories or historical memories about other cultures could stem from layers of stereotypes, myths, and micro aggressions (or subtle, culturally offensive comments about a specific cultural group) about cultural groups that were passed down from generation to generation (Sue, 2010).

Memories, myths, and shared narratives can also give rise to direct prohibitions by family members against specific racial groups. An example of this can be when family members tell their children or grandchildren to not bring home anyone who is Black or who is not Catholic. Families can also presume that their children are straight and usher in an ideology of heteronormativity and not entertain any discussion of LGBTQIA romances (Ingraham, 2009; Warner, 1993; Yep, 2003). These prohibitions can take on the form of verbal rejections (as theorized by Gordon Allport, 1954) and/or micro aggressions (Sue, 2010).

Our friendships also may play into the accumulated historical memories, myths, and narratives about cultural groups. While the surrounding zones of context may delimit which cultural group members we are exposed to, to what degree we establish intercultural friendships with certain cultural group members and how we make sense of these friendships relates to historical memories and myths. For instance, you may befriend an individual of a different cultural background but hold that person as an exception to the rule. Termed as "refencing" in Gordon Allport's (1954) work, the sense-making logic that has us view a cultural group member as different from his or her cultural group (the exception) and thus not of that culture at all, illustrates the power of historical memories, myths, and stereotypes that we have inherited from our families and society. Thus, we can be friends with a lesbian, a Latino, and or a Muslim person who may stand as

Same-sex marriages have been prohibited in the past but are gaining recognition in several countries such as Argentina, Belgium, Canada, Mexico, New Zealand, South Africa, Sweden, United Kingdom, and U.S.A.

"exceptions to the rule" in our minds but still can be pointed to as representing specific cultural groups when questioned about the diversity of our network of friends. Exceptions to the rule represent a response to circumvent (and yet ironically reinforce) prevailing and circulated historical memories about cultural groups.

Structural Influences of Power

Structures of power have formalized harmful measures against intercultural relationships, namely intercultural marriages. Up until 1967, marriages between Whites and non-Whites (Blacks, Native Americans, Asians) were prohibited in the United States in terms of state laws. In what are known as anti-miscegenation laws, these statutes were formed in the late 17th century.

Thus, intercultural marriages were prohibited until the *Loving v. Virginia* landmark case in which the statues were deemed unconstitutional in prohibiting a White male from marrying a non-White female.

Same-sex marriages have also historically been prohibited and outlawed in the past. It wasn't until 2001 when the Netherlands allowed same-sex marriage (Gerstmann, 2017). Then, from that point on, several countries followed suit in recognizing gay marriage, such as Argentina, Belgium, Canada, Mexico, New Zealand, South Africa, Sweden, the United Kingdom, Sweden, and the United States, among others.

State and federal governmental structures therefore have a long history of directly intervening in the creation of intercultural marriages (Gerstmann, 2017). What

Individuals in intercultural relationships may increase their cultural capital or gain a social advantage in their own cultural community or society because of the racial/ethnic background of their romantic partner. But such a social advantage could also be decreased if that individual is in a more privileged position in society than her/his/their romantic partner.

should be a private one-on-one union is very much structured by power in terms of legal statutes and governmental definition. The formal recognition of a union between culturally different persons is an important right, which has been denied to intercultural couples for centuries.

Cultural Capital

Another factor that plays a role in who and of which specific cultural group we select for intercultural relationships is cultural capital. We frame cultural capital in terms of intercultural relationships as the social advantage or leverage one gains when dating or marrying someone of a particular cultural, racial, ethnic background. Gaining social advantage or leverage means that an individual is positively perceived by society or accepted more by society for who that person dates or marries. This advantage or leverage is based on the larger power hierarchy among cultural groups in a particular context. This notion of cultural capital is similar to critical scholar Pierre Bourdieu's (1985) concept of social capital, which refers to the social networks (relationships, recognitions) that an individual possesses and the resources that these afford that person.

For instance, when a Black/African American male dates and/or marries a White/European American female, that male will be more positively perceived in society because aligning himself with a White/European American woman—who is widely accepted and framed as the center of the racial hierarchy in the United States—affords him that

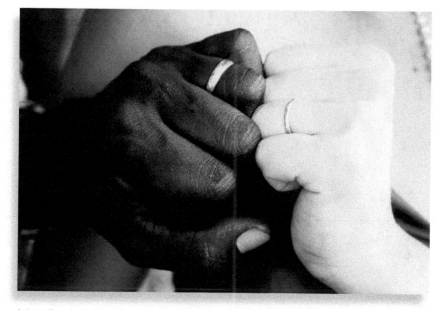

Intercultural relationships are still subject to societal judgment and the reproduction of stereotypes especially in terms of cultural capital.

acceptance. An Asian woman who enters in a romantic relationship with a White/European American man also gains a sense of dominance and social advantage by aligning with someone of a White dominant position.

Cultural capital also helps an individual gain a social advantage and leveraged position within one's own cultural community. That Black/African American male who dates and/or marries a White/European American woman may do so because he feels as if it increases his social and economic power among his racial and ethnic peers. This is also known as dating or marrying up or class passing.

However, while individuals may gain a type of social advantage or positive perception, this leverage is tempered by intracultural resentment and social disdain. Intercultural resentment occurs when cultural group members view marrying up or out as an affront to maintain their cultural identity and being true to that identity. Some Black/African Americans may view an intercultural marriage between a Black man and White woman as culturally offensive and may judge that Black male harshly. He would be deemed as a sell-out or as someone wanting to be White. Thus, given the racial hierarchy sediments between Blacks and Whites in the United States and the historical memory of slavery, outmarriage will always stand as a contested notion within both of these communities.

For instance, in the movie, *Something New*, an upper-class Black/African American female accountant falls in love with a middle-class White/European American male landscaper. She is negatively perceived as not being truly Black and being with someone below her social class (a double whammy). In the television film, *The Wedding*, a wealthy Black/African American family struggles with the impending nuptials between their daughter and a working-class White/European American male. The family worked hard to attain class distinction in White society and did not want to lose that by marrying down in terms of social class (which means that race or Whiteness on its own did not provide enough cultural capital).

Such intracultural resentment is often coupled with social disapproval or rejection. In Spike Lee's classic *Jungle Fever*, when an African American male starts up an extramarital affair with an Italian-American woman in New York City, both of these respective communities express disdain for the intercultural relationship. The boundaries of cultural membership come into play as these communities scoff at marrying out and what that means to their cultural identity. There is also societal judgment about the appropriateness of such an intercultural relationship. In the groundbreaking film *Guess Who's Coming to Dinner*, an African American father is disappointed and angry that his daughter brought home a White/European American male fiancée. His anger results from his need to be culturally and racially true to his identity and his historical distrust of Whiteness.

Other examples of societal judgment impacting intercultural relationships can be seen in specific Hollywood movies. In the film *How to be a Latin Lover*, a Latino male pursues affluent White/European American women in order to gain cultural capital and affluence. This portrait of intentional class passing as a strategy reproduces the Latin lover stereotype and highlights the pursuit of cultural and economic capital in some intercultural relationships. The movie *The Big Sick* portrays a romantic courtship and relationship between a Pakistani male and White woman whose families initially struggle with the relationship. This intercultural relationship then faces intense societal and cultural scrutiny that throws the relationship into question.

Thus, cultural capital refers to the increase in social advantage or leverage by which one interculturally dates or marries. This concept relies on and stems from the surrounding contexts of power—the racial hierarchy, economic placement of groups, historical memories, and legacies around groups.

Intercultural Desire

For the fourth narrative for this chapter, meet Seth and Ani. Seth is a 36-year-old White/European American tech entrepreneur in Silicon Valley. He is married to Ani, a 34-year-old Japanese American female business owner. They met each other in college in Boston. Seth remembers the day they met.

He explains, "It was a business class. I was in the middle row and she came in and I thought she was so beautiful. I had never seen many girls like her. Especially coming from Maine where it's mostly Whites. I needed to meet her.

Ani remembers their first meeting a little differently. "Seth was in my class. I walked in and I caught him staring at me. After class, I headed out the door and he was right there and asked if I was in his other class. He just was always around and was persistent. Then we went on a date and the rest is history."

Seth remembers that Ani's beauty stuck out. "She was just unique looking. Very exotic and beautiful that way." Ani had dated other White/European American men

throughout high school. Seth had a great sense of humor and passion for business. She loved that about him.

They dated throughout college and were both business majors. After college graduation, Seth and Ani attended business school together and then settled down in the Silicon Valley.

Their families integrated with each other well. Both Seth and Ani came from upper-middle class backgrounds. Their families joined together and became a larger one together.

However, some of Ani's Asian-American friends have always joked around with Seth about his "Asian fetish." When he first heard those words, Seth did not understand what that meant. He didn't see himself as going for Ani because she was Asian or that he had an "Asian fetish." Seth chose Ani because she had all the qualities that he was looking for. So, those "Asian fetish" comments confused Seth and, later on, made him angry. To make matters worse, oftentimes when Seth and Ani would walk around in Asian-dominated areas, they would be subject to comments like "Asian fetish" or "Yo, she's not your geisha."

Seth and Ani seemed to face some level of social commentary about why they were together. The intercultural relationship between Seth and Ani represents one that is impacted by intercultural desire and larger social perceptions about that desire. Intercultural desire refers to the longing or attraction one has for a person. Such intercultural desire is formed by a number of different factors such as exposure to media or societal images and societal views of what is desirable, among other factors.

Seth's desire for Ani was judged as being an exoticization of Asian women or an Asian fetish. Their friends and those around them—Asian Americans and others—negatively evaluated such a desire and saw it as stereotypical and exploitative. The comment, "She's not your geisha" also raises the notion that Seth's Asian fetish could also be a desire for

Asian subservience. The power dynamic of White male dominance-Asian female submission is wrapped up in this notion of the Asian fetish. Thus, our romantic desire for certain people and certain cultural group members may also involve power issues with regard to wanting a specific power arrangement and/or actualizing a stereotype that elevates one's self.

In addition, by growing up in similar socioeconomic classes, Seth and Ani were able to meet because they were in the same zones of contact (same university and major). This then means that the Asian fetish image gets reproduced as more White males and Asian females enter relationships and marry. In fact, according to a Pew Research Center Report by Livingston & Brown (2017), "Just over one-third (36%) of Asian newlywed women have a spouse of a different race or ethnicity, while 21% of Asian newlywed men do. A substantial gender gap in intermarriage was also present in 1980, when 39% of newly married Asian women and 26% of their male counterparts were married to someone of a different race or ethnicity" (p. 1). Thus, it appears then that more of these couples exist, which risks reifying and confirming the Asian fetish and desire for Asian women (Marchetti, 1994; Zheng, 2016).

Or what came first? This particular intercultural combination (White male, Asian female)? Or the Asian fetish and desire for Asian women? Or, is it impossible to trace these as separate from one another? Our desires may come from seeing couples around us or from the media. But desire may also stem from both unconscious and conscious modes of life.

This notion of intercultural desire represents an intricate area of power that impacts our intercultural relationships.

Intercultural desire represents an internal mechanism in our hearts, minds, and bodies or how we feel, think, and act toward others in our lives. When considering our romantic attraction to others, desire is not something that we fully know or create. In fact, we may not fully know how our desire is shaped or how it came to be. All we may know is how we feel toward others and our powerful preferences for traits, qualities, attributes, and physical markers of people.

Desire is something that develops unconsciously and consciously. Our social experiences and what we are exposed to (through the media and the community) may contribute to the formation of our desire.

Our intercultural desire is formed by the following:

- Type of access we have to other cultural groups (more access to one group may shape a positive feeling toward that group or less access to a cultural group may create an increased desire for that group)

- Exposure to media images of specific cultural groups and how those groups were depicted (images of femininity, beauty, masculinity, of couples and their dynamics)

- Cultural views of what is desirable (skin color, body type, gender, race or ethnicity)

Our own intercultural desire is shaped by historical and structural influences of power.

Cultural or Racial Fetish

A key element that influences and shapes our intercultural desire is cultural (or racial) fetish. A **cultural or racial fetish** can be defined as a type of stereotype one has for a cultural group in terms of its physical appearance and what that means or is associated with. For example, being attracted to an Asian American female (and only this group in terms of dating patterns) because of her exotic beauty is an example of a racial fetish and one that connects Asian females with exoticism and the expectation of Asian female subservience (Marchetti, 1994). Zheng (2016) points out that the dominance and prevalence of the Asian fetish can be seen in the following cited example:

"UrbanDictionary.com, the premier source for user-generated documentation of contemporary slang, boasts no less than 27 definitions of yellow fever, the hit blog 'Stuff White People Like' lists 'Asian women' as #11 on a list containing over a hundred items" (Zheng, 2016, p. 400). Likewise, Halualani (1995) argues that the Asian female fetish can be seen in Asian mail-order bride catalogs and how these forms commodify a sexually and racially differentiated power relationship between Anglo male consumers and Filipina female products. We also see the preponderance of such a fetish in popular culture, movies, television, and specific Asian female-seeking dating web sites.

When someone (female or male) is attracted to Black males (and at the exclusion of other males), there may be a cultural or racial fetish at work. Black males have been fetishized historically in terms of their bodies (and physical attributes, such as their penis size) and such physicality has been associates as hyper masculine and hypersexual. This association was created historically as a stereotype and characterization of Black slaves wanting to sexually assault White women (and wives of slave masters).

Likewise, White males are often attracted to Latina women for their beauty and exotic appearance. However, Latina females and the way they look (or deemed as supposed to look) with darker features, sensual lips and hips, and a disarming linguistic accent, have created a larger stereotype and cultural fetish that objectifies Latina culture. There's also a fetishization of mixed race women. Mixed race (or "hapa") women are desired for their exotic looks. Part White and part-Asian/Black/Latina women are sought after because of their ethnic looks as mixed with White or Anglo features.

Postcolonial scholar Homi Bhaba (1983) stresses that racial fetishes represent colonialistic tools of

Cultural or racial fetishes play a role in shaping our intercultural desire and engaging in intercultural relationships. White males who are attracted to Asian and Asian American females may be influenced by an Asian fetish and the images, fantasies, myths, and stereotypes that have been widely and historically circulated about Asian women.

domination and objectification that "otherizes" cultural groups. Anne McClintock (2013) extends this argument further by highlighting how in 1837 through 1901, such fetishization of cultural groups (and specifically of colonized Black and Brown women and men) occurred through the framing, marketing, and consumption of specific commodities or products such as milk cartons, sauce bottles, tobacco tins, whiskey bottles, biscuits, toothpaste, toffee boxes, and match boxes, among others. She also underscores the point that racial fetishes objectify race, gender, and socioeconomic class all at the same time and in relation to (and opposition with) one another. Thus, by connecting fetishes to colonialism and the marginalization of specific groups, Homi Bhaba and Anne McClintock illustrate that cultural or racial fetishes were created, reproduced, and enacted by White power interests as a way to make exotic, objectify, and gain power over specific racially and gender-marked groups.

Latina women like Sofia Vergara (with her darker features, curvaceous body, and linguistic accent) are often framed in terms of a racial/cultural fetish that objectifies Latina culture.

These cultural or racial fetishes always seem to place a White person in a position of power (socially, culturally, economically, representationally), while making inferior the fetishized cultural group member (McClintock, 2013).

Many have argued that they do not fetishize other groups but that they are naturally attracted to those groups or they attain their desired qualities. Cultural fetishes are not traceable; you can't pinpoint the origin of one (or if you have one) because it represents an accumulation of images, fantasies, myths, and stereotypes that have been widely and historically circulated for ages and across contexts and cultural forms (media, books, popular culture, music, jokes).

Robin Zheng (2016) goes further to argue that rather than looking for the origins or causes of racial fetishes, we should consider the effects of these fetishes on the cultural groups at hand. She argues that "Asian women across the globe experience negative psychological effects and burdens due to 'yellow fever' or an Asian female based racial fetish" (p. 417). This fetish otherizes these women and makes them feel inferior in terms of both their racial or cultural identity and gender. She argues that such fetishes are byproducts and effects of the larger system and structure of racial difference and power.

Thus, the impact of cultural or racial fetishes on the actual cultural groups and gendered counterparts is significant and potentially damaging in the long term. (Cultural or racial fetishes are also typically framed as compliments but actually objectify cultural groups and genders.) Understanding the impact of how fetishes constitute and shape our intercultural desires is important in unpacking how power enters into our intercultural relationships.

Macro Layers and Intercultural Relationships

These macro layers touch on and reach into our intercultural relationships. Taken together, these macro layers influence our private moments and personal connections in ways that we never could imagine. These macro layers also move through the past and present intercultural relationships of this book's author.

This book's author, Rona Tamiko Halualani, grew up in a predominantly White/European American neighborhood (San Mateo) in Northern California. Her family (a multiracial and multiethnic one) represented one of the only Asian American and Pacific Islander families in the area. Rona and her brothers were the only part Native Hawaiian individuals at her school and in her neighborhood. Rona mostly had White/European American friends, with some individuals of Asian and African American backgrounds. Because she lived in a predominantly White/European American area, her family became involved in a Japanese American Youth Basketball League (JYO) through which she played basketball alongside other Asian Americans. This is where Rona started to develop more friendships with Asian Americans and her family members interacted with Asian-American families from Hawai'i (where her parents came from). But, other than through this basketball league and her weekly Japanese school class, Rona had mostly White/European American friends and this continued into high school. She only dated White/European American males as well. When she entered college, Rona noticed that the setting had many more people and that White/European Americans only seemed to date each other and not non-Whites. In fact, Rona always felt that White/European American males were not attracted to her: a multiethnic female. She was introduced to the Asian American scene through her college roommate (and good friend from childhood who was also Japanese American). Rona was fascinated at how Asian-American clubs, fraternities, and sororities created a specific social community through which ethnically similar individuals could interact and date one another. She dated a Korean American male in college and then met her husband (Chinese American) from mutual friends in this Asian-American scene. Her zones of contact shifted and varied over time, and this shaped her intercultural relationships. Rona was always expected (implicitly and explicitly) to date anyone except individuals who were African American or Filipinos; however, she did not carry these framings once she entered high school and college. Rona just wanted to meet and interact with kind people. She was always struck by how her own parents—a Japanese-American mother and a part Native Hawaiian and White father—themselves had an intercultural marriage that faced scrutiny from traditional Japanese-American grandparents. Even though her parents faced pressure from her mother's family about intermarrying and discrimination from society, Rona still heard retellings of historical memories and shared narratives about other groups in her family. Memories of the past and who to marry persist over generations even for multiracial and multiethnic cultural members.

Summary

This chapter highlights how power relations and ideologies impact our one-on-one intercultural relationships and private exchanges. In subtle and obvious ways, power is embedded in our one-on-one intercultural relationships. It is important to understand how zones of contact, historical memories, myths, shared narratives, structural influences of power, cultural capital, and intercultural desire all shape the nature of (and even the existence of) our intercultural relationships.

Keywords

Cultural capital
Cultural/Racial fetish
Exceptions to the rule
Historical memories
Intercultural desire
Intercultural friendship
Intercultural marriage
Intercultural relationship

Intercultural romantic relationship
Intercultural work relationship
Micro aggressions
Myths
Shared narratives
Social capital
Structural influences of power
Zones of contact

Questions and Activities

REFLECTION activity: Reflecting on your own intercultural relationships:
Answer all of the following questions:

- To what extent have you experienced an intercultural relationship (friendship, romantic relationship)? What was that experience like?

- How would you characterize your zones of contact from childhood to the present? How did these affect the way you see your intercultural friendships?

- What kinds of historical memories, myths, or shared narratives about cultural groups did you hear, growing up to the present? How did these affect the way you see your intercultural friendships?

- How do you think we as a society should approach intercultural relationships so that true harmony, happiness, and bridge-building can be possible across all cultures and backgrounds?

- Talk about how zones of contact, historical memories, myths, shared narratives, and structural influences of power impacted your intercultural relationships.

- Why is the notion that "love should be enough" somewhat naive? How does this notion guise what we have been learning about intercultural communication throughout the semester? Fully explain. Share your views and connect this to course material.

REFLECTION activity: Friendship inventory exercise:

- Write down the initials of six of your closest friends (not to be family members or relatives) in a list, and then next to those initials write down the gender, age, race/ethnicity, sexual orientation, highest educational level earned, if disabled, and marital status of each person.

- Then, reflect on the characteristics of your closest friends. What do you notice? Are your friends diverse in a particular area? To what extent do your friends share the same characteristics as you? What do you make of these observations?

- What role do you think zones of contact, historical memories, myths, shared, narratives and structural influences of power play in your friendships?

REFLECTION activity: Symbolic presence and absence of intercultural relationships in popular culture:

- Identify the kind of intercultural relationships that are featured in television shows and movies that you watch and in books that you read.

- What do you notice about these intercultural relationships? How are they depicted? Which cultural groups are represented? Which are not? (These questions relate to the presence of intercultural relationships and the absence of intercultural relationships and the kinds of meanings that exist in the presences and absences.)

- What kind of pressure do these intercultural relationships have? From individuals? From larger societal perceptions and structures of power?

- What do you make of all of this?

DISCUSSION activity: Viewing *Bride and Prejudice*:
Answer all of the following questions:

- View any of the television show *Bride and Prejudice* video clips: www.youtube.com/watch?v=nFYwqts1_Tl

- Discuss why you think it is that intercultural relationships (whether they be across religious, cultural, racial, and sexual orientation backgrounds) can be so tense and complicated, especially when it comes to family acceptance?

DISCUSSION activity:
Intercultural relationships as our hope or our despair?

- How might intercultural relationships (friendships and romantic relationships) serve as important vehicles to bring cultural groups together? How so? Why?

- How might these relationships continue to divide cultural groups?

Chapter 11

Re-Imagining Your Role in Intercultural Communication

Learning Objectives

> To reflect on the previous chapters of this book and envision your role in this intercultural world

> To identify how you can engage in intercultural action through the ACT framework for intercultural justice as introduced in chapter 1 and referenced throughout this book

> To conceptualize individual and collective actions that you may want to take up to create transformative positive change for our intercultural world

Introduction: Janis and Intercultural Justice

Janis is finishing up her intercultural communication course for her senior year in college in San Antonio, Texas. It is the last course she has to complete before graduation. She is very excited and yet intrigued at this course that has pushed her to rethink her own cultural views and explore the power issues around culture and intercultural communication. Thinking about power is so draining and depressing. Her professor keeps highlighting how becoming aware of power is a significant action step in and of itself and to think about what the next steps are for actuating change. Janis has not really thought about it before. Life is so busy with her internship, part-time job at a rec center, and school. But, the course raised so many important issues that she saw in her own life: how cultural identity is important and yet changing due to globalization and diaspora (she has experienced this through her own German and Asian background and her family's diasporic move to South Africa and then Canada). Janis also is struck by the inequality that she has seen around her—in South Africa, Canada, and in the United States. She wonders what she could do about it. How can she help in the fight against poverty and injustice? Where would she begin? Perhaps the problem is too big for her to make any kind of difference. What does it mean to be an intercultural communication scholar for positive, transforma-tive change in the world?

Janis's situation may be familiar to you. She is uncertain about the kind of change that she can engage in for the intercultural world in which she lives. Is there a way to make a difference? Or, is this all futile, especially with the critical intercultural communication (power-based) per-spective through which we have been seeing the

world in this entire course? This chapter seeks to reiterate how we can envision our role as intercultural communicators in terms of making positive change in the world. We will revisit the ACT framework for intercultural justice that was discussed in chapter 1 and throughout the book. Individual and collective actions will be unpacked in terms of providing potential ideas for action by all of us.

What Now?

Now that we have moved through each chapter from understanding critical intercultural perspective and using this to see anew culture, communication, ideology, history, repre-sentation and speaking, identity, race and racialization, globalization, and intercultural relationships, the question becomes "What now?" We also should ask, "What do we do with this information and this perspective?" This final chapter highlights the next steps to use and apply all the critical insights and information from this book. The ACT framework for intercultural justice provides a module through which to think about the kind of individual and collective actions we can take up.

The ACT Framework for Intercultural Justice

Agency

Chapter 1 introduced the notion of **agency,** or the socially shaped capability to act and make a difference against a structure of power or practice of domination. As we conclude our journey through this book, understanding how we can enact our agency in a world framed by power is important. Remember that the critical intercultural perspective underscores that we all have agency (albeit in delimited structural conditions and con-texts of power) in this world and we can work to change the power forces in our lives. The **ACT framework for intercultural justice** represents a model for agency in our intercultural world.

As covered in chapter 1, the "A" in the framework speaks to the need to continually increase our awareness of the ways in which power shapes culture, our identities, and experiences. This area of awareness sounds straightforward, but it actually requires a great deal of energy and strength to really unpack and uncover all the power issues and implications in our everyday lives and today's world (as well as that of yesterday). You may have even thought to yourself the following:

- "Wow, this is so depressing!"
- "I can't think about this because it just seems too big to change."
- "Life isn't that bad, so why think about all these negative thoughts?"
- "I feel powerless to change anything. It is hopeless. We are screwed."

Given these thoughts (which we all experience when being introduced to a critical perspective), awareness is a major step to this framework, and one that requires resilience. We should remember that just because we are uncovering overwhelming information (and perspectives) about power in our lives that does not mean all hope is lost or that there is nothing we can do. Instead, truly knowing what we are working with is key. Wouldn't you rather see and understand all facets of power in our lives so that we can focus our energies on making change that will matter and chip away at hardened (but not closed off) structures and ideologies of power? Or, would you rather not know (like Althusser's notion of false consciousness, as highlighted in Chapter 4) and live your days in a particular version of reality that may seem good but has harmful and or unjust areas that need your help to change and transform? Our desire to not want to know about power will not change or erase power from our lives. To ignore and or refuse awareness about power, then, brings harm to ourselves, our families and communities, and to surrounding cultural groups across the globe. But, to be aware and fully in the know about power is to honor the power of the human spirit to rise, challenge, transcend, and demand a better tomorrow. This "A" or awareness step is pivotal and the most difficult in this framework.

"C" refers to the need to contemplate, consider, and critique specific concepts and contexts of power before one acts. Structures of power are complex and formidable and therefore require close attention. In moving from the previous "A" or awareness step, the focus in this "C" step is to feel empowered to move from awareness to full-fledged reflection and critique of all of the aspects of power around us (and those that we cannot fully see). So, after shaking ourselves out of the heaviness of the initial awareness brought forth by the critical intercultural communication perspective, this step gives us the space to do the full work of examining our everyday lives and contexts in terms of exposing power dimensions. We will be able to deploy newly gained concepts

With the "A" or "Awareness" step of the ACT Framework, becoming fully aware of relations of power around culture and intercultural communication in one's life can surprise and disarm individuals.

of power (as highlighted throughout this book—structures of power, ideologies, representations, speaking for others, historical memories, historical remembering and historical amnesia, social/structural and personal layers of identity, authenticity, race, racialization, globalization, glocalization, hybridity, intercultural relationships, macro layers that impact intercultural relationships, and agency, among many others) and apply these without abandon. The "C" step can often be accompanied by a sense of exhilaration at deconstructing the world through a new critical (power-based) lens and unrelenting need to keep doing so. You may even feel removed from your family members, friends, and loved ones in this step because this critical intercultural view of the world is not widely shared (in fact, it is a historically underused perspective in the larger scheme of the world and its population). But, such a step is time consuming and fueled with the passion to know and uncover more and more. This breathless stage is vital for the life blood of the critical intercultural communication perspective and its continued relevance in the world.

"T" stands as the step through which we think about and engage the best course of action to break down a structure of power or dominant power interest. Action requires constant reflection on what to do, how it will affect others, and how it will resist a dominant power. Recall that in chapter 4 we discussed the importance of speaking for, about, and with culturally different others. Acting without thinking about how such action will impact cultural group members experiences and without including their voices would constitute an act of oppression and symbolic violence (which would be antithetical to the goal of intercultural justice). In fact, trying to immediately take up action to help a cultural group (while good in intention), without thoughtful reflection of the utility and impact of such action, could potentially be worse than doing nothing at all. In individualistic, Western societies, the tendency to push for an immediate solution to a problem reveals the limited (and hasty) approach to confronting and transforming aspects of power. (Such a tendency highlights the refusal to fully consider the historical effects and legacies of societal problems that are not easily fixable.)

This entire book has toured you through the "A" (awareness) and "C" (contemplate, consider, and critique) steps. It has presented information about various contexts and concepts related to culture, intercultural communication, and power. Because these steps take so much time and energy (and in different ways for each, in and of themselves), this book has not fully explored this "T" step. How do we create thoughtful, mindful, and purposeful action to change the course of power in the world? That is the larger question. As such, we need to highlight examples and ways of engaging in this "T" (think and act) step.

Specific examples of "T" steps in terms of individual and collective actions, should be highlighted:

Individual Actions
Some individual actions are as follows:

- Interacting with many people with different cultural backgrounds, experiences, and identities and reflecting on these interactions in terms of the role of power in

The culturally different individuals in this photo engage in a deep and meaningful conversation. This represents the "T" ('Think and Act') step of the ACT Framework and can enable us to see intercultural relations in new ways.

framing the interaction, the resulting perceptions, and the expression of identities. Asking questions and providing thoughtful insight (after reflection) are important activities in which we can all partake on a daily basis.

- Engaging in deep, meaningful conversations with culturally different persons than yourself, will expose you to new, different ways of looking at the world and other cultures. These exchanges stand as key forms of knowledge that can expand and/or alter your sense-makings or perceptions of a cultural group. Keep in mind that while conversation, communication, and dialogue are important in connecting to and understanding different power positionalities and cultural groups, dialogue may not be enough (as critical education scholar Paul Gorski (2009) argues) and it may require us to deeply immerse ourselves in our own privilege and positionality and to understand others' historically created disadvantages and oppressions.

- Seeking out knowledge and perspectives on status quo or dominant ideas (or those that are widely held that privilege certain power interests over others). This can happen in educational settings and or trainings and workshops or even through books, blogs, and videos and or live interactions.

- Posing new questions about cultural groups and structures of power; questions that have never crossed your mind. These questions may throw off and challenge your past perceptions and belief systems. However, this may be a necessary step

Communication graduate scholar Ravinder Kaur created a blog that engages issues of power, critical pedagogy, and social issues in order to share critical insights with people across all contexts.

to develop and advance your understanding of culturally different persons and the complex nature of culture and power.

- Advocating for a cultural group's perspective or cause. When one speaks up for or defends a cultural group that is framed negatively or mistreated, we often describe such an act as advocacy. For example, a Chicano male student speaks up in class and corrects a professor's description of his culture and the terms he uses about persons with disabilities. Another example can be seen when a female teenager informs her peers that the oft-used phrase "that is so gay" is offensive and hurtful to LGBTQIA persons. Advocacy is that much more powerful when an individual speaks up for a group or community that is external to and different from his or her own. We refer to this notion of acting or speaking out on behalf of others as "allyship." Intercultural scholar Sara DeTurk (2011) explains that becoming an ally requires a full and continuous commitment, strategic thinking, and fortitude to make significant social change. Reflecting on one's positionality in relation to the cultural group one helps, is important. We learned in chapter 5 from Linda Alcoff (1995) that we need to be mindful of the effects on other cultural groups through both our actions and non-actions.

- Creating music, a social media campaign, a blog, or a video that highlights a key issue of inequality and power to make others more aware and inspired to take action

- Initiating a social justice nonprofit group that helps local immigrant communities in terms of job training, legal aid, and survival knowledge to make it in the host society

- Participating in an economic boycott of companies and/or organizations that exploit and or oppress specific cultural groups around the world (e.g., refusing to purchase any phone or computer made by a technology company that economically and physically exploits cultural workers in another country).

- Volunteering in your surrounding community to help specific cultural groups in terms of skill acquisition and/or social support.

- Creating a creative product (art, performance, exhibition) that draws attention to a key power problem in the community (e.g., creating a free performance that highlights the experiences of the homeless and of veterans and ways to change our perceptions while also identifying ways to change the system to help these groups or creating a free performance that highlights sexual orientation in communities of color and reaching out to LGBTQIA members of every community to dismantle cultural stigmas against LGBTQIA members).

These individual actions are all examples of micro practices (as discussed in the area of cultural studies which examines the relationship among culture, society, and power in specific contexts) that contribute to action and social change (or the challenging of status quo norms, beliefs, practices, and structures). These micro practices should never be underestimated or characterized as small or inconsequential. Instead, micro practices speak to the everyday acts on a one-on-one level that we have across all settings that are taken for granted but can make a lasting impact on a person.

Collective Actions

Some collective actions (meaningful work completed by a large group) are as follows:

- Joining a grassroots group that works on behalf of disenfranchised people in terms of civil rights, injustices, and inequalities (worker rights, gender justice, racial justice, human rights, LGBTQIA rights).

- Creating your own group or community to address or challenge a status quo structure or practice of power (e.g., creating a community organization that helps single mothers of color and their families in terms of resources, job placement, and child care).

- Identifying and participating in organizations that push for the environmental rights of indigenous peoples and environmental conservation of natural resources (e.g., locating collectives that connect environmental issues to indigenous peoples' struggles for land and water rights).

- Having your student club or organization (made up of a diverse group of individuals—Whites/European American, Latin, Asian American, Pacific Islander, Black/African American, Muslim, and Jewish students, among others) take up a racial or global justice cause and passionately spread the word about the cause and design a campaign for action to help this cause

- Convening a critical mass of individuals to work together on a specific cause or need in society (e.g., female business owners who assemble to help unemployed and homeless women with skill acquisition, resume writing, and professional networking).

- Pulling together other individuals who are as passionate as you are for a specific cause or commitment and working together locally to address needs and provide solutions (e.g., gathering a group of other business owners who could create a mentoring program for immigrant business owners in order to help establish their businesses and fill the need for more business owners from other cultures).

There are countless individual and collective action examples that can make a difference in our intercultural world and ones that you can uniquely design with your insights and talents. Know that agency and action as an intercultural communication scholar can be in abundance and will always be important given that agency and action will always be tied to and situated in histories, conditions, contexts, and structures of power. Thus, there will not be boundless or free-flowing action, but instead it will be connected to power. This makes our agency and action via the ACT framework for intercultural justice more impressive and essential because we are confronting power issues head on. A critical intercultural communication perspective does just this: It gives us a space to confront and intervene in key power challenges in the intercultural world and make our world a better and more just one for all cultural groups. This notion of using our intercultural knowledge and applying it to transform our world in terms of dismantling power inequalities beyond the classroom is **praxis**. As critical intercultural scholars, we should strive to engage in praxis and positively impact the intercultural world we are in.

This book's author has established her own goals for intercultural justice via a critical intercultural communication approach and the ACT framework for intercultural justice. As a university professor of intercultural communication of 21 years, Rona Tamiko Halualani has asked herself on a daily basis: Am I making a difference in the world? If so, how and in what ways? Because her world revolves around her family and her students (and her departmental home), the classroom has become a primary site through which Rona tries to expose and share information, perspectives, and tools through which awareness, critique, and action could be taken up. Her students over the last 21 years have been so inspiring; their insights and unique perspectives have been important for Rona. Rona's students have also identified and created pathways for action in terms of positive intercultural change through creating community organizations, social justice non-profits, and intercultural dialogue training programs. But, in the last two years, Rona has also realized that she needs to move beyond the classroom as only a specific segment of individuals (and of the larger population) go to college. Last year, she took the first steps in creating a regional and international forum of intercultural scholars (as a learning community) through which they

With the T (or "Think and Act") step of the ACT Framework, joining a social movement or grassroots group for a social cause or a human rights issue stands as a type of collective action. Collective action forges a space to create a critical consciousness among a community and to parlay this into directed action to help change the status quo.

On March 14, 2018, thousands of high school students across multiple states walked out of class to highlight the need to act on gun safety in the U.S.

can help make a difference beyond their educational institutions. One goal is to create a framework for community conversations about cultural difference, power issues, and micro aggressions. This would entail having intercultural scholars develop a framework to share in neighborhood meetings, homeowner association meetings, block parties, and in settings where individuals of all economic, racial, and ethnic backgrounds are located. Rona is not yet sure what these community conversations will look like, but the goal is to challenge misperceptions of cultures and/or facilitate important conversations about difference, power, and connection. These conversations would represent a first step, to be followed by intercultural activities that groups and communities can participate in together (clean-up campaigns, skills training summits, networking, economic summits). She also wants to do more about intercultural awareness (and gender awareness) and behavioral change for police departments and city and state governmental entities in terms of micro aggressions and intercultural obstacles. Rona wants to—like you—positively contribute to the world, disrupt power relations and structures of power, and create meaningful change. She is a critical intercultural communication scholar and together we all can connect with one another, raise the difficult but important questions, and help to change the conditions, contexts, and structures around us to improve our lives and reimagine a just society.

Let's revisit Janis from the beginning of this chapter and how she applies the ACT framework for intercultural justice. A month before she graduated, she decided to fully jump into the ACT framework from her critical intercultural communication course. Because the course pushed her through the "A" (awareness) step and "C" (contemplate,

As the utmost collective action, individuals work in a group or community to design a plan of action and execute that action to transform the status quo for a cultural group or multiple groups.

consider, and critique) step, Janis had the remaining steps to complete. She decided to put her energy into addressing an issue for her home country, Canada, and her community in that country (Chinese Canadians). As a mixed Chinese and German Canadian, Janis wanted to do something for her community in her home country. She knew two issues back at home impacting Chinese Canadians were poverty and legal injustice.

Janis wanted to help the newly arrived Chinese immigrants and those who had been in Canada for awhile. But, through the "A" (awareness) and "C" (consider, contemplate, critique), she found out that this was not for a lack of trying as these community members worked hard. However, the system of getting an education and jobs training was geared for non-immigrants. In this sense, Janis knew she had to provide support to the Chinese-Canadian immigrant community and work to change the system as well. She understood that change needed to happen in multiple ways.

Over a period of six months, Janis called two social agencies that provided services to the Chinese immigrant community in Canada (Toronto, Calgary) and asked what help they needed. Agency representatives told her that they needed help with job training and language training. As a former business major, Janis knew what to do. She called her business contacts and asked their workforce development directors if they could volunteer some time to provide dedicated workshops on resume building, applying for jobs, and interviewing. She also reached out to language studies graduate students and professors to help teach English language skills on a volunteer basis. These were the skill areas that the community needed most and they needed to be translated into Chinese and offered directly in the communities (their enclaves, restaurants, gathering places)

The Chinese emigrated to Canada and experienced hardships in their new home site. In relation to the ACT framework, Janis (of mixed Chinese and German Canadian background) decided to focus on this Chinese immigrant community in Canada.

as many Chinese immigrants stayed in areas that made them comfortable. Janis was maximizing her social capital (or her network of social relationships and resources) in order to help this community.

On the other end, Janis had to tackle the systemic issue of poverty for Chinese Canadian immigrants. She had two friends who were interested in helping—one was a law student (Lisa, a Chinese American now living in Canada) and the other (Ted, a White Canadian) was working in a Canadian media company. Janis and Lisa decided to join an already existing legal rights and services consortium but to extend its outreach and yield. They built a communication campaign in multiple Chinese dialects for the Chinese Canadian community. They even hosted workshops on legal rights in the community.

Janis and Ted started work on the impossible: providing more employment opportunities (and not just trainings) for Chinese Canadian immigrants. They approached Canadian companies and asked if these businesses had any needs that needed to be filled by multilingual workers. Moreover, these workers would need to be trained for entry-level jobs. In this way, Janis and Ted were trying to create a need for and space within extant businesses for immigrants in Canada (who could speak multiple languages and could learn on the job). The training workshops that Janis had helped to expand would not be as impactful if there also weren't built-in opportunities for immigrants within the job sector. Because businesses cannot target specific groups, the strategy had to be creative. Also, businesses would be interested in doing this in order to promote a larger image of social responsibility and communal caring to their shareholders and the general public.

After four years, with the help of her friends, contacts, and countless agencies, businesses, and people, Janis was able to serve and help Chinese Canadians (and other immigrants as well) in a way that improved their lives, helped them fight injustice, and provided spaces for their valued skill sets. It took a lot of work, but Janis loved helping her community in Canada and it even pushed her to become an entrepreneur for her own company that would also have a workforce of at least 50% newly settled Canadians from other countries. Janis engaged in the ACT framework for intercultural justice and used it as a model for living and contributing to the world.

From Janis's narrative, we must remember that positive societal change is possible. And, such change is even more possible now that we know about and understand the structures, conditions, and arrangements of power that are at play.

Summary

As critical intercultural communication scholars, we face the challenge of contributing positively to our intercultural world. Because power is a central focus and yet not fully unpacked by larger society, engaging in transformative action has never been more important. The ACT framework for intercultural justice provides a guiding structure through which to act, consider and critique, and thoughtfully act toward creating a more just world for all cultural groups. Through individual and collective actions, we can perform praxis or thoughtfully apply our intercultural knowledge to bring about positive change. We can actualize our agency and make a difference in the intercultural world.

Keywords

ACT framework for intercultural justice
Action
Agency
Awareness
Collective action

Critique
Individual action
Micro practices
Praxis

Questions and Activities

REFLECTION activity:

Think about this course and how we are now positioned for the future in terms of transforming our intercultural world. Answer all of the following questions:

- Based on your reading of this chapter, how do you define intercultural justice? What does it look and feel like? How can we practice it?
- How do you see yourself practicing the ACT framework for intercultural justice?
- Which individual actions and collective actions do you see yourself as possibly taking up?

DISCUSSION activity: Designing action assignment:

- Identify a specific and significant action that you would like to take that will help transform our intercultural world in terms of dismantling and/or remaking unequal power relations.
- Identify each step of the ACT framework for intercultural justice in going about this action.
- Specify what you will need (resources, knowledge, connections with others, timeline) to execute such an action.
- Share with a classmate in a dyad share exercise.
- Debrief and share with the rest of the class.

Glossary

ACT framework for intercultural justice: The guiding framework to work toward intercultural justice, with each letter representing a specific component and step as delineated:

A refers to the steps in raising one's awareness. This requires us to revisit certain contexts and structures in our lives that we have taken for granted.

C speaks to the next step of considering, questioning, and **critiquing** invisible dimensions of power.

T addresses the stage of **thoughtfully taking action**, individually and collectively.

Action: The stage to think about and engage the best course of action to break down a structure of power or dominant power interest.

Agency: The socially shaped capability to act and make a difference against a structure of power or practice of domination.

Alliances: An association or partnership among individuals, groups, and organizations with a shared goal, experience, or viewpoint.

Allies: Individuals committed to helping and advocating for one another and especially for marginalized groups and causes.

Authenticity: The notion of what it means to be a true, real, or native member of a cultural group.

Awareness: The stage to reflect on and uncover all the power issues and implications in our everyday lives and today's world (as well as that of yesterday).

Collective action: Those acts that can be achieved with others in a formal or informal organization, collective, or association in order to challenge a structure of power and advocate for and assist a cultural group in terms of their needs and struggles.

Colorblindness: An ideology that claims that racial difference and race do not factor into how society is lived and organized. It presumes that society is a neutral and equal playing field in which all groups can prosper depending on their effort and perseverance.

Communication position: The specific vantage point from which to view and approach culturally different people. This vantage point is established by historical factors such as past relations between cultural groups, as well as sociopolitical factors such as the current societal view of the cultural groups of the people involved and the racial order and economic placement of those groups. Such a vantage point includes how one's motivation and willingness to interact with a culturally different person in the first place is historically and sociopolitically shaped.

Communication: An exchange that is affected by the historical contexts and sociopolitical contexts that surround each interlocutor and his or her cultural groups. It is *not* a neutral channel between two people in the immediate moment.

Contexts of power: The settings that are constituted by larger, unseen power forces that help to demarcate how we understand and approach culturally different persons and communities. These contexts of power include the economic context, the governmental context, the legal context, the educational context, the family context, the media context, and the tourism context.

Critical intercultural communication approach (or a critical approach to intercultural communication): A perspective that explores and views intercultural communication encounters through a specific focus on power and how cultural groups are positioned in different ways through larger, unseen sociopolitical structures, histories, and conditions.

Critical race theory (CRT): An area of study that focuses on the relationship between race and power in the arena of law. It is a field of study that aims to critique how race constitutes and shapes American-based legal theory, doctrine, and practice in such a way that a bias toward whiteness and rigid racial or gender hierarchies is strongly upheld.

Critique: The stage to contemplate, consider, and examine specific concepts and contexts of power before one acts.

Cultural capital: The social advantage or leverage one gains when dating or marrying someone of a particular cultural, racial, or ethnic background.

Cultural homogenization: The view of globalization as a massive reproduction of Western institutions and cultural formations over the rest of the world and thus, homogenizing places in terms of Western values and capitalism.

Cultural hybridity: The view of globalization as the creator of a dynamic set of unpredictable, chaotic, disjointed, and multidirectional cultural flows that bring about new forms of cultural expression and cultural identities.

Cultural insider: A person that belongs to and is accepted in a cultural group.

Cultural outsider: A person that does not belong to and is not perceived as a member of a cultural group.

Cultural/Racial fetish: A type of stereotype one has for a cultural group in terms of its physical appearance and what that means or is associated with.

Culture: A system of meanings and representations created in an entangled field of forces through which differently positioned entities (e.g., dominant governmental, legal, economic, mediated, institutional, and educational structures), groups, and persons compete for the power to define, represent, and even own a culture and its resources (land, artifacts, cultural practices).

Culture as a site of struggle (also culture as a field of forces): The process whereby competing interests (dominant structures and cultural communities) shape different representations of culture from different positionalities of power.

Diaspora: The migration or movement of one cultural group to at least one to two sites of settlement.

Discourse: A language of signs and symbols that frames how a cultural issue or group is discussed and understood; it sets into place the who of a cultural group or a topic and how we come to know, see, and act toward that group.

Discursive context: The fields of power that surround representations and discourses and carry different consequences for different cultural groups; refers to the tight-knit, interlocked relationship between representation and power.

Discursive formation: A discourse (or a set of words, statements, utterances, images, memories, and myths) that takes on such great narrative authority or truth value that it dominates the range of knowledge and understanding on a cultural issue, topic, or group.

Divine birthright: The notion that only a few by birthright are destined to be rulers while the masses should be ruled.

Dominant ideology: A world view that aligns with the reigning or dominant ideology and status quo perspective.

Dominant party: A group that possesses the legal, economic, and governmental authority to enforce rules, laws, policies, and taxes and fees onto others.

Exceptions to the rule: The logic that has us view a cultural group member as different from his or her cultural group (the exception) and thus not of that culture at all.

False consciousness: When people accept and absorb a false set of ideas that are perpetuated by the dominant political force and absorbed by societal members. These ideas are deemed false because they do not benefit those societal members. Individuals that are in false consciousness are often referred to as dupes.

Global flows: The rapid, persistent, and uneven movement of people, goods, money, and meanings across national borders and spaces, which is dominated by specific forces. These global flows can also create new opportunities to recreate cultural identities and forms of expression.

Global North: Refers to the power and influence accumulated by the United States, Canada, Western Europe, Hong Kong, South Korea, Singapore, Taiwan, Japan, Israel, Australia, and New Zealand. The Global North (with only one-fourth of the world's population) is characterized has having more wealth, resources, and development and thus dominates the world's income.

Global South: Refers to the poor, less developed, and more populated (with three-fourths of the world's population) but generating less of the world's income.

Globalization: The interplay between structural and economic forces and the cultural meanings of people and groups that result from economically influenced shifts. It refers to the intensified flow of people, goods, money and meanings across national borders and spaces.

Glocalization: The adaptation of global brands to the local and ethnic identities, tastes, and preferences of its market.

Hegemony: The means whereby the dominant groups in society maintain their dominance by securing the supposed spontaneous, willing, or free consent of subordinate groups. Subordinate groups consensually accept the ideas, values, and leadership of the dominant group, even though those ideas and values may partly conflict with their own interests.

Historical amnesia: A selective forgetting or denial of the past.

Historical context: Those past events, moments, crises, perceptions, and experiences that have affected specific cultural groups. Such happenings from the past do not merely disappear as time passes.

Historical frames: The lenses that are shaped by the past and that inform our emotions,

motivations, and views of others before, during, and after intercultural interactions.

Historical memories: The remembrances of culture, nations, and the world that are circulated in the media, news, history textbooks, and public memorials and shape our intercultural relationships.

Historical memory: A remembrance of the past as shared by a group or nation (also known as collective memory).

Historical myth: A widely circulated explanation about the past that may derive from stereotypes and false information.

History as a field of power: The framing of history as a collection of events, images, experiences, sentiments, relations, and perceptions (memories) for a specific nation, culture, or group that are all influenced and shaped by structures of power.

Human agency: The capacity to act, make decisions about, and protest the surrounding societal structures of power.

Identities as politicized: The notion that our identities are political in that each construction is created and spoken from different positionalities (through structures of power, by communities themselves) and in response to past and present discourses of identity.

Identity: Stands as a multilayered arena of defining who we are through two specific key layers: (1) our personal view or declaration of our own identity (the personal layer) and (2) others' framings of our identities or of who we are (the social/structural layer).

Identity politics of authenticity: A larger hierarchy of cultural membership that determines and shapes whose cultural identity is deemed more authentic than another's.

Ideological state apparatus (ISA): Those structures (such as educational institutions, churches or religious institutions, family, media, and popular culture) that create and reproduce dominant viewpoints more subtly through social, everyday institutions and practices and not by force or repression such as in the case of the RSAs.

Ideology: A set of meanings that structure a cultural group's view of the world. However, ideology is not innocent or neutral; it always speaks from the vantage point of a specific power position. Ideology is an instrument of power because it becomes attached to the private and personalized area of selfhood and identity.

Individual action: Those acts that you can plan and enact on your own in terms of pushing for a change in the status quo.

Intercultural desire: The longing or attraction one has for a culturally different person. Such intercultural desire is formed by a number of different factors such as exposure to media or societal images or societal views of what is desirable, among other factors.

Intercultural friendship: An ongoing exchange between two individuals who have a positive affinity for one another (common interests, shared settings).

Intercultural justice: The notion of taking action to help culturally different communities, groups or persons (of your own or outside of your group) whose identities and lives are negatively impacted by structures of power.

Intercultural marriage: A formally recognized union between two individuals of different cultural backgrounds (nationality, race, ethnicity, language, sexual orientation, religion, disability, among other aspects).

Intercultural relationship: An ongoing exchange between two individuals who are from culturally different backgrounds (via gender, race or ethnicity, nationality, religion, socioeconomic class, sexual orientation, among other identity aspects).

Intercultural romantic relationship: A relationship of a romantic nature (dating, long term) between two culturally different members (whether international or interracial or interethnic).

Intercultural work relationship: A connection to culturally different others whom one works with in a professional or organizational setting; these people may occupy the same work team or division for a larger organizational goal.

Interlocuter: A person who participates in a conversation, interaction, or dialogue.

Law or legal scholarship as neutral/objective: The presumed notion that the legal arena ensures the promise of neutrality, fairness, and justice in its procedures, processes, and outcomes.

Legal rationality: The logic that racial bias is deemed as not existing in the first place and/or when it did exist, it showed up as an obvious, extreme, direct, intentional, and out-of-the ordinary act.

Meritocracy: A specific social system through which an individual's talent, ability, and work effort determine success, wealth, position, and social status.

Micro aggressions: Subtle, culturally offensive comments about a specific cultural group.

Micro practices: The everyday acts on a one-on-one level that contribute to action and social change (or the challenging of status quo norms, beliefs, practices, and structures). These acts can occur across all settings and can make a lasting impact.

Misrecognition: The erroneous naming or representation of a cultural group by a structure of power (or a dominant party).

Multiculturalism: An ideology that presumes that all cultural groups are already in equal positions relative to one another and that power is not an issue. It also reduces culture and diversity to an oversimplified encoding of demographic presence.

Myths: Stories about cultural groups that become larger stereotypes and prejudgments of groups over time.

Nationalism: An ideology that naturalizes the superiority of a culture's (a nation's) beliefs, practices, and priorities.

Negotiated ideology: A world view that combines a dominant ideology but inflects it to one's own unique experiences and identity.

Oppositional ideology: A world view that directly challenges, refuses, and rejects the dominant ideology or world view of a culture or society.

Perpetrator perspective: The understanding of racial discrimination as a series of actions inflicted on a victim by a perpetrator. Thus, conditions of the victims are not considered here; rather, the focus is primarily on what the perpetrators did to the victims.

Post-racial society: An ideology that took hold after the election of former President Barack Obama that posits that all racial groups—as evidenced by the leadership of Barack Obama—could succeed and prosper.

Power-based perspective: The view of intercultural communication through the concrete structural pressures, demands, and realities of individuals and cultural groups in their intercultural communication relationships and encounters.

Power: The constraining force by which larger dominant structures, groups, and individuals are able to gain in position and achieve their aims over or against the will of others. It can also be a creative, enabling force through which individuals and social groups can contribute to society and make positive societal change.

Praxis: The notion of using our intercultural knowledge and applying it to transform our world in terms of dismantling power inequalities beyond the classroom.

Private memories: The collective images, histories, and narratives expressed and shared by individuals and communities to represent who they are. Communities create private memories in order to imagine a shared experience of identification with those to whom they are in some way historically, politically, and culturally connected.

Race: A social category or classification created for specific cultural groups in terms of how and what a group is, who is a member, the criteria for belonging, and what it means to be in the group. These classifications of race have often deemed some groups more superior over others based on their skin color, cranial capacity, IQ score, educational status, and blood lineage or the intelligence level, potential mobility, morality, and productivity of cultural groups. Race therefore differentiates, categorizes, and classifies who we are based on a hierarchy of differences (with some being deemed superior over others).

Race as a social construct: The notion that race is a concept that has changed over time (while seemingly meaning one or two things) and been reproduced by structures of power and groups in specific historical periods.

Racial discrimination: The notion that is assumed to be merely the misguided actions of a few in a world in which there is colorblindness and equal opportunity for all.

Racial order: A distinct hierarchy in which groups are positioned relative to one another based on deemed racial categories and meanings.

Racial power: The larger system of economic, social, and cultural processes that reproduce racial categories and re-inscribe a dominant White system or status quo.

Racial state: A structural apparatus made up of local, state, and federal governmental structures and backed by the courts of law, military power, public policy, public educational institutions, local, regional, and national media that construct and delimit what race is.

Racialization: The deployment and assignment of race by various structures and interests of power as a construct or marker to differentiate groups and place them in a hierarchy of value. A hierarchy of value refers to the unequal or asymmetrical positioning of groups for a society through which those at the top of the hierarchy are positively and distinctively valued over those lower in the scale (and deemed as inferior, weak, less than, and underdeveloped).

Racist act: The framing of racism as an obvious, extreme, direct, intentional, and out-of-the ordinary behavior.

Representation: A specific process of giving meaning to things through language.

Repressive state apparatus (RSA): Those structures (such as the police, court systems, military, prison systems) that enforce a dominant ideology in everyday life, especially when it is threatened by deviant or resistive action. RSAs thus work through the constraining power of repression and coercion.

Shared narratives: Stories about other cultures that are passed down in cultural communities.

Social capital: The social networks (relationships, recognitions) that an individual possesses and the resources that this affords that person.

Social justice: The ways to positively transform society by working toward the redistribution of advantages, disadvantages, benefits, and resources to those in need or left without these forms.

Social location: The notion that we all have different identities, backgrounds, and group affiliations and thus are placed differently in relation to one another with regard to our backgrounds. Social location refers to the power positionality and placement of an individual in a society in terms of key demographics such as gender, race, ethnicity, socioeconomic class, sexual orientation, nationality, regional origin, and language, among others.

Sociopolitical context: The contemporary landscape of power in which the government, legal system, economy, institutions and media act toward cultural groups in disproportionate ways.

Speaking as a native member (inside): When you are asked to represent your own cultural group when traveling to another country or when situated in contexts where you stand as one of the few representatives of that group.

Speaking as a non-native (outsider): When you are an outsider and in a position to speak on behalf of or for a cultural group of which you are not a member.

State ideologies: Dominant views endorsed by a governmental or national body

Strategic nationalism: The use of nationalistic appeals in order to redress a colonialist past and restore power that was taken away by an oppressor nation.

Structural framings of identity (social/structural layer): The framings of who we are by surrounding historical conditions and structures of power.

Structural influences of power: Formal harmful measures against intercultural relationships.

Subordinate party: Defined in opposition to that of a dominant party. A subordinate party does not possess the larger authority to make and enforce laws (and imprison individuals), impose fees, control media content, nor does it have the great financial and political resources of a dominant party at its feet to exert influence over society. A subordinate party (an individual, a group, or community) instead is often the one who is at the other end (and who experiences the brunt) of the dominant party's full reach of power and authority and who must creatively use its own resources to fight domination and being marginalized in society.

Symbolic absence: The actual symbols, images, or narratives that are obscured from our view and rendered invisible.

Symbolic presence: The actual symbols, images, or narratives that are shared, told, and made visible.

Traditional model of communication: The view of communication as a direct, immediate, and easy-to-read channel of expression and meaning between two or more individuals. This model frames communication as direct, linear, and on the surface (meaning that what transpires during the communication process defines the entire communication process).

Transnationalism: The uneven movement of global capitalism beyond and between single nation-states.

Unseen or invisible structures of power: Hidden governmental, institutional, mediated, and social forces that embed our lives.

Victim perspective: The understanding of racial discrimination through the inflicted on person's vantage point in terms of the set of actual, objective conditions of lower class existence (lack of jobs, money, housing) and the position resulting from such conditions (lack of choice, of individuality) that surround that person.

Zones of contact: The set of surrounding settings or contexts of possible interactions with other cultural groups that we are exposed to by virtue of where we live, work, or are situated through our histories and those of our family members.

References

Alcoff, L.M. (1995). The problem of speaking for others. In J. Roof & R. Wiegman (Eds.), *Who can speak? Authority and critical identity* (pp. 97–119). Urbana, IL: University of Illinois Press.

Alger, H. (1985). *Ragged Dick; and, struggling upward.* New York, NY: Penguin.

Allen, B. J. (2017). Standpoint theory. In *International encyclopedia of intercultural communication*, Vol. 1. Hoboken, NJ: Wiley.

Allport, G. W. (1954). *The nature of prejudice.* New York, NY: Basic Books.

Althusser, L. (1969). *For Marx* (B. Brewster, trans.). London, UK: Verso.

Althusser, L. (1971). Ideology and ideological state apparatuses (Notes toward an investigation). In B. Brewster (Trans.), *Lenin and philosophy and other essays* (pp. 121–173). London, UK: New Left Books.

Anderson, B. (2006). *Imagined communities: Reflections on the origin and spread of nationalism.* London, UK: Verso.

Anten, T. (2006). Self-disparaging trademarks and social change: Factoring the reappropriation of slurs into Section 2 (a) of the Lanham Act. *Columbia Law Review, 106*(2), 388–434.

Ashcroft, B., Griffiths, G., & Tiffin, H. (2013). *Post-colonial studies: The key concepts.* New York, NY: Routledge.

Balsamo, A., & Treichler, P. A. (1990). Feminist cultural studies: Questions for the 1990s. *Women and Language, 13*(1), 3.

Barker, C. (2000). What is globalization? In J. Beynon & D. Dunkerley (Eds.), *Globalization: The reader* (pp. 42–44). New York, NY: Routledge.

Barker, C. (2003). *Cultural studies: Theory and practice.* Thousand Oaks, CA: SAGE.

Barker, C., & Jane, E. A. (2016). *Cultural studies: Theory and practice* (5th ed.). Los Angeles, CA: SAGE.

Bauman, Z. (1998). *Globalization: The human consequences.* New York, NY: Columbia University Press.

Bean, F. D., & Bell-Rose, S. (Eds.). (1999). *Immigration and opportunity: Race, ethnicity, and employment in the United States.* New York, NY: Russell Sage Foundation Publications.

Bell, J. A. (2017). *The challenge of social mobility: Habitus among low-income and working-class students in higher education* (Doctoral dissertation). Boston, MA: University of Massachusetts, Boston.

Beynon, J., & Dunkerley, D. (Eds.) (2014). *Globalization: The reader.* New York, NY: Routledge.

Bernstein, R., & Edwards, T. (2008). An older and more diverse nation by midcentury. *US Census Bureau News, 14.*

Bhaba, H. K. (1983). The other question: Difference, discrimination and the discourse of colonialism. *Screen, 24*(6), 18–36.

Blackwell, M. (2016). ¡*Chicana power!: Contested histories of feminism in the Chicano movement*. Austin, TX: University of Texas Press.

Bonvillain, N. (2016). *Native nations: Cultures and histories of Native North America*. Lanham, MD: Rowman & Littlefield.

Borgen, L., & Rumbaut, R.G. (2011). Coming of age in 'America's finest city': Transition to adulthood among children of immigrants in San Diego. In M.C. Waters, P.J. Carr, N.J. Kefalas, & J. Holdaway (Eds.), *Coming of age in America* (pp. 133–168). Berkeley, CA: University of California Press.

Bourdieu, P. (1986). The forms of capital (English version). In J. G. Richardson (Ed.), *Handbook of theory and research for the sociology of education* (pp. 241–258). Westport, CT: Greenwood.

Bower, L. C., Goldberg, D. T., & Musheno, M. C. (Eds.). (2001). *Between law and culture: Relocating legal studies*. Minneapolis, MN: University of Minnesota Press.

Brewer, C.A., & Suchan, T.A. (2001). *Mapping census 2000: The geography of U.S. diversity*. Redlands, CA: ESRI Press.

Brown, M. (2015). BrandZ top 100 global brands. *Milward Brown*. Retrieved from http://www.millward-brown.com/brandz/top-global-brands/2017

Brummett, B. (2014). *Rhetoric in popular culture*. Los Angeles, CA: SAGE.

Burd-Sharps, S., & Rasch, R. (2015, June). Impact of the US housing crisis on the racial wealth gap across generations. *Social Science Research Council*, 12.

Busse, K., & Lothian, A. (2017). Debating queer sex, gay politics and media fan cultures. In C. Smith & F. Attwood (Eds.), *The Routledge companion to media, sex and sexuality* (pp. 117–X129X). New York, NY: Routledge.

Cha, A. E., & McLaughlin, K. (1999, April 14). Shift to foreshadow changes in state, U.S. *San José Mercury News*, pp. 1A, 20A.

Chambers, S. A. (2003). Telepistemology of the closet; or, the queer politics of Six Feet Under. *The Journal of American Culture, 26*(1), 24–41.

Chan, S. (2016, January 29). Historical figures, campus controversies. *New York Times*. Retrieved from https://www.nytimes.com/interactive/2016/01/29/education/college-symbol-controversies.html

Chang, E. T., & Leong, R. C. (Eds.). (2017). Los Angeles—*Struggles toward multiethnic community: Asian American, African American, and Latino perspectives*. Seattle, WA: University of Washington Press.

Chang, G. H. (2001). *Asian Americans and politics: Perspectives, experiences, and prospects*. Palo Alto, CA: Stanford University Press.

Chang, I. (2012). *The rape of Nanking: The forgotten holocaust of World War II*. New York, NY: Basic Books.

Chen, K. H., & Morley, D. (Eds.). (2006). *Stuart Hall: Critical dialogues in cultural studies*. New York, NY: Routledge.

Chou, R. S., & Feagin, J. R. (2015). *Myth of the model minority: Asian Americans facing racism*. New York, NY: Routledge.

Chung, L. C., & Ting-Toomey, S. (1999). Ethnic identity and relational expectations among Asian Americans. *Communication Research Reports, 16*(2), 157–166.

Clifford, J. (1994). Diasporas. *Cultural anthropology, 9*(3), 302–338.

Cobas, J. A., Duany, J., & Feagin, J. R. (2015). *How the United States racializes Latinos: White hegemony and its consequences*. New York, NY: Routledge.

Coombe, R. J. (1998). *The cultural life of intellectual properties: Authorship, appropriation, and the law*. Durham, NC: Duke University Press.

Crenshaw, K., Gotanda, N., Peller, G., & Thomas, K. (Eds.) (1995). *Critical race theory: The key writings that formed the movement*. New York, NY: The New Press.

Cross, J. A. (2017). East Asians in America: Chinese, Japanese, and Southeast Asian ethnic landscapes. In *Ethnic Landscapes of America*. Cham, SUI: Springer.

Cumings, B. (1984). The legacy of Japanese colonialism in Korea. In R. Myers & M. Peattie (Eds.), *The Japanese colonial empire 1895–1945* (pp. 478-496). Princeton, NJ: Princeton University Press.

De Certeau, M. (1984). *The practice of everyday life*. Minneapolis, MN: University of Minnesota Press.

Delgado, R., & Stefancic, J. (2017). *Critical race theory: An introduction*. New York, NY: New York University Press.

DeTurk, S. (2001). Intercultural empathy: Myth, competency, or possibility for alliance building? *Communication Education, 50*(4), 374–384.

DeTurk, S. (2007). The power of dialogue: Consequences of intergroup dialogue and their implications for agency and alliance building. *Communication Quarterly, 54* (1), 33–51.

DeTurk, S. (2011). Allies in action: The communicative experiences of people who challenge social injustice on behalf of others. *Communication Quarterly, 59*(5), 569–590.

Diawara, M. (Ed.). (1993). *Black American cinema*. New York, NY: Routledge.

Dippel, C. (2014). Forced coexistence and economic development: Evidence from Native American Reservations. *Econometrica, 82*(6), 2131–2165.

Dotson, K. (2011). Tracking epistemic violence, tracking practices of silencing. *Hypatia, 26*(2), 236–257.

Dudden, A. (2006). Japan's colonization of Korea: Discourse and power. Honolulu, HI: University of Hawai'i Press.

During, S. (2004). *Cultural studies: A critical introduction*. New York, NY: Routledge.

Eagleton, T. (2014). *Ideology*. New York, NY: Routledge.

Ellen, I. G., & O'Regan, K. M. (2011). How low income neighborhoods change: Entry, exit, and enhancement. *Regional Science and Urban Economics, 41*(2), 89-97.

Ehrenreich, B., & A. R. Hochschild (Eds.) (2002). *Global woman: Nannies, maids, and sex workers in the new economy*. New York, NY: Metropolitan Books.

Fabian, J. (2014). *Time and the other: How anthropology makes its object*. New York, NY: Columbia University Press.

Fanon. F. (1961). *The wretched of the earth*, (C. Farrington, trans.). New York, NY: Grove Weidenfeld.

Fischer, E. F., & Brown, R. M. (1996). *Maya cultural activism in Guatemala*. Austin, TX: University of Texas Press.

Fiske, J. (1992). British cultural studies and television. In R. C. Allen (Ed.), *Channels of discourse, reassembled: Television and contemporary criticism* (pp. 284–326). Chapel Hill, NC: University of North Carolina Press.

Fleischauer, S. (2007). The 228 incident and the Taiwan independence movement's construction of a Taiwanese identity. *China Information, 21*(3), 373–401.

Fouad, N. A., & Byars-Winston, A. M. (2005). Cultural context of career choice: Meta-analysis of race/ethnicity differences. *Career Development Quarterly, 53*(3), 223–233.

Foucault, M. (1972). *The archaeology of knowledge and the discourse on language* (A. M. Sheridan Smith, trans.). New York, NY: Pantheon.

Foucault, M. (1973). *The birth of the clinic: An archaeology of medical perception* (A. M. Sheridan-Smith, trans.). New York, NY: Pantheon.

Foucault, M. (1978a). *The history of sexuality, vol. 1: An introduction* (R. Hurley, trans.). New York, NY: Pantheon.

Foucault, M. (1978b). Politics and the study of discourse. In (A. M. Nazzaro, trans.) (revised by C. Gordon) *Ideology & Consciousness, 3* (Spring), 7–26.

Foucault, M. (1980). C. Gordon (Ed.), *Power/knowledge*. New York, NY: Pantheon.

Freeman, A. D. (1995). Legitimizing racial discrimination through antidiscrimination law: A critical review of Supreme Court doctrine. In K. Crenshaw, E. Gotanda, G. Peller, and K. Thomas (Eds.), *Critical race theory: The key writings that formed the movement* (pp. 29–45). New York, NY: The New Press.

Freeman, D. (1983). *Margaret Mead and Samoa*. Cambridge, MA: Harvard University Press.

Friedman, T. L. (2015). *The world is flat: A brief history of the twenty-first century*. London, UK: Macmillan.

Gates, G. J., & Cooke, A. M. (2010). *United States census snapshot, 2010*. Williams Institute. Available from https://williamsinstitute.law.ucla.edu/wp-content/uploads/Census2010Snapshot-US-v2.pdf

Gerstmann, E. (2017). *Same-sex marriage and the Constitution*. Cambridge, MA: Cambridge University Press.

Gibson, M. (2007). *Culture and power: A history of cultural studies*. New York, NY: Bloomsbury.

Gill, R. (2015). *Gender and the media*. Cambridge, UK: Polity Press.

Gilroy, P. (1993). *The black Atlantic: Modernity and double consciousness*. Cambridge, MA: Harvard University Press.

Gilroy, P. (2013). *There ain't no black in the union jack*. New York, NY: Routledge.

Giroux, H. A. (2006). Academic freedom under fire: The case for critical pedagogy. *College Literature, 33* (4), 1–42.

Goldberg, D. T. (1993). *Racist culture: Philosophy and the politics of meaning*. Oxford, UK: Blackwell.

Goldberg, D. T. (1994). *Multiculturalism: A critical reader*. Oxford, UK: Blackwell.

Goldberg, D. T. (1997). Taking stock: Counting by race. In *Racial subjects: Writing on race in America* (pp. 27–58). New York, NY: Routledge.

Goldberg, D. T. (2002). *The racial state*. Malden, MA: Blackwell.

Goldberg, D. T. (2016). Racial subjects: Writing on race in America. New York, NY: Routledge.

Gonzalez, R. J. (2004). *Anthropologists in the public sphere: Speaking out on war, peace, and American power*. Austin, TX: University of Texas Press.

Goodyear-Ka'ōpua, N., Hussey, I., & E. Kahunawaika'ala Wright (Eds.) (2014). *A nation rising: Hawaiian movements for life, land, and sovereignty*. Durham, NC: Duke University Press.

Gordon, A. F., & Newfield, C. (1996). *Mapping multiculturalism*. Minneapolis, MN: University of Minnesota Press.

Gorski, P. C. (2009). Intercultural education as social justice. *Intercultural Education, 20*(2), 87–90.

Gotanda, N. (1996). Multiculturalism and racial stratification. In A. F. Gordon and C. Newfield (Eds.), *Mapping multiculturalism* (pp. 238–502). Minneapolis, MN: University of Minnesota Press.

Gramsci, A. (1971). *Selections from the prison notebooks of Antonio Gramsci*. London, UK: Lawrence and Wishart.

Grossberg, L. (1996a). Identity and cultural studies: Is that all there is? In S. Hall and P. du Gay (Eds.), *Questions of cultural identity*, (pp. 87–107). Thousand Oaks, CA: SAGE.

Grossberg, L. (1996b). History, politics and postmodernism. *Stuart Hall*, 151.

Grossberg, L. (2014). *We gotta get out of this place: Popular conservatism and postmodern culture*. New York, NY: Routledge.

Guilbault, I. (2006). On redefining the "local" through world music. *The World of Music, 35*(2), 33–47.

Guidotti-Hernández, N. M. (2011). *Unspeakable violence: Remapping US and Mexican national imaginaries*. Durham, NC: Duke University Press.

Guzmán, I. M., & Valdivia, A. N. (2004). Brain, brow, and booty: Latina iconicity in US popular culture. *The Communication Review, 7*(2), 205–221.

Hall, S. (1979). Race, articulation and societies structured in dominance. In UNESCO, *Sociological theories: Race and colonialism* (pp. 305–345). Paris, France: UNESCO.

Hall, S. (1980a). Encoding/Decoding. In S. Hall, D. Hobson, A. Lowe, & P. Willis (Eds.), *Culture, media, language* (pp. 128–139). London, UK: Hutchinson.

Hall, S. (1980b). Cultural studies: Two paradigms. *Media, Culture, and Society, 2,* 57–72.

Hall, S. (1985). Signification, representation, ideology: Althusser and the poststructuralist debates. *Critical Studies in Mass Communication, 2,* 91–114.

Hall, S. (1986). The problem of ideology: Marxism without guarantees. *Journal of Communication Inquiry, 10* (2), 28–43.

Hall, S. (1989). Ideology and communication theory. In B. Dervin et al. (Eds.), *Rethinking communication, vol. 1, paradigm issues* (pp. 40–52). Newbury Park, CA: SAGE.

Hall, S. (1992). The question of cultural identity. In S. Hall, D. Held, & J. McGrew (Eds.), *Modernity and its futures* (pp. 274–316). Hoboken, NJ: Wiley.

Hall, S. (1996a). New ethnicities. In K. H. Chen and D. Morley (Eds.), *Stuart Hall: Critical dialogues in cultural studies* (pp. 441–449). New York, NY: Routledge.

Hall, S. (1996b). Race, articulation, and societies structured in dominance. In H. A. Baker Jr., M. Diawara, & R. Lindeborg (Eds.), *Black British cultural studies: A reader* (pp. 16–60). Chicago, IL: University of Chicago Press.

Hall, S. (1996c). Cultural studies and its theoretical legacies. In K. H. Chen and D. Morley (Eds.), *Stuart Hall: Critical dialogues in cultural studies* (pp. 262–275). New York, NY: Routledge.

Hall, S. (1997a). The local and the global: Globalization and ethnicity. *Cultural politics, 11,* 173–187.

Hall, S. (1997b). The work of representation. In S. Hall (Ed.), *Representation: Cultural representations and signifying practices* (pp. 13–74). London, UK: SAGE.

Hall, S. (Ed.). (1997c). *Representation: Cultural representations and signifying practices* (Vol. 2). London, UK: SAGE.

Hall, S., & Du Gay, P. (Eds.). (2006). *Questions of cultural identity.* Thousand Oaks, CA: London office.

Halualani, R. T. (1995). The intersecting hegemonic discourses of an Asian mail-order bride catalog: Pilipina "oriental butterfly" dolls for sale. *Women's Studies in Communication, 18*(1), 45–64.

Halualani, R. T. (2000). Rethinking 'ethnicity' as structural-cultural project(s): Notes on the interface between cultural studies and intercultural communication. *International Journal of Intercultural Relations, 24,* 579–602.

Halualani, R. T. (2002). *In the name of Hawaiians: Native identities and cultural politics.* Minneapolis, MN: University of Minnesota Press.

Halualani, R. T. (2006). 'This is the way things are!': Making sense of gender roles in cultures. In M. K. Lustig & J. Koester (Eds.), *AmongUs: Essays on identity, belonging, and intercultural competence* (2nd ed.) (pp. 104–108). New York, NY: Pearson.

Halualani, R. T. (2008). How do multicultural university students define and make sense of intercultural interaction: A qualitative study. *International Journal of Intercultural Relations, 32,* 1–16.

Halualani, R. T. (2010). Interactant-based definitions of intercultural interaction at a multicultural university. *Howard Journal of Communications, 21,* 247–272.

Halualani, R. T. (2011a). Abstracting and de-racializing diversity: The articulation of diversity in the post-race era. In M. Lacy and K. Ono (Eds.), *Critical rhetorics of race* (pp. 247–63). New York, NY: NYU Press.

Halualani, R. T. (2011b). In/visible dimensions: Framing the intercultural communication course through a critical intercultural communication framework. *Intercultural Education, 22*(1), 43–54.

Halualani, R. T., Fassett, D. L., Morrison, J., & Dodge, P. S. W. (2006). Between the structural and the personal: Raceless diversity, racial pivoting, and situated sense-makings of "Race." *Communication and Critical/Cultural Studies, 3* (1), 70–93.

Hamamoto, D. Y. (1994). *Monitored peril: Asian Americans and the politics of TV representation.* Minneapolis, MN: University of Minnesota Press.

Hamamoto, D. Y., & Liu, S. (Eds.). (2000). *Countervisions: Asian American film criticism* (Vol. 174). Philadelphia, PA: Temple University Press.

Harding, S. G. (Ed.). (2004). *The feminist standpoint theory reader: Intellectual and political controversies.* New York, NY: Routledge.

Harris, T. M., & Kalbfleisch, P. J. (2000). Interracial dating: The implications of race for initiating a romantic relationship. *Howard journal of Communication, 11*(1), 49–64.

Hartsock, N. (1983). The feminist standpoint. In S. Harding & M. B. Hintikka (Eds.), *Discovering reality* (pp. 283–310). London, UK: D. Riedel.

Harvey, D. (2006). *Spaces of global capitalism.* Brooklyn, NY: Verso.

Hasian, M. A., Jr. (1998). Intercultural histories and mass-mediated identities: The re-imagining of the Arab-Israeli conflict. In J. N. Martin, T. K. Nakayama, & L. A. Flores (Eds.), *Readings in cultural contexts* (pp. 97–103). Mountain View, CA: Mayfield.

Hearn, J., & Parkin, W. (2001). *Gender, sexuality and violence in organizations: The unspoken forces of organization violations.* London, UK: SAGE.

Hecht, M. L., Collier, M. J., & Ribeau, S. A. (1993). *African American communication: Ethnic identity and cultural interpretation.* Thousand Oaks, CA: SAGE.

Hewstone, M. E., & Brown, R. E. (1986). *Contact and conflict in intergroup encounters.* Hoboken, NJ: Blackwell.

Hill Collins, P. (2000). *Black feminist thought: Knowledge, consciousness, and the politics of empowerment.* New York, NY: Routledge.

Hobsbawm, E., & Ranger, T. (1983). *The invention of tradition.* Cambridge, MA: Cambridge University Press.

Hochschild, A.R. (2002). Love and gold. In B. Ehrenreich & A. R. Hochschild (Ed.), *Global woman: Nannies, maids, and sex workers in the new economy* (pp. 15–30). New York, NY: Henry Holt.

Hoewe, J. (2016). Loving v. Virginia. In Stone, J., Dennis, R. M., Rizova, P. S., Smith, A. D., & Hou, X. (Eds.). (2016). The Wiley Blackwell encyclopedia of race, ethnicity, and nationalism (Vol. 1). John Wiley & Sons, pp. 1-2.Hofstede, G. (2003). *Culture's consequences: Comparing values, behaviors, institutions, and organizations across nations* (2nd ed.). Thousand Oaks, CA: SAGE.

Hutton, P. H. (1993). *History as an art of memory.* Hanover, MA: University Press of New England.

Hwang, D. H.(1999). Facing the mirror. In K. Aguilar-San Juan (Ed)., *The state of Asian America: Activism and resistance in the 1990s* (pp. ix-xii). Boston, MA: South End Press.

Hwang, J. Y. (2016). Transitional justice in postwar Taiwan. *Handbook of contemporary Taiwan.* New York, NY: Routledge.

Hwang, J., & Sampson, R. J. (2014). Divergent pathways of gentrification: Racial inequality and the social order of renewal in Chicago neighborhoods. *American Sociological Review, 79*(4), 726–751.

Ingraham, C. (2009). *White weddings: Romancing heterosexuality in popular culture.* New York, NY: Routledge.

Irwin-Zarecka, I. (2017). *Frames of remembrance: The dynamics of collective memory.* New York, NY: Routledge.

Jenness, V. (1999). Managing differences and making legislation: Social movements and the racialization, sexualization, and gendering of federal hate crime law in the US, 1985-1998. *Social Problems, 46*(4), 548–571.

Johnson, C. S., Olson, M. A., & Fazio, R. H. (2009). Getting acquainted in interracial interactions: Avoiding intimacy but approaching race. *Personality and Social Psychology Bulletin, 35*(5), 557–571.

Johnson, H. B. (2014). *The American dream and the power of wealth: Choosing schools and inheriting inequality in the land of opportunity.* New York, NY: Routledge.

Johnson, R., & Dawson, G. (1982). Popular memory: Theory, politics, method. In R. Johnson, G. Mclennan, B. Schwarz, & D. Sutton (Eds.), *Making histories: Studies in history-writing and politics* (pp. 205–252). New York, NY: Routledge.

Johnson, R., McLennan, G., Schwartz, B, & D. Sutton (Eds.) (2013), *Making histories: Studies in history-writing and politics*. New York, NY: Routledge.Kame'eleihiwa, L. (1992). *Native land and foreign desires*. Honolulu, HI: Bishop Museum Press.

Kaplan, H. R. (2011). *The myth of post-racial America: Searching for equality in the age of materialism*. Lanham, MD: Rowman & Littlefied.

Katriel, T. (2013). *Performing the past: A study of Israeli settlement museums*. New York, NY: Routledge.

Kauanui, J. K. (2007). Diasporic deracination and "off-Island" Hawaiians. *The Contemporary Pacific, 19*(1), 138–160.

Kim, C. (2000). *Bitter fruit: The politics of Black-Korean conflict in New York City*. New Haven, CT: Yale University Press.

Kim, C. J. (1999). The racial triangulation of Asian Americans. *Politics & Society, 27*(1), 105–138.

Kim, C. J. (2004). Imagining race and nation in multiculturalist America. *Ethnic and Racial Studies, 27*(6), 987–1005.

Kitwana, B. (2006). *Why white kids love hip hop: Wankstas, wiggas, wannabes, and the new reality of race in America*. New York, NY: Basic Civitas Books.

Kiuchi, Y. (Ed.). (2016). *Race still matters: The reality of African American lives and the myth of postracial society*. Albany, NY: SUNY.

Kochhar, R., & Fry, R. (2014). Wealth inequality has widened along racial, ethnic lines since end of great recession. *Pew Research Center, 12*, 1–15.

Kraidy, M. (2017). *Hybridity, or the cultural logic of globalization*. Philadelphia, PA: Temple University Press.

Kroska, A. (2007). Gender ideology and gender role ideology. In Ritzer, G., Ryan, J.M., & Thorn, B. (Eds.), *Blackwell encyclopedia of sociology*, Volume 1. Hoboken, NJ: Wiley.

Kula, S. M., & Paik, S. J. (2016). A historical analysis of Southeast Asian refugee communities: Post-war acculturation and education in the US. *Journal of Southeast Asian American Education and Advancement, 11*(1), 1–23.

Kwon, S. A. (2006). Youth of color organizing for juvenile justice. In S. Ginwright, P. Noguera, & J. Cammorota (eds.), *Beyond resistance* (pp.215–228). New York, NY: Routledge.

Laclau, E. (1977). Towards a theory of populism. In *Politics and ideology in Marxist theory* (pp. 143–200). Brooklyn, NY: Verso.

Laclau, E., & Mouffe, C. (2001). *Hegemony and socialist strategy: Towards a radical democratic politics*. Brooklyn, NY: Verso.

Lavie, S., & Swedenburg, T. (Eds.) (1996). *Displacement, diaspora, and geographies of identity*. Durham, NC: Duke University Press.

Lee, J. (2017, March 17). Palo Alto: Two schools named after eugenics advocates to get new names. *Mercury News*. Retrieved from https://www.mercurynews.com/2017/03/17/palo-alto-eugenics-controversy-spurs-school-name-changes/

Lee, J., & Zhou, M. (2014). The success frame and achievement paradox: The costs and consequences for Asian Americans. *Race and Social Problems, 6*(1), 38–55.

Lee, J., & Zhou, M. (2015). *The Asian American achievement paradox*. New York, NY: Russell Sage Foundation.

Lees, L. (2016). Gentrification, race, and ethnicity: Towards a global research agenda? *City & Community, 15*(3), 208-214.

Legewie, J. (2016). Racial profiling and use of force in police stops: How local events trigger periods of increased discrimination. *American Journal of Sociology, 122*(2), 379–424.

Levin, S., Taylor, P. L., & Caudle, E. (2007). Interethnic and interracial dating in college: A longitudinal study. *Journal of Social and Personal Relationships, 24*(3), 323-341.

Lipsitz, G. (1990). *Time passages: Collective memory and American popular culture.* Minneapolis, MN: University of Minnesota Press.

Livingston, G., & Brown, A. (2017, May 18). Intermarriage in the US 50 years after *Loving v. Virginia. Pew Research Center Report.* Retrieved from http://www.pewsocialtrends.org/2017/05/18/intermarriage-in-the-u-s-50-years-after-loving-v-virginia/

Lobo, S., Talbot, S., & Carlston, T. M. (2016). *Native American voices.* New York, NY: Routledge.

Loewen, J. W. (2008). *Lies my teacher told me: Everything your American history textbook got wrong.* New York, NY: The New Press.

Logan, J. (2000). Still a global city: The racial and ethnic segmentation of New York. In Marcuse, P. & van Kempen R. (Eds.) *Globalizing cities: a new spatial order?* (pp. 158–185). Malden, MA: Blackwell.

Lowe, L. (1996). *Immigrant acts: On Asian American cultural politics.* Durham, NC: Duke University Press.

MacCannell, D. (1999). *The tourist: A new theory of the leisure class.* Berkeley, CA: University of California Press.

Madison, D. S. (1993). "That was my occupation": Oral narrative, performance, and black feminist thought. *Text and Performance Quarterly, 13*(3), 213–232.

Marchetti, G. (1994). *Romance and the "yellow peril": Race, sex, and discursive strategies in Hollywood fiction.* Berkeley, CA: University of California Press.

Martin, J. N., & Nakayama, T. K. (1997). *Intercultural communication in contexts.* Mountain View, CA: Mayfield.

Martin, J. N., & Nakayama, T. K. (1999). Thinking about culture dialectically. *Communication Theory, 9*(1), 1–25.

Martin, J. N., & Nakayama, T. K. (2006). Communication as raced. In G. J. Shepherd, J. St. John, & T. Striphas (Eds.), *Communication as . . .: Perspectives on theory* (pp. 75–83). Thousand Oaks, CA: SAGE.

Martin, J. N., Bradford, L. J., Drzewiecka, J. A., & Chitgopekar, A. S. (2003). Intercultural dating patterns among young white US Americans: Have they changed in the past 20 years? *Howard Journal of Communication, 14*(2), 53–73.

Marx, K. (2000). *Karl Marx: Selected writings.* Oxford, UK: Oxford University Press.

Mau, W. C. (2000). Cultural differences in career decision-making styles and self-efficacy. *Journal of Vocational Behavior, 57*(3), 365–378.

McClennen, S. A. (2006). The geopolitical war on U.S. higher education. *College Literature, 33*(4), 43–75.

McClintock, A. (2013). *Imperial leather: Race, gender, and sexuality in the colonial contest.* New York, NY: Routledge.

McKay, J. (2016). Native American DNA: Tribal belonging and the false promise of genetic science by Kim Tallbear. *The American Indian Quarterly, 40*(2), 175–179.

Mead, M. (1971, reprint). *Coming of age in Samoa.* New York, NY: Harper Perennial.

Mendoza, S. L. L. (2002). *Between the homeland and the diaspora: The politics of theorizing Filipino and Filipino American identities: A second look at the poststructuralism-indigenization debates.* New York, NY: Routledge.

Mendoza, S. L., & Strobel, L. M. (Eds.). (2015). *Back from the crocodile's belly: Philippine Babaylan studies and the struggle for indigenous memory.* Createspace Independent Publishing Platform.

Mendoza, S. L., Halualani, R. T., & Drzewiecka, J. A. (2003). Moving the discourse on identities in intercultural communication: Structure, culture, and resignifications. *Communication Quarterly, 50 (3/4)*, 312–327.

Mercer, K. (1999). *Welcome to the jungle: New positions in black cultural studies.* New York, NY: Routledge.

Meyer, D. S., Whittier, N., & Robnett, B. (Eds.). (2002). *Social movements: Identity, culture, and the state.* New York, NY: Oxford University Press.

Minh-Ha, T. T. (2009). *Woman, native, other: Writing postcoloniality and feminism.* Bloomington, IN: Indiana University Press.

Minh-Ha, T. T. (2014). *When the moon waxes red: Representation, gender and cultural politics.* New York, NY: Routledge.

Mio, J. S., & Fu, M. (2017). Poverty in the Asian/Pacific Islander American community: Social justice-related community responses. *Social Issues in Living Color: Challenges and Solutions from the Perspective of Ethnic Minority Psychology, 3 Volumes*, 75.

Moon, D. G. (1996). Concepts of 'culture': Implications for intercultural communication research. *Communication Quarterly, 44(1)*, 70–84.

Moon, D. G., & Holling, M. A. (Eds.). (2017). *Race(ing) intercultural communication: Racial logics in a colorblind era.* New York, NY: Routledge.

Nakayama, T. K. (2000). Dis/orienting identities: Asian Americans, history, and intercultural communication. In Gonzalez, A., M. Houston, & V. Chen (Eds.). *Our voices: Essays in culture, ethnicity, and communication.* New York, NY: Oxford University Press.

Ngo, B., & Lee, S. J. (2007). Complicating the image of model minority success: A review of Southeast Asian American education. *Review of Educational Research, 77(4)*, 415–453.

Nguyen, T. H. (2014). *A view from the bottom: Asian American masculinity and sexual representation.* Durham, NC: Duke University Press.

Olick, J. K. (2013). *The politics of regret: On collective memory and historical responsibility.* New York, NY: Routledge.

Omi, M. (1996). Racialization in the post-civil rights era. In A. F. Gordon and C. Newfield (Eds.), *Mapping multiculturalism* (pp. 238–502). Minneapolis, MN: University of Minnesota Press.

Omi, M., & Winant, H. (2012). Racial formation rules. In D.M. Hosang, O. LaBennett, & L. Pulido (Eds.) *Racial formation in the twenty-first century* (pp. 302–330). Berkeley, CA: University of California Press.

Omi, M., & Winant, H. (2014). *Racial formation in the United States.* New York, NY: Routledge.

Ong, A. (1999). *Flexible citizenship: The cultural logics of transnationality.* Durham, NC: Duke University Press.

Ono, K. A. (Ed.). (2004). *A companion to Asian American studies.* Hoboken, NJ: Wiley-Blackwell.

Orbe, M. P., & Harris, T. M. (2013). *Interracial communication: Theory into practice* (3rd edition). Los Angeles, CA: SAGE.

Pacific Islanders in Communications (Producer), & Lucas, P. (Director). (1996). *Storytellers of the Pacific: Identity* (Documentary). Lincoln, Neb.: Vision Maker Video.

Paine, E. (2000, October). The road to the Global Compact: Corporate power and the battle over global public policy at the United Nations. In *Global Policy Forum* (pp. 104-129).

Parker, L. S. (1996). *Native American estate: The struggle over Indian and Hawaiian lands.* Honolulu, HI: University of Hawai'i Press.

Parnell, S., & Oldfield, S. (Eds.). (2014). *The Routledge handbook on cities of the global south.* New York, NY: Routledge.

Parrenas, R. S. (2002). The care crisis in the Philippines: Children and transnational families in the new global economy. In B. Ehrenreich & A. R. Hochschild (Eds.), *Global woman: Nannies, maids, and sex workers in the new economy* (pp. 39–54). New York, NY: Metropolitan Books.

Passel, J. S., Cohn, D., & Lopez, M. H. (2011). *Hispanics account for more than half of nation's growth in past decade*. Washington, DC: Pew Hispanic Center.

Pearson, E. M. (2017). Native American injustice and the mathematics of blood quantum. In E. Sieh & J. McGregor (Eds.), *Human dignity* (pp. 301–317). London, UK: Macmillan.

Pettigrew, T. F., & Tropp, L. R. (2005). Allport's intergroup contact hypothesis: Its history and influence. In J. Dividio, P. Glick & L. Budman (Eds.), *On the nature of prejudice: Fifty years after Allport* (pp. 262–277). Malden, MA: Blackwell.

Pieterse, J. N. (2009). *Globalization and culture: Global mélange*. Plymouth, UK: Rowman & Littlefield.

Popular Memory Group (1982). Popular memory: Theory, politics, method. In R. Johnson, G. McLennan, B. Schwarz, and D. Sutton (Eds.), *Making histories: Studies in history-writing and politics* (pp. 205–252). London, UK: Centre for Contemporary Cultural Studies.

Qin, A. (2018, February 11). NBC Apologizes after Japan comment draws anger in South Korea. *New York Times*. Retrieved from https://www.nytimes.com/2018/02/11/world/asia/nbc-apology-japan-korea.html.

Reiter, M. J., & Gee, C. B. (2008). Open communication and partner support in intercultural and interfaith romantic relationships: A relational maintenance approach. *Journal of Social and Personal Relationships*, 25(4), 539–559.

Richter, D. H. (Ed.). (1998). Multiculturalism and the canon wars: The politics of literature. In *The Critical Tradition: Classic Texts and Contemporary Trends*. Boston, MA: Bedford Books.

Ritzer, G. (Ed.). (2009). *McDonaldization: The reader*. Thousand Oaks, CA: SAGE.

Roberts, J. T., & Parks, B. (2006). *A climate of injustice: Global inequality, north-south politics, and climate policy*. Cambridge, MA: MIT Press.

Romano, D. (2008). *Intercultural marriage: Promises and pitfalls*. Boston, MA: Nicholas Brealey Publishing.

Rubio, D. (2017). Historical amnesia is undermining European democracy [blog post]. *LSE European Politics and Policy (EUROPP)*. Retrieved from http://blogs.lse.ac.uk/europpblog/2017/05/03/historical-amnesia-is-undermining-european-democracy/

Safran, W. (1991). Diasporas in modern societies: Myths of homeland and return. *Diaspora: A journal of transnational studies*, 1(1), 83–99.

Said, E. W. (1978). *Orientalism*. New York, NY: Vintage Books.

Said, E. W. (2012). *Culture and imperialism*. New York, NY: Vintage Books.

Sailes, G. A. (2017). Social myths and stereotypes. *African Americans in Sports*, 183.

Samovar, L. A., Porter, R. E., McDaniel, E. R., & Roy, C. S. (2015). *Communication between cultures* (8th edition). Boston, MA: Cengage.

Sassen, S. (1991). *The global city*. Princeton, NJ: Princeton University Press.

Sassen, S. (1998). *Globalization and its discontents: Essays on the new mobility of people and money*. New York, NY: The New Press.

Sassen, S. (2018). The global city: Strategic site, new frontier. In L. Ferro, M. Smagacz-Poziemska, M. V. Gomez, S. Kurtenbach, P. Pereira, & J. J. Villalón (Eds.), *Moving cities—Contested views on urban life* (pp. 11–28). Wiesbaden, Germany: Springer.

Schachter, J. (2015). A nation rising: Hawaiian movements for life, land, and sovereignty. *Canadian Journal of Native Studies*, 35(1), 170.

Schaefer, R. T. (2004). *Racial and ethnic groups* (9th edition). Upper Saddle River, NJ: Prentice Hall.

Scommegna, P. (2004, April). U.S. growing bigger, older, and more diverse. *Population Reference Bureau*. Retrieved from ttps://www.prb.org/usgrowingbiggerolderandmorediverse/.

Shilts, R. (2014). *Conduct unbecoming: Gays and lesbians in the US military*. New York, NY: Griffin.

Shome, R., & Hegde, R. S. (2002). Culture, communication, and the challenge of globalization. *Critical Studies in Media Communication*, 19(2), 172–189.

Siapera, E. (2010). *Cultural diversity and global media: the mediation of difference*. Hoboken, NJ: Wiley-Blackwell.

Silva, Noenoe K. (2004). *Aloha betrayed: Native Hawaiian resistance to American colonialism*. Durham, NC: Duke University Press.

Slack, J. D. (1996). The theory and method of articulation in cultural studies. In D. Morley & K. Chen (Eds.). *Stuart Hall: Critical dialogues in cultural studies* (pp. 112–127). New York, NY: Routledge.

Spivak, G. C. (1988). Can the subaltern speak? In C. Nelson & L. Grossberg (Eds.), *Marxism and the interpretation of culture* (pp. 271–313). Urbana, IL: University of Illinois Press.

Stapleton, K. R. (1998). From the margins to mainstream: The political power of hip-hop. *Media, Culture & Society, 20*(2), 219–234.

Starosta, W. J., & Chen, G.M. (2001, November). *A fifth moment in intercultural communication? A dialogue*. Paper presented at the meeting of the National Communication Association. Atlanta, GA.

Starosta, W. J., & G. M. Chen. (2003). *Ferment in the intercultural field: Axiology/value/praxis—international and intercultural communication annual, 26*. Thousand Oaks, CA: SAGE.

Storey, J. (2016). Popular Culture. In A. Malinowska & K. Lebek (Eds.), *Materiality and popular culture: The popular life of things*. New York, NY: Routledge.

Strinati, D. (2004). *An introduction to theories of popular culture*. New York, NY: Routledge.

Sue, D. W. (2010). *Microaggressions in everyday life: Race, gender, and sexual orientation*. Hoboken, NJ: Wiley.

Swedenburg, T. (Ed.). (1996). *Displacement, diaspora, and geographies of identity*. Durham, NC: Duke University Press.

TallBear, K. (2013). *Native American DNA: Tribal belonging and the false promise of genetic science*. Minneapolis, MN: University of Minnesota Press.

Tang, E. (2000). Collateral damage: Southeast Asian poverty in the United States. *Social Text, 18*(1), 55–79.

Taylor, C. (2011). *Multiculturalism* (expanded paperback edition). Princeton, NJ: Princeton University Press.

Thompson, J. B. (1990/2013). *Ideology and modern culture: Critical social theory in the era of mass communication*. Cambridge, UK: Polity Press.

Thorbecke, E., & Charumilind, C. (2002). Economic inequality and its socioeconomic impact. *World Development, 30*(9), 1477–1495.

Tomlinson, J. (1999). *Globalization and culture*. Chicago, IL: University of Chicago Press.

Trevino, M., Kanso, A. M., & Nelson, R. A. (2010). Islam through editorial lenses: How American elite newspapers portrayed Muslims before and after September 11, 2001. *Journal of Arab & Muslim Media Research, 3*(1-2), 3-17.

Tukachinsky, R., Mastro, D., & Yarchi, M. (2017). The effect of prime time television ethnic/racial stereotypes on Latino and black Americans: A longitudinal national level study. *Journal of Broadcasting & Electronic Media, 61*(3), 538–556.

United States Census Bureau (2017, May). Asian Pacific American Heritage Month (2017, May). *Facts for Features*.

Van Dijk, T. A. (2015). Critical discourse studies: A sociocognitive approach. *Methods of Critical Discourse Studies* [e-book], 63–74.

Waisman, C. H. (2015). *Modernization and the working class: The politics of legitimacy*. Austin, TX: University of Texas Press.

Waldman, C. (2014). *Encyclopedia of Native American tribes*. New York, NY: Checkmark Books.

Wang, F. H. (2017, October 5). 'Never again is now': Japanese-American theater group finds new relevance supporting Muslims. *NBC News*. Retrieved from https://www.nbcnews.com/news/asian-america/never-again-now-japanese-american-theater-group-finds-new-relevance-n805771.

Warner, M. (Ed.). (1993). *Fear of a queer planet: Queer politics and social theory* (Vol. 6). Minneapolis, MN: University of Minnesota Press.

Washington, M. (2012). Interracial intimacy: Hegemonic construction of Asian American and black relationships on TV medical dramas. *Howard Journal of Communications, 23*(3), 253–271.

Waters, M. C. (1990). *Ethnic options: Choosing identities in America*. Berkeley, CA: University of California Press.

Whelan, Y. (2016). Heritage, memory and the politics of identity: New perspectives on the cultural landscape. New York, NY: Routledge.

Wildman, S.M. (2002). Interracial Intimacy and the Potential for Social Change, Available at: https://digitalcommons.law.scu.edu/facpubs/622Wilkins, D. E., & Stark, H. K. (2017). *American Indian politics and the American political system*. Plymouth, UK: Rowman & Littlefield.

Wilson, J. K. (2015). *Patriotic correctness: Academic freedom and its enemies*. New York, NY: Routledge.

Wolf, R. (2017, October 10). Children of Japanese American legal pioneers from World War II fight travel ban. *USA Today*. Retrieved from https://www.usatoday.com/story/news/politics/2017/10/10/children-japanese-american-legal-pioneers-world-war-ii-fight-travel-ban/740910001/

Wong Lau, K. (1998). Migration across generations: Whose identity is authentic? In Martin, J. N., Nakayama, T. K., & Flores, L. A. (Eds.), *Readings in cultural contexts* (pp. 127-134). Mountain View, CA: Mayfield Publishing.

Wright, H. K. (2003). Cultural studies as praxis: (Making) an autobiographical case. *Cultural Studies, 17*(6), 805–822.

Yep, G. A. (2003). The violence of heteronormativity in communication studies: Notes on injury, healing, and queer world-making. *Journal of Homosexuality, 45*(2–4), 11–59.

Young, R. J. (2005). *Colonial desire: Hybridity in theory, culture and race*. New York, NY: Routledge.

Zheng, R. (2016). Why yellow fever isn't flattering: A case against racial fetishes. *Journal of the American Philosophical Association, 2*(3), 400–419.

Zhou, M. (2004). Are Asian Americans becoming "White?" *Contexts, 3*(1), 29–37.

Name Index

Subject Index

economic competition, 9, 37, 66, 72

economic context of power, 12
    globalization and, 184–187

economic shifts, 194, 195

educational context of power, 14–15

educational status, 120, 162

educational stereotypes, 113

educational structures, 38, 46

Egypt, 191

El Salvador, 194

"Encoding/Decoding" (Hall), 53

England, 17, 88, 122, 185, 189, 193

entitlement, 38, 142, 154

episteme, 99

ethnic enclaves, 11, 12

Europe, 34, 125, 140, 161, 182, 187

Europeans. *See* White/European Americans

exceptions to the rule, 214

Exxon Mobil, 185

F

Facebook, 9, 143, 182, 192, 198

Facetime, 182

false consciousness, 79–80

family context of power, 15–16

Family Tree DNA, 131

fasting rituals, 194

femininity, 90, 219

feminist standpoint theory, 102

Fiji, 19

Filipino movement, 34–35

Fishburne, Laurence, 77

Forbes, 192

Ford, 185

foreign films, 191

French, 2, 4, 15, 27, 28, 89, 151, 154, 191

French pop, 2, 4

friendships, 32

G

gay persons. *See* LGBTQIA

gender discrimination, 14

gender groups, 5, 10, 14

gender ideology, 212

General Electric, 185

General Motors, 185

genetics, 131, 132, 162

gentrification, 9, 11

German migrants, 194

Germany, 76, 149, 151, 163, 192, 194, 227, 237, 238

Ghana, 78

Glenn, John, 149

global age, 183

global brands, 182, 185–186, 192–194

global capitalism, 4, 196–199

global culture, 4, 184, 192–194

global flows, 192–193, 195–196

globalization, 181–199
    capitalism and, 196–199
    conditions of intercultural context created by, 188
    cultural authenticity and, 195–196
    cultural images moving across boundaries by, 190–192
    defined, 183–184
    economic power and, 184–187
    flows of global commodities, 192–193, 195–196
    geographic place of cultural groups changed by, 187–188
    key attributes of, 184–199
    migration and, 194–195
    narrative, 181–183

    power dynamics in, 187, 199
    technological advancements created by, 189–190
    transnationalism and, 196–197
    Western consumerism and commodities spread by, 193–194

global migration, 194–195

Global North, 91, 187, 192, 193

Global Policy Forum, 185

Global South, 91, 187

glocalization, 42, 193–194, 230

GM, 185

Google, 185, 192, 193, 198

Google Hangout, 182

Google maps, 181

Google Play, 191

governmental context of power, 12–13

Graceful Crane theater troupe, 152–153

Great Britain, 80, 88, 194, 197

Greece, 17, 42, 133–134

Guam, 19, 121

Guess Who's Coming to Dinner (movie), 217

H

hair texture, 159–160, 162

Harlem in New York, 1, 9

hate crimes, 13–14, 63

haves and have nots, 33, 187, 198

Hawaiian Homes Commission Act (HHCA), 126

Hawaiianness, 43–44, 133

Hawaiians, 35, 41, 43–44, 103, 126–127, 133

Hawaii Five-O (TV series), 44

heathen groups, 78, 126

hegemony, 85–87

Hemingway, Ernest, 15

heteronormative romance ideology, 212, 213

heterosexual marriage, 83

Hidden Figures (film), 149

hierarchy of power, 8–9

hierarchy of value, 165

Hinglish films, 196

hip-hop, 5, 50, 96, 182, 196

historical amnesia, 149–151, 230

historical context, 56–62

historical memory, 145–154

   historical amnesia, 149–151, 230

   intercultural communication and, 153–154

   intercultural relationships and, 210–214

   myths, 210–214

   narratives, 139–140, 210–214

   outdated historical narratives in textbooks, 145–146

   power of, 146–149, 153–154

   private memory, 153

   remaking, 151–152

   symbolic absences, 150

   symbolic presence, 149–150

history. *See also* historical context

   biased perspectives of, 143–145

   defined, 140

   dominant interests advanced by, 142

   as field of power, 140–145

   intercultural communication encounters connected to, 56–62

   myths of cultural groups, 59–61, 211–214

   political moment, 114–115

of representations for cultural groups of focus, 112–114

   work to (re)produce, 143

Hitler, Adolf, 151

Hmong, 30, 66, 99

Hollywood celebrity culture, 106

Hollywood films, 190

homosexuality, 86–87, 112–113, 163. *See also* LGBTQIA

homosexual persons. *See* LGBTQIA

Hong Kong, 78, 132, 142, 185, 187, 188, 197, 198

Hong Kong pop, 2, 4

How to be a Latin Lover (movie), 217

Hulu, 191

human agency, 75, 84

hybridity, cultural, 195–196, 197, 199

I

IBM, 90, 185

identity

   in cultural studies, 122–123, 128

   misrecognition, 129, 130–131

   narrative, 119–121

   personal/group constructions of, 121, 128–131

   as politicized, 127

   politics of authenticity, 131–135

   power and, 121–122

   structural framings of, 121, 122–127, 128, 131

   understanding, 121–122

identity layers, 119–135

   colliding dynamics between, 130–135

   personal, 121, 128–131

social/structural, 121, 122–127, 128, 131

identity politics of authenticity, 131–135

ideological state apparatus (ISA), 81, 82–83

ideology, 71–92

   cultural views as, 73–74

   defined, 74–75

   dominant, 76–80

   false consciousness and, 79–80

   hegemony, 85–87

   of heteronormativity, 212, 213

   Japanese way of life (narrative), 71–73

   of Manifest Destiny, 78

   meritocracy and, 91–92

   nationalistic, 87–89

   negotiated, 84–85

   oppositional, 85

   of race, 166–169

   as representation, 79

   superstructure and, 80–84

   surrounding culture, 87–92

independent/interdependent contexts of power, 11

India, 42, 78, 112, 182, 185

Indian Bhangra fusion, 4

indigenous peoples, 18, 78, 108, 121, 153, 188, 234

individual actions, in ACT framework, 22, 230–233

individualism, 90, 91, 197

Indochina, 154

Instagram, 2, 182, 192

institutional racism, 14

intelligence level, 161

intercultural activities, 236

intercultural communication

   connecting, 3–7

   contexts of power in, 7–19

   critical approach to (*See* critical intercultural

communication approach)

cultural representation and, 95–115

encounters (See intercultural communication encounters)

in everyday life (narrative), 1–3

globalization and, 181–199

historical memory and, 153–154, 210–214

identity layers and, 119–135

ideology and, 71–92

locating, 3

portrait of (narrative), 49–51

racialization and, 159–176

intercultural communication encounters

historical context of, 56–62

sociopolitical context of, 63–68

intercultural desire, 208, 217–222

cultural or racial fetish in, 220–222

defined, 219

formation of, 219

intercultural friendship, 51, 206, 207, 208, 213

intercultural justice. See also ACT framework for intercultural justice

defined, 21

narrative, 227–228

intercultural marriage, 5, 6, 207, 214–216, 222–223

intercultural relationships, 205–223. See also macro layers of power

cultural capital and, 105, 208, 215–217

exceptions to the rule, 214

historical memory and, 210–214

intercultural desire and, 208, 217–222

intercultural friendships, 51, 206, 207, 208, 213

intercultural marriage, 5, 6, 207, 214–216, 222–223

intercultural romantic relationships, 206

intercultural work-relationships, 206–207

shared narratives, 205–206, 211–214

types of, 206–207

intercultural resentment, 216

intercultural romantic relationships, 206

intercultural work-relationship, 206–207

interlocutor, 49–68

from critical perspective, 51–53

cultural group experiences with, 63–64

current view of, 64–65

economic positioning of, 65–67

family experiences with, 58–59

of focus, cultural representation for, 112–114

geographic place of, globalization and, 187–188

from historical context, 56–62

historical myths of, 59–61

past cultural relations between/among, 61

perception of, over time, 56–57

portrait of intercultural communication (narrative), 49–51

position of, in society, 67–68

from power-based perspective, 53–55, 68

productivity of, 161

society's historical treatment of, 61–62

from sociopolitical context, 63–68

International Labor Organization, 185

iPhone, 2, 4, 192

IQ scores, 161, 162

Iran, 182, 191

Iraq, 13, 74, 75, 98

Ireland, 192

Irish migrants, 194

Israel, 187

Israelis, 154

Italy, 76

iTunes, 191

J

Jackson, Mary, 149

Jamaican reggae, 2, 4

Japanese, 194, 196, 217, 222–223, 30152–154

Japanese Americans, 11, 13

Japanese American Youth Basketball League (JYO), 222

Japanese migrants, 194, 196

Japantown, 11

Jewish migrants, 194

Johnson, Katherine, 149

Jolie, Angelina, 106

Jordan, 80

Jordan, David Starr, 147–148

Jungle Fever (movie), 217

K

Kamehameha, King, 44

Keller, Helen, 146

Kentucky Fried Chicken, 194

Kim, Daniel Dae, 44

Korean migrants, 194

Korematsu, Fred, 153

natural order of things, 80
Nazi Germany, 149, 163
NBA, 182
negotiated ideology, 84–85
Nepal, 17
Netflix, 182, 191
Netherlands, 185, 192, 214
network television, 190–191
neutrality, 13
New Zealand, 187, 193, 214
Nguyen, Madison, 134
Nike, 182
9/11 terrorist attacks, 97–98, 154
Nisqually people, 121
North Korea, 17, 75

O
Obama, Barack, 105, 169, 170
Office of Hawaiian Affairs (OHA), 126
oppositional ideology, 85
oppositional memory, 153
Orientalism, 125

P
Pacific Islanders, 15
Pakistan, 182, 217
Palo Alto, California, 147–148, 149
Patriot Act, 97
Pentagon, 97–98, 154
perpetrator perspective, 174
personal/group construc-tions of identity, 121, 128–131
Pew Research Center Report (Livingston & Brown), 219
physical markers, 160, 162, 219
police
    force and brutality during peaceful protests, 35

intercultural awareness for, 236
protection for immigrants, 175
protection for under-re-sourced areas, 9
as RSAs, 81–82
Polish, 133
political competition, 37, 61
politicized, identities as, 127
politics of authenticity, 131–135
popular memory, 153
Popular Memory Group, 151–152
post-racial society, 169, 170, 171
potential mobility, 161
power. See also contexts of power; macro layers of power
characteristics of, 32–36
as constraining, 34–35, 36
cultural perspective based on, 28–32
dominant forms of, 35–36, 166
as enabling and creative, 35–36
in haves and have nots, 33, 187, 198
hierarchy of, 8–9
of historical memory, 145–149, 153–154
history as field of, 140–145
identity and, 121–122
intercultural relationships and, 208
material as, 33–34
structural influences of, 214–215
struggle for, 10
unseen or invisible struc-tures of, 6–7, 8, 32–33
power-based perspective

of communication, 53–55, 68
of culture, 28–32, 38
power distance, 90
power inequalities, 92, 208, 234–235
praxis, 235
Princeton University, 147
private memory, 153
privilege capitalism, 193
productivity of cultural groups, 161
Proposition 187, 86
Puerto Ricans, 2, 5, 41
Puerto Rico, 19, 78

Q
queer persons. See LGBTQIA

R
race. See also critical race theory (CRT); racialization
attributes of, 162–165
creating, in context of power, 163–164
defined, 161–162
described, 161
as identity marker, 164
narrative on, 159–160
naturalized over time, 165
racial state, 166
as social construct, 162–163
state ideologies of colorblindness and mul-ticulturalism, 166–169
structural formations of, 166–176
racial discrimination, 13–14, 171–176
racial/ethnic groups, 4, 12, 15, 16
racial/ethnic interests, 9
racial fetish, 220–222

Photo Credits

Fig 4.4: Copyright © ...ns_of_ ...es_of_Norway.svg. house 2010 by Stephen Mich-...owicz, (CC BY-SA 2.0) at https://commons.wikimedia.org/wiki/File:Riot_Police_Marching_towards_John_and_Richmond_(4740548755).jpg.

Fig 4.6: Copyright © 2011 by Depositphotos/sepavone. Reprinted with permission.

Fig 4.7: Copyright © 2013 by Depositphotos/aruba2000. Reprinted with permission.

Chapter 5

Fig. 5.0: Copyright © 2014 by Depositphotos/zhykova. Reprinted with permission.

Fig 5.1: Copyright © 2015 by Depositphotos/ASphoto777. Reprinted with permission.

Fig 5.2a: Copyright © 2014 by Depositphotos/kasto. Reprinted with permission.

Fig 5.2b: Copyright © 2018 by Depositphotos/IgorVetushko. Reprinted with permission.

Fig 5.2c: Copyright © 2017 by Depositphotos/EdZbarzhyvetsky. Reprinted with permission.

Fig 5.3: Copyright © 2010 by Shotgun Spratling, (CC BY-SA 2.0) at https://commons.wikimedia.org/wiki/File:Barack_Obama_speaking_at_USC_on_Oct._22,_2010._(Shotgun_Spratling-Neon_Tommy)_(5105577361).jpg.

Fig 5.4: Copyright © 2012 by Iggy Roberts, (CC BY 2.0) at https://www.flickr.com/photos/foreignoffice/8612210069.

Fig 5.5a: Source: https://commons.wikimedia.org/wiki/File:Margaret_Mead_NYWTS.jpg.

Fig 5.5b: Source: https://commons.wikimedia.org/wiki/File:Coming_of_age_in_Samoa_title_page.jpg.

Fig 5.6: Copyright © 2016 by Depositphotos/Rawpixel. Reprinted with permission.

Fig 5.7: Copyright © 2008 by Madame Tussauds, (CC BY 2.0) at https://commons.wikimedia.org/wiki/File:Bruce_Lee_(Madame_Tussauds).JPG.

Fig 5.8: Source: https://pixabay.com/en/protest-blm-black-lives-matter-sign-1567028/.

Chapter 6

Fig. 6.0: Copyright © 2016 by Depositphotos/encrier. Reprinted with permission.

Fig 6.2: Source: http://www.censusscope.org/us/map_multiracial.html.

Fig 6.3: Source: https://www.census.gov/2010census/news/releases/operations/cb12-146.html.

Fig 6.4: Source: https://commons.wikimedia.org/wiki/File:Duke_Kahanamoku_and_his_troupe_3a40900u.jpg.

Fig 6.5: Copyright © 2011 by Fibonacci Blue, (CC BY 2.0) at https://commons.m.wikimedia.org/wiki/File:Join_the_Impact_at_the_Twin_Cities_Pride_Parade_2011_(5873840105).jpg.

Fig 6.7: Source: https://commons.wikimedia.org/wiki/File:A_prayer_and_presentation_of_colors_at_a_Colorado_Springs_Native_American_Inter_Tribal_Powwow_and_festival_in_that_central_Colorado_city_LCCN2015633356.tif.

Fig 6.8a: Copyright © 2009 by Daryl Davis, (CC BY 2.0) at https://commons.wikimedia.org/wiki/File:San_Jose_Tet_parade,_2009.jpg.

Chapter 7

Fig. 7.0: Copyright © 2017 by Depositphotos/demerzel21. Reprinted with permission.

Fig 7.1: Copyright © 2011 by Depositphotos/fotoduki. Reprinted with permission.

Fig. 7.2: Source: https://pixabay.com/en/character-tibet-ethnic-ms-2535231/.

Fig.7.3: Source: https://commons.wikimedia.org/wiki/File:1890sc_Pears_Soap_Ad.jpg.

Fig.7.4: Source: https://archive.org/details/libraryofamerica04ellirich.

Fig.7.5: Copyright © 2016 by Peter Hvizdak / New Haven Register, (CC BY 2.0) at https://www.flickr.com/photos/fibonacciblue/29527939373.

Fig.7.7: Source: https://commons.wikimedia.org/wiki/File:Katherine_Johnson_at_NASA,_in_1966.png.

Chapter 8

Fig. 8.0: Copyright © 2014 by iStockphto/nullplus. Reprinted with permission.

Fig 8.2a: Copyright © 2013 by Depositphotos/donscarpo. Reprinted with permission.

Fig 8.2b: Copyright © 2016 by Depositphotos/ fotoquique. Reprinted with permission.

Fig 8.2c: Copyright © 2015 by iStockphoto/basar17. Reprinted with permission.

Fig 8.3: Source: https://www.23andme.com/.

Fig 8.4: Copyright © 2017 by Depositphotos/Wavebreakmedia. Reprinted with permission.

Fig 8.5: Copyright © 2016 by Chensiyuan, (CC BY-SA 3.0) at https://commons.wikimedia.org/ wiki/File:Day124ckoreatown.JPG.

Fig 8.6: Source: https://commons.wikimedia.org/wiki/ File:FEMA_-_39841_-_Official_portrait_of_ President-elect_Barack_Obama_on_Jan._13. jpg.

Fig 8.7: Source: https://pixabay.com/en/ black-lives-matter-african-american-1011597/.

Fig 8.8: Copyright © 2014 by Depositphotos/Jan-Pietruszka. Reprinted with permission.

Chapter 9

Fig. 9.0: Copyright © 2010 by Depositphotos/sumners. Reprinted with permission.

Fig 9.1a: Source: https://commons.wikimedia.org/ wiki/File:Coca-Cola_logo.svg.

Fig 9.1b: Source: https://commons.wikimedia.org/ wiki/File:Logo_NIKE.svg.

Fig 9.1c: Source: https://commons.wikimedia.org/ wiki/File:Netflix_logo.svg.

Fig 9.2: Source: https://www.businesswire.com/news/ home/20170925006062/en/Interbrand-Releas-es-2017-Global-Brands-Report-Apple.

Fig 9.3: Source: https://commons.wikimedia.org/wiki/ File:Global_North_and_Global_South,_ according_to_the_Wikimedia_Foundation. svg.

Fig 9.4: Source: https://getting-it-together.moadoph. gov.au/national-story/people-and-places/ resource-3.html.

Fig 9.5: Source: https://pixabay.com/en/ bollywood-posters-poster-bollywood-995224/.

Fig 9.6a: Source: https://commons.wikimedia.org/ wiki/File:Coca-Cola_logo.svg.

Fig 9.6b: Source: https://commons.wikimedia.org/ wiki/File:Disney-logo.jpg.

Fig 9.6c: Source: https://commons.wikimedia.org/ wiki/File:McDonald%27s_Golden_Arches.svg.

Fig 9.6d: Source: https://pixabay.com/en/ apple-logo-mac-macintosh-computer-311246/.

Fig 9.6e: Source: https://en.wikipedia.org/wiki/File:-Googlelogo.png.

Fig 9.6f: Source: https://commons.wikimedia.org/ wiki/File:Amazon_logo_plain.svg.

Fig 9.7a: Copyright © 2009 by Flying Cloud, (CC BY 2.0) at https://commons.wikimedia.org/wiki/ File:India_Trip_2009_(3991752867).jpg.

Fig 9.7b: Copyright © 2007 by Colipon, (CC BY-SA 3.0) at https://commons.wikimedia.org/wiki/ File:KFC_in_Hohhot.jpg.

Fig 9.8: Source: https://commons.wikimedia.org/ wiki/File:Japanese_immigrant_family_in_ Brazil_02.jpg.

Fig 9.9a: Source: https://pixabay.com/id/ washington-dc-dc-kota-jalan-245333/.

Fig 9.9b: Copyright © 2008 by ONewYork, (CC BY-SA 3.0) at https://commons.wikimedia.org/wiki/ File:HK_Shum_Shui_Po_Un_Chau_Street_ Cha_Chaan_Teng_Pratas_Street.JPG.

Fig 9.10: Copyright © 2014 by Depositphotos/mj0007. Reprinted with permission.

Chapter 10

Fig. 10.0: Copyright © 2015 by Depositphotos/Rawpixel. Reprinted with permission.

Fig 10.1: Copyright © 2017 by Depositphotos/ SashaKhalabuzar. Reprinted with permission.

Fig 10.2: Copyright © 2016 by Depositphotos/Rawpixel. Reprinted with permission.

Fig 10.3: Copyright © 2016 by Depositphotos/yacob-chuk1. Reprinted with permission.

Fig 10.4: Copyright © 2011 by Jose Antonio Navas, (CC BY 2.0) at https://www.flickr.com/photos/ joseanavas/5984377111.

Fig 10.5: Copyright © 2015 by Depositphotos/tiagoz. Reprinted with permission.

Fig 10.6: Source: https://pixabay.com/en/ couple-marriage-relationship-1246304/.

Fig 10.7a: Copyright © 2012 by Depositphotos/odua. Reprinted with permission.

Fig 10.7b: Copyright © 2016 by Depositphotos/lon-dondeposit. Reprinted with permission.

Fig 10.8: Copyright © 2016 by Udarmudar, (CC BY-SA 4.0) at https://commons.wikimedia.org/

Chapter 11

CPSIA information can be obtained
at www.ICGtesting.com
Printed in the USA
FSHW021909021219
64675FS